Edexcel AS/A level
Drama and Theatre

John Davey | Phil Cleaves | John Johnson

ActiveBook included

PEARSON

Published by Pearson Education Limited, 80 Strand, London, WC2R 0RL.

www.pearsonschoolsandfecolleges.co.uk

Copies of official specifications for all Edexcel qualifications may be found on the website: www.edexcel.com

Text © Pearson Education Limited 2016
Designed by Elizabeth Arnoux for Pearson
Typeset by Tek-Art
Produced by Hart McLeod Ltd
Cover design by Elizabeth Arnoux for Pearson
Picture research by Rebecca Sodergren
Cover photo/illustration © Getty Images/Tom Van Heel @ Sapphire&Steel

The rights of John Davey, Phil Cleaves and John Johnson to be identified as authors of this work have been asserted by them in accordance with the Copyright, Designs and Patents Act 1988.

First published 2016

19 18 17 16
10 9 8 7 6 5 4 3 2 1

British Library Cataloguing in Publication Data
A catalogue record for this book is available from the British Library

ISBN 978 1 292 15062 8

Acknowledgements
We are grateful to the following for permission to reproduce copyright material:

Text
Quote on page 28 from Equus, Penguin Classics (Schaffer P. 2007) pp. 18, 20, 21, 25, 28, 59, 60, 61, 63, 79, 82, 87, Penguin; Quote on page 30 from Machinal, Nick Hern Books (Treadwell S. 1995) Episode 6, Nick Hern Books; Quote on page 36 from Machinal, Nick Hern Books (Treadwell S. 1995) Scene 2, Nick Hern Books; Quote on page 36 from Colder than Here, Oberon Modern Plays (Wade L. 2005) Scene 8, Oberon; Quote on page 37 from That Face, Faber & Faber (Stenham P. 2008) Faber & Faber; Quote on page 37© Dario Fo, 1987, Accidental Death of an Anarchist, Bloomsbury Methuen Drama, an imprint of Bloomsbury Publishing Plc.; Text on page 42 from Machinal, Nick Hern Books (Treadwell S. 1995) Nick Hern Books; Extract on page 43 from Review of Equus, The Guardian, 27/07/1973 (Billington M.), Guardian News and Media Ltd; Extract on page 43 from Review of Equus, The Guardian, 28/02/2007 (Billington M.), Guardian News and Media Ltd; Extract on page 45 from Review of That Face, The Telegraph, 26/04/2007 (Spence C.), Telegraph Media Group Ltd; Extract on page 45 from Review of That Face, The Guardian, 12/05/2008 (Billington M.), Guardian News and Media Ltd; Extract on page 46 from Polly Stenham on 'That Face', Time Out (McGinn C. 2008), Time Out; Quote on page 46 from That Face, Faber & Faber (Stenham P. 2008) Scene 3, Faber & Faber; Extract on page 47 from The Lively Years 1920-1973, Association Press (Brooks Atkinson and Albert Hirshfield 1973) Rowman and Littlefield; Extract on page 48 from The soul of the machine, The Independent, 17/10/1993 (Taylor P.), Independent News and Digital Media Ltd; Extract on page 48 from Machinal, Nick Hern Books (Treadwell S. 1995) Scene 1, Nick Hern Books; Extract on page 49 from Fences - A review, The Guardian, 27/06/2013 (Billington M.), The Guardian; Quotes on page 50 from Fences, Penguin Books Ltd (Wilson A. 1991) Troy, Act 1, Penguin; Extract on page 51 from Colder than Here - review, The Guardian, 02/08/2012 (Hickling A.), The Guardian; Extract on page 51 from Theatre review of Colder than Here by Philip Fisher, February, 2005, http://www.britishtheatreguide.info/reviews/colderthanhere-rev, British Theatre Guide; Extract on page 51 from Re:play 2015 : Colder Than Here – Home, Manchester, http://www.thereviewshub.com/replay-2015-colder-than-here-home-manchester/, The Reviews Hub; Quote on page 52 from Colder than Here, Oberon Modern Plays (Wade L. 2005) Scene 1, Scene 8, Oberon Books; Extract on page 54 from Accidental Death of an Anarchist, The Guardian, 27/02/2003 (Billington M.), The Guardian; Quote on page 54 © Dario Fo, 1987, Accidental Death of an Anarchist (Act 2, Scene 1), Bloomsbury

Methuen Drama, an imprint of Bloomsbury Publishing Plc.; Quote on page 57 from That Face, Faber & Faber (Stenham P. 2008) Scene 6, Faber & Faber; Quotes on pages 57–58 from Colder than Here, Oberon Modern Plays (Wade L. 2005) pp. 54–57, Oberon; Quote on page 59 from Machinal, Nick Hern Books (Treadwell S. 1995) Episode 3, pp. 21–24, Nick Hern Books; Quotes on pages 59–60 © Dario Fo, 1987, Accidental Death of an Anarchist (Act 1, Scene 2), Bloomsbury Methuen Drama, an imprint of Bloomsbury Publishing Plc.; Quote on page 61 from Fences, Penguin Books Ltd (Wilson A. 1991) Act 2 Scene 4, Penguin; Quotes on pages 61–62 from Equus, Penguin Classics (Schaffer P. 2007) Scene 27, Penguin; Quote on page 63 from Fences, Penguin Books Ltd (Wilson A. 1991) Scene 4, Penguin; Quote on page 64 from Colder Than Here, Oberon Modern Plays (Wade L. 2005) pp. 75–78; Quote on page 66 from Fences, Penguin Books Ltd (Wilson A. 1991) Act 2, Scene 2, Penguin; Quote on page 68 from from Colder Than Here, Oberon Modern Plays (Wade, L. 2005) Scene 8; Quote on page 71 from That Face, Faber & Faber (Stenham P. 2008) Scene 3, Faber & Faber; Quotes on pages 72 © Dario Fo, 1987, Accidental Death of an Anarchist (Act 1, Scene 2) Bloomsbury Methuen Drama, an imprint of Bloomsbury Publishing Plc; Quote on page 74 from Colder than Here, Oberon Modern plays (Wade L. 2005) Scene 6, Oberon Books Ltd; Quote on page 75 from Machinal, Nick Hern Books (Treadwell S. 1995) Episode 7, Nick Hern Books; Quote on page 77 from Fences, Penguin Books Ltd (Wilson A. 1991) Act 1, Scene 1; Quotes on page 99–100 from Waiting for Godot, Faber & Faber (Beckett, S. 2006) Faber & Faber; Quote on page 160–161 from Waiting for Godot, Faber & Faber (Beckett, S. 2006) pages 18–20, Faber & Faber.

The author and publisher would like to thank the following individuals and organisations for permission to reproduce photographs:

(Key: b-bottom; c-centre; l-left; r-right; t-top)

Alamy Images: GL Archive 120, **Used by permission of Bloomsbury Methuen Drama, an imprint of Bloomsbury Publishing Plc.** © Design United 25; **Complicite:** 110; **Getty Images:** Bettman 108, Nat Jag 9l, Martinie 104, Stuart Wilson 106; **Kneehigh:** 113; **Linda Nylind:** vi; **Photostage Ltd:** 44, 46, 50, 52, 54, Donald Cooper 10; **Punchdrunk:** 117; **Rex Shutterstock:** Associated Newspapers 115, Geraint Lewis 3, Alastair Muir 5, 9r; **TopFoto:** Johan Persson / ArenaPal 13, Richard Midenhall / ArenaPAL 48, The Stanislavski Centre / Rose Bruford College / ArenaPAL 121

Cover images: *Front:* **Getty Images:** Tom Van Heel @ Sapphire&Steel

All other images © Pearson Education

Contents

Foreword

I wrote my first full-length play while studying A level Drama. It was a story about a teenage girl growing up in Sheffield – so quite autobiographical. The play tried to describe what it was like to be 17, and how bewildering, funny and sad the world seemed. I wrote a few pages a night after my homework, and once it was done I sent a copy to my local theatre, the Crucible. A few months later they put on the play with actors from their youth theatre company. Seeing my play performed in front of a live audience was the most exciting moment of my life up to that point.

If I read it now I'd find it hopelessly naïve; I've had to track down and kill everyone who saw it. But it was through writing that play that I realised what I wanted to do with my life.

I was really inspired by the plays I read on the A level course, and over the years they've become old friends. I loved learning how to read a play – over and over again sometimes, looking between the lines to work out how the playwright had built it. Like taking a car apart with a spanner, then

trying to put it back together again. I came to love the idea of a play not just as words on a page, but as a blueprint for a live event that can happen over and over again, never quite the same, meaning something different to everyone who performs it or watches it. I think about those plays all the time.

You can use your discoveries to make new work of your own. Drama trains and tones your imagination, and great plays help us understand each other. They make us consider what it means to be human.

You might not want to work in the performing arts as a career, but the skills you'll learn on the course will serve you well whatever you choose to do later. I can't think of a better way to spend your time. Turn the page – you're about to make some new friends.

Laura Wade, writer of *Colder than Here*

How to use this book

Introduction: how to use this book

The content in this book can be used to help you study for either the Edexcel AS or the A level Drama and Theatre courses, as there is much similar content between the two specifications. The book focuses on helping you to prepare for the exam component: Theatre Markers in Practice, but the content and activities suggested may help you with other parts of your course too.

As there is overlap between the content in AS and A level, most of the sections in the book will be relevant to you, but where content is specific to either the AS exam or the A level exam, we have clearly marked it using these features:

Where you see exam tips, these give useful advice that is relevant to both of the courses.

Exam tip

Where you see exam tips, these give useful advice that is relevant to both of the courses.

AS level course overview

AS level exam guidance

AS content is always shown in a blue-coloured box.

AS Drama and Theatre course overview

Component 1: Exploration and Performance

60% of the AS level – 96 marks

As a performer or a designer you will work in a group to create a performance of one key extract from a performance text informed by the methodology of one influential practitioner. The performance or design realisation of your extract is worth 32 marks.

The analysis and evaluation of both development and performance will be presented as a written or recorded/verbal portfolio worth 48 marks.

As a performer or a designer you will create a monologue or duologue of one key extract from a different text. This performance or design realisation is worth 16 marks.

Component 2: Theatre Makers in Practice

40% of the AS level – 48 marks

1 hour 45 minutes, written exam

Section A: Live theatre evaluation

This section will ask you to analyse and evaluate a live theatre performance that you have seen during the course. You are allowed to bring 500 words of notes into the exam to help you respond to the questions. This section is worth 16 marks.

Section B: Page to stage: Realising a performance text

This section will ask you to answer two extended response questions on how you would interpret and realise an extract in performance from a performance text that you have studied. The performance text will be chosen by your teacher and you will practically explore the whole text in preparation for the exam. You will not be able to take your text into the exam, but you will be given an extract from the text to help you respond to the questions. This section is worth 32 marks.

A level course overview

A level exam guidance

A level content is always shown in a green-coloured box.

A level Drama and Theatre course overview

Component 1: Devising

40% of the A level – 80 marks

As a performer or a designer you will create and develop an original piece of drama using one key extract from a performance text and a theatre practitioner as stimuli. The performance or design realisation of your devised drama is worth 20 marks.

The analysis and evaluation of both development and performance will be presented as a written or recorded/verbal portfolio worth 60 marks.

Component 2: Text in Performance

20% of the A level – 60 marks

As a performer or a designer you will work in a group to create a performance of one key extract from a performance text. The performance or design realisation of your extract is worth 36 marks.

As a performer or a designer you will create a monologue or duologue of one key extract from a different text. This performance or design realisation is worth 24 marks.

Component 3: Theatre Makers in Practice

40% of the A level – 80 marks

2 hours 30 minutes, written exam

Section A: Live theatre evaluation

This section will ask you to analyse and evaluate a live theatre performance that you have seen during the course. You are allowed to bring 500 words of notes into the exam to help you respond to the questions. This section is worth 20 marks.

Section B: Page to stage: Realising a performance text

This section will ask you to answer two extended response questions on how you would interpret and realise an extract in performance from a performance text that you have studied. The performance text will be chosen by your teacher and you will practically explore the whole text in preparation for the exam. You will not be able to take your text into the exam, but you will be given an extract from the text to help you respond to the questions. This section is worth 36 marks.

Section C: Interpreting a performance text

This section will ask you to answer an extended response question on how you would re-imagine a production concept of a section from a performance text. You will need to explain how you will communicate ideas to a contemporary audience and outline how a theatre practitioner has influenced your production concept. You are able to take clean copies of this performance text into the exam. This section is worth 24 marks.

SECTION A
Live theatre evaluation

Overview

This section will explore the evaluation of live theatre, which is the first part of the exam paper for Component 3 Theatre Makers in Practice. Watching live theatre is an important part of your course. Not only can you learn from experiencing the work of other theatre makers and collect ideas to use in your own work, but also, through your critical analysis, you can use it as an opportunity to show everything you have learned throughout your course.

Choosing a performance

The live theatre experience will be at the centre of your response and you will need to demonstrate your understanding by referring to the work of one or more of the following theatre makers in your answer:

- directors
- performers
- designers.

You may have seen a number of live theatre productions during the course, but you must choose only one to prepare for this examination. The production you choose to write about must fit within the criteria below.

- Live theatre means being in the same performance space as the performers. You cannot use filmed versions of a stage production in the exam.
- The performance must not be sung through in its entirety.
- The production can be amateur or professional, but it cannot be the work of other students.
- The performance cannot be a performance text on the prescribed lists for your AS or A level specification.
- Your chosen performance should give you enough to talk about! It should include a range of production elements – for example, costume, set, sound, lighting – and opportunities to discuss the work of key theatre makers – for example, directors, performers and designers.

> **Top tip**
>
> Try to see as much live theatre as possible. Being able to critically analyse and evaluate productions effectively will only come with practice.

Taking notes

You are allowed to take in one set of theatre evaluation notes of up to a maximum of 500 words to inform your response. Your teacher will guide you on this and provide you with the official form to use, which will accompany your notes. Five hundred words may seem like plenty, but there is a skill in condensing your thoughts into this word limit. These are **notes** that do not, for example, need to be written in continuous prose. Once you have practised writing your notes, you will find them very useful when it comes to answering the live theatre evaluation question in the exam.

> **Exam tip**
>
> The name of performance seen, date of performance seen and venue of performance seen do not count towards your maximum of 500 words.

These notes must include the title, venue and date of the production you have seen and are going to focus on in this section of the examination.

The purpose of the notes is to help you to demonstrate knowledge and understanding as an **informed member of a theatre audience** and therefore to support your response in the examination.

> **Top tip**
>
> To help you become an informed member of the audience you should draw on:
>
> - your own experience in preparing work for performance
> - your research – both practical and theoretical – into the work of theatre makers throughout your course
> - experiences outside the course, such as theatre visits, related work experience or involvement in theatre companies
> - knowledge from background reading, for example, reading the text of the play you are going to see, as well as reading what others have written about the play and the production.

The exam paper

For both AS and A level Specifications, Assessment Objective four **(AO4)** is the focus of this section for the examination in Component 2 for AS level and Component 3 for A level.

(AO4) is: Analyse and evaluate their own work and that of others.

Specifically, in Section A you are being assessed on your ability to analyse and evaluate the work of others.

In both the AS and A level exams, you will have a choice of two questions in Section A. You will need to consider the demands of both questions before deciding which one you are going to answer. Although they are very similar in tone and structure, the specific demands of the questions are different and the clue to finding the focus of the question will be through the key words used in the question. Below are examples of the sorts of questions you will be asked to answer.

In the AS exam questions, you will be asked to analyse and evaluate the performance by focusing on the role of one theatre maker or one production element. For example:

> **AS level exam question**
>
> Analyse and evaluate the contribution of the **costume designer** and their use of colour in the performance you have seen.
>
> In your answer you should consider:
>
> - key moments in the performance
> - your response as an informed member of the audience.
>
> Your answer must give **balanced consideration** between your analysis **and** your evaluation.
>
> **(16 marks)**

In the A level exam questions, you will be given a thought-provoking statement and asked to analyse and evaluate the performance by giving your response to the statement and referring to contributions by two or more theatre makers.

> **A level exam question**
>
> Analyse and evaluate the live performance you have seen in light of the following statement:
>
> 'Live performance has nothing to say to a young audience.'
>
> Your answer should:
>
> - include analysis and evaluation of key moments from the performance you have seen and the contribution made by different theatre makers
> - offer **balanced consideration** between your analysis and evaluation of the performance and your response to the statement.
>
> **(20 marks)**

AS level exam guidance

Component 2 is worth 48 marks and up to 40% of the total AS level mark. Section A carries up to 16 marks in total and is based on your experience of a live theatre performance.

A level exam guidance

Component 3 is worth 80 marks and up to 40% of the total A level mark. Section A carries up to 20 marks in total and is based on your experience of a live theatre performance.

A level exam guidance

For the A level exam, find the specific demands in the statement that lead each question. The statement should be at the heart of your response.

For the purpose of this section, notes based on the National Theatre Production of *Othello*, which played at the Olivier Theatre, London, have been used as a model. It will imagine that you are preparing to watch the live performance of this production of *Othello* and will offer a guide to the areas of the production that you should be thinking about as an informed member of the audience.

An image of Rory Kinnear as Iago and Adrian Lester as Othello in the National Theatre production of *Othello* in 2013.

Taking it further

The specification clearly states that the answer in Section A must be based on a live theatre performance. However, in order to practise before going to see a performance you might want to use an online resource such as National Theatre On Demand in Schools. This includes various recorded productions, including *Othello*, which we have based our model guide on. National Theatre On Demand is available to educational establishments and is a free resource. Your teacher can find further details on the National Theatre website.

Analysing and evaluating live theatre

For the purposes of the specifications for both AS and A level, **analyse** and **evaluate** can be defined as:

- analysis: picking out key ideas or concepts and being able to say how these were explored by the directors, performers or designers
- evaluation: forming a judgement about whether an idea or performance element has worked or not with effective supporting evidence.

This component comes at the end of the course and there will be a range of experiences you can draw on to help you shape your response to the performance.

Before the performance

Before you watch a performance, there are a few things you might like to do in order to prepare for the experience.

- Read the play.
- Read reviews on the production.

- Research other productions that the director and designers have produced.
- Look into the style or practitioners that may have influenced the director, performers and designers.
- Research previous productions of the play.
- Think about elements you have learned about performance throughout your course to remind you of points to look out for.

Note your expectations – what are you expecting the production to be like?

> **Exam tip**
>
> You might like to structure your notes under three headings:
>
> - Before the performance
> - During the performance
> - After the performance.
>
> This will help you when you come to prepare your 500 words for the final exam, as you will be able pick out the important elements from each section and you may also be able to see any common threads or ideas as well as whether your own evaluative views on the section changed at any point.

You may wish to make a prompt list of the different elements to look out for at the performance. This list may depend on the production you are going to see, but might include the following.

Directors	Performers	Designers
<ul><li>Directorial style</li><li>Staging</li><li>Target audience</li><li>Choice of theatre</li><li>Use of text (cuts and edits)</li><li>Practitioner influence</li><li>Interpretation/concept</li></ul>	<ul><li>Acting style</li><li>Movement</li><li>Physicality</li><li>Vocals</li><li>Facial expressions</li><li>Delivery of text</li><li>Characterisation</li><li>Use of proxemics/stage space</li></ul>	<ul><li>Set</li><li>Lighting</li><li>Sound</li><li>Costume</li><li>Stage make-up/special effects</li><li>Projections/multimedia</li><li>Props</li><li>Stage space</li></ul>

This student has decided to watch *Othello* at the National Theatre in the Olivier Theatre. Below is a prompt list written by the student before they see the production.

Glossary

Naturalistic/naturalism
A style of drama that developed in the late 19th century. It attempts to represent real life on stage. There is an emphasis on the influence of environment, plus human behaviour and psychology. The presentation uses everyday speech and movement.

- The size and make-up of the audience
- The staging used
- The overall style of the production
- The interpretation of a classical text
- The modern setting
- The **naturalistic** style
- The use of costume and light

It may be that you also want to make a list of points to look out for, or specific questions to ask yourself, at the performance about the production you are about to see.

> *Othello* at the National Theatre in the Olivier Theatre on 4 October 2013
>
> What is the setting and context chosen by director Nicholas Hytner and has this worked?
>
> How has Rory Kinnear approached the character of Iago?
>
> How have Adrian Lester (Othello) and Olivia Vinall (Desdemona) developed their relationship on stage?
>
> How did the audience respond to the first time they saw Othello, Desdemona, Brabantio and the Senators?
>
> How were the key scenes staged: such as the moment when Othello begins to believe Iago ('Beware the Green Eyed Monster') or the scene when Othello murders Desdemona (Act 5 Scene 2)?
>
> How has the lighting/set/costume/sound designer had an impact on the performance?

Othello and Desdemona played by Adrian Lester and Olivia Vinall.

You may want to consider characters' relationships and how these are portrayed by the actors in performance, such as Othello and Desdemona played here by Adrian Lester and Olivia Vinall.

During the performance

During the performance you should focus on the impact of the director, the performers and the designers as this will be important in your answers. You should also consider the impact of the performance on an audience.

You might find these questions are useful when preparing your notes for Section A and these are areas that you should be considering when visiting the theatre.

- Where are you sitting and how does this fit with the general layout of the audience seating?
- What type of staging/audience positioning is used (end-on/proscenium arch, traverse, in-the-round, apron).
- What type of theatre space is it (e.g. a modern space, a Victorian theatre or a black box studio)?
- What is the audience make-up? Are you surrounded by other students or is the audience a mix of ages?
- Does the theatre seem full?
- What is the atmosphere directly before the performance? Is this audience excited? Is there a sense of anticipation?
- How are those around you responding to the performance and what kind of comments do you hear after the performance?

AS level exam guidance

For the AS paper, you should consider the impact of and relationship between the use of stage space and the audience.

A level exam guidance

For the A level paper, you might want to extend your observations to the audience and audience reaction.

Exam tip

Notice how the student's notes above use performers' names rather than characters. For both the AS and A level exam it is good practice to write about the performers rather than the characters, and the production rather than the play.

Top tip

It may be useful to consider that immediate reactions during and straight after the performance might differ from considered reactions after the event. You may have an initial response that is based on where you are sitting or the audience immediately around you, for example. After the event, however, your response may be more considered when you reflect on your experience as a whole.

Later on in this section we will be looking at structuring notes and the areas to cover. One of those areas will include analysing and evaluating 'key moments' from the performance, so taking into account the preparation before the performance will be important. During the performance itself, it would be advisable to pay close attention to those key moments that you might eventually write about in your exam answer.

After the performance

It may be useful to write notes straight after the performance on your own to capture your initial, personal response before discussing the performance with your class. It is important to remember that both the AS and A level questions are looking for a **personal** response and it is important not to be swayed too much by the thoughts or opinions of others.

In order for your theatre evaluation notes to be useful, they need to be accessible. The theatre evaluation notes in themselves are not the answer to the response and, once you have written them and submitted them to your teacher, you will not see them again until you are in the examination room. When structuring your notes, it is likely that your individual response to the live theatre experience will have been shaped and informed as a result of wider discussions following the performance, but the notes that you take into the examination must be your own unaided work.

It is worth considering, therefore, how you structure your notes in order to make them accessible in the examination room. You may see the live performance in March, for example, and compile your notes almost immediately. The examination might not be until May/June, so you might consider using subheadings, different colours for different aspects of the performance, a size of font that makes specific references stand out on the page, and key words and phrases to remind you of the experience.

Your notes after the performance may include reference to:

- the director's concept/interpretation and the chosen performance style
- performers, including performers in specific roles
- design considerations, including the use of costume, set, lighting and sound
- impact on the audience, including, specifically, on you, and how this was achieved
- the use of the theatre space
- how ideas were communicated during the performance.

Structuring your notes

In order to prepare for writing a response, you need to organise the notes you will be taking into the exam with you. This is important, as time will be a key factor in the exam and therefore **well-organised, well-structured** and **relevant** notes will help you in writing your response.

There is a word limit on the notes, not a page limit, so there may be ways you can structure your notes that suit your particular learning style. It is important to remember that you will be accessing the information under examination conditions and that you do not want to waste precious time in the exam trying to find key points in your notes to support your response.

You may also include sketches, drawings and diagrams to support the response to the question if required, but no pre-published material, including programmes and photographs, may be taken into the examination or form part of your notes.

Your notes may be handwritten or word-processed, but the total word limit must not be exceeded.

Consider, for example, the set of notes on page 8, which reflects on the National Theatre production of *Othello*, and how useful these might be to you in the exam.

Top tip

One way to help you in the exam is to colour-code your notes to differentiate between moments of analysis or evaluation, or positive and negative critique. With time at a premium in both the AS and A level papers, any way that you can help speed up the process for yourself is advisable. This may take the following form:

Red = negative critique   Green = positive critique

Blue = analysis   Orange = evaluation

The use of lighting at this point lacked imagination and was very basic …

The use of floor lighting was effective as it created a shadow on the **cyclorama** …

The costume seemed to suggest the lack of status of the performers …

The costume worked to some extent as it allowed the audience to understand …

Try this method in your note-taking task.

Glossary

Cyclorama
A fabric drop hung from a curved or segmented batten, or a curved wall at the back of the stage, on which light can be cast to create effects (cyc for short).

Building a vocabulary for analysing and evaluating

There is no doubt that you will need to be able to evaluate and analyse with the right level of language and vocabulary. As an activity, start to build up a 'bank' of words that you draw on when you come to write your notes or even that you can use to revise with before the exam.

ACTIVITY

The idea is to use this list as a starting point and to add your own vocabulary – particularly language that is suited to the performance you have seen. In preparation for Section A for both AS and A level papers, try building your own list/bank of vocabulary that you can draw on in the exam.

Some words have been outlined in the table below as a starting point:

Vocabulary that might be used in a convincing performance	Vocabulary that might be used in an unconvincing performance
Accomplished	Basic
Enhanced the performance	Inconsistent
Exemplary use of	Variable
Sophisticated	Lacked development
Highly effective	Poor
Impressive	Cursory
Creative	Vague
Thought-provoking	Patchy
Powerful	Little evidence of
Inspired	Dull
Innovative	Lacking creativity

In both the A level and AS level examinations you need to be able to offer informed opinions that demonstrate your ability to:

- formulate and justify personal judgements of how ideas, meaning and impact are created by the director(s), performers, and/or designers
- offer a sophisticated and in-depth personal response
- evaluate how dramatic elements have been used to create theatrical impact, such as set, lighting, costume, sound, staging and acting
- present evaluation of key theatre makers, their collaboration and the contribution they have made to specific aspects of the production
- show sensitive reasoning, interpretation and engagement with the statement (for A level)
- offer a perceptive evaluation, demonstrating an accomplished ability to formulate and justify personal judgements of how ideas, meaning and impact are created by different theatre makers' use of production values and dramatic elements.

Examples of structuring your notes

Theatre evaluation notes – key people – example 1

Othello at the National Theatre in the Olivier Theatre on 4 October 2013

Production: key people	Performance: key people
Director: Nicholas Hytner	Othello: Adrian Lester
Designer: Vicky Mortimer	Iago: Rory Kinnear
Lighting: Jon Clark	Desdemona: Olivia Vinall
Music: Nick Powell	Roderigo: Tom Robertson
Sound: Gareth Fry	Cassio: Jonathan Bailey
Fight Direction: Kate Waters	Brabantio: William Chubb
	Bianca: Rokhsaneh Ghawam-Shahidi
	Emilia: Lyndsey Marshal

There are 49 words here, listing key people associated with the production. As stated in the previous section, there is an expectation at this level of study that you are able to reference theatre makers by name in your response so, from that point of view, the list is useful, particularly to remind you of the experience in the examination, which may be weeks or even months after you have seen the production. There may be other ways of presenting the list – grouping actors together for key scenes in the example below, or by order of appearance in the third example might be useful. However, by putting the production team first in every example, you are more likely to write about the play in performance rather than just the play, just as in the example below from a student answer.

Student answer

'In the production of *Othello*, directed by Nicholas Hytner, I was fascinated with the use of sound designed by Gareth Fry, which created a sense of …'

Gareth Fry with his Olivier Award in 2009 for his sound design for *Black Watch* with the National Theatre of Scotland.

Black Watch 2010 National Theatre of Scotland production.

This set of notes starts with the production team before outlining the performers.

Theatre evaluation notes – key people – example 2

Othello at the National Theatre in the Olivier Theatre on 4 October 2013

<u>Production: key people</u>

Director: Nicholas Hytner

Designer: Vicky Mortimer

Lighting: Jon Clark

Music: Nick Powell

Sound: Gareth Fry

Fight Direction: Kate Waters

<u>Performance: key people and key scenes</u>

Opening (Act 1 Scene 1)

Iago: Rory Kinnear; Roderigo: Tom Robertson; Brabantio: William Chubb

Othello and the Senators (Act 1 Scene 2)

Iago: Rory Kinnear; Brabantio: William Chubb; Duke of Venice: Robert Demeger;

Othello: Adrian Lester

'I hate the Moor' (Act 1 Scene 3)

Iago: Rory Kinnear; Roderigo: Tom Robertson

Cassio Drunk Scene (Act 2 Scene 3)

Roderigo: Tom Robertson; Cassio: Jonathan Bailey; Iago: Rory Kinnear

Top tip

Starting your notes with the production team will help you to make sure that you are writing about the production rather than the play when you come to answer Section A at both AS and A level.

Note this example takes up more words than the previous one, but could be a way of you linking the key scenes with the key performers.

Theatre evaluation notes – key people – example 3

Othello at the National Theatre in the Olivier Theatre on 4 October 2013

<u>Production: key people</u>

Director: Nicholas Hytner

Designer: Vicky Mortimer

Lighting: Jon Clark

Music: Nick Powell

Sound: Gareth Fry

Fight Direction: Kate Waters

<u>Performance: key people (in order of appearance)</u>

Iago: Rory Kinnear

Roderigo: Tom Robertson

Brabantio: William Chubb

Duke of Venice: Robert Demeger

Othello: Adrian Lester

Desdemona: Olivia Vinall

Cassio: Jonathan Bailey

Bianca: Rokhsaneh Ghawam-Shahidi

Emilia: Lyndsey Marshal

This example will help you if you remember the play chronologically (from Scene 1 onwards), but you will need to make sure all key characters are covered.

Now that you have started your notes with the production and performance key people you need to structure the remainder of your words (most likely to be around 400 words remaining). In both examples you would be aiming to cover **key performance values**, such as acting style, lighting, set/stage, costume/props, sound/music and audience. How many notes you write for each key performance value will depend on the type of play that you see. Those writing about Frantic Assembly's version of *Othello* (2014/2015) may write more about the set with the 'moving walls' used in Laura Hopkins' design (image below), whereas a student writing about the National Theatre production might write about the naturalistic directorial style of Nicholas Hytner. As well as key performance values, notes should also cover **key performance moments**. Both of the examples that follow cover these, but with different structures.

Frantic Assembly's production of *Othello* in 2014/15 with Laura Hopkins' imaginative 'moving walls' and pool table set design.

Theatre evaluation notes – key performance values and key performance moments – example 1

Othello at the National Theatre in the Olivier Theatre on 4 October 2013

<u>Acting style</u>
Modern setting (Afghanistan/Allied Forces)
Naturalistic
Emotional and psychological approach to character (Iago in particular)
Use of breaking the **fourth wall** with **asides** and **soliloquys**
Speaking of text is made to fit modern setting
Poetical nature and imagery of the language is conveyed with vocal delivery

<u>Lighting</u>
Use of window lighting – gobos (pub Scene 1)
Natural lighting (Othello Senators Scene Act 1 Scene 3)
Use of shadow and steel gels for Othello's arrival in Cyprus (Act 2 Scene 1)
Blue wash for night time (Cassio's Drunk Scene Act 2 Scene 3)
Use of spotlight and darkness (with Rodrigo and Iago Act 4 Scene 2)
Blue wash and onstage floods to create sense of night and naturalism (Desdemona's 'Willow' song Act 4 Scene 3)
A single candle in Othello's soliloquy to the sleeping Desdemona (Act 5 Scene 2)

<u>Set/stage</u>
The street and outside of the pub (Act 1 Scene 1)
The boardroom (Othello Senators Scene (Act 1 Scene 3)
The outside of the army base (various scenes)
The 'mess' room (Act 2 Scene 3)
Iago and Othello's office (Act 3 Scene 3)
Prefabricated/temporary army base
Afghanistan – modern-day setting
Male toilets where Othello is sick (Act 4 Scene 1)

<u>Costume/props</u>
British army uniform
War uniform (bullet-proof vests, etc.)
Badges (showing status)
Modern dress (suits, etc. in Act 1 Scene 1/Scene 3)
Desdemona – modern dress (leather jacket, smart trousers and blouse, gilet, vests)
Officials wearing cream suits – no ties, official yet relaxed
Guns
Computers
Handkerchief
Beer cans
Army hats and equipment

<u>Sound/music</u>
Opening rock/electric guitar style music
Loud, modern music (Act 2 Scene 3)
'Soldier's' chant (Act 2 Scene 3)
Guitar music to underscore ('Hell and Night must bring … Iago Act 1 Scene 3)
Guitar music/mixed with sound of helicopter and dock door opening (Act 2 Scene 1)

<u>Audience</u>
Mixed/lots of tourists
Lots of school groups
Full/sell out
Mix of ages of audience
Audience watched quietly but reacted to moments of comedy (Cassio's 'drunk' lines)
Sense of shock at blood and gunshots at the end of the play
Act 4 Scene 1 – the audience response to Iago's 'Work on my medicine' (with his glass)
Clear understanding of the classical text

Glossary

Fourth wall
An imaginary wall at the front of the stage that the audience 'sees' through, usually when the stage is set in a traditional proscenium arch.

Aside
Lines spoken by an actor to the audience and not supposed to be overheard by other characters on stage.

Soliloquy
A speech in which an actor, usually alone on stage, speaks the inner thoughts of their character aloud.

This example uses a little under 400 words, so is around the amount of space available. There are some elements that are more in-depth than others (lighting and audience, for example), though this is perhaps the nature of this particular performance. So how might a student convert these notes into a written response? Some examples based on these notes can be found below.

Turning your notes into a written response

Now you have made your notes, you will need to think clearly about how you will turn these into evaluation and analysis.

> **Top tip**
>
> Remember:
>
> - analysis is picking out key ideas or concepts and being able to say how these were explored by the director, performers or designers
>
> - evaluation is you forming a judgement about whether an idea or performance element has worked or not with effective supporting evidence.

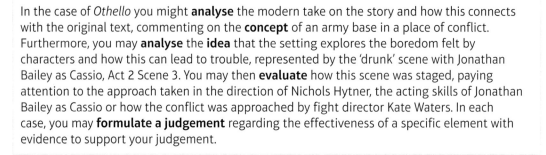

> **Taking it further**
>
> In the case of *Othello* you might **analyse** the modern take on the story and how this connects with the original text, commenting on the **concept** of an army base in a place of conflict. Furthermore, you may **analyse** the **idea** that the setting explores the boredom felt by characters and how this can lead to trouble, represented by the 'drunk' scene with Jonathan Bailey as Cassio, Act 2 Scene 3. You may then **evaluate** how this scene was staged, paying attention to the approach taken in the direction of Nichols Hytner, the acting skills of Jonathan Bailey as Cassio or how the conflict was approached by fight director Kate Waters. In each case, you may **formulate a judgement** regarding the effectiveness of a specific element with evidence to support your judgement.

An example of how analysis and evaluation might read in an answer may be as follows. To help: 'analysis' has been coloured **blue** and 'evaluation' orange.

Sample answer that uses analysis and evaluation using *Othello*

In *Othello* at the Olivier Theatre, it was clear that the character of Iago was well thought out and had depth in the interpretation given to the character through Rory Kinnear's portrayal. His use of voice, for example, showed a distinct use of tonality to show a vulgarity in the way that he referred to Othello as a 'barbarous horse' in Act 1 Scene 1. Kinnear made use of a slight speech impediment, giving Iago a slight tick in the way that he spoke his lines, particularly in front of Othello. This added to the devious nature of the role and worked well in creating a 'Machiavellian' side to the character as we, the audience, would see Kinnear delivering a speech with great power and clarity ('I hate the Moor' in Act 1 Scene 3) and then stuttering on his words as he spoke to Othello in Act 3 Scene 1 'Defend from jealousy'. Kinnear coupled his use of facial expressions and gesture with his vocal **tone** at this point to convey the character clearly to the audience. It must be said that this worked effectively, grabbing the attention of those watching as the character developed throughout the performance to become a hateful and hated role, which was in no small part down to the devious portrayal of Iago.

> **Glossary**
>
> **Tone**
> Choice of the mood or emotion of delivery.

The sample answer above shows a student analysing and evaluating the performance they have seen and there are examples of good practice for both the AS and A level specification. The student has used the performer's name, and there are specific moments mentioned with the use of quotes from the text in support. Most importantly, and in keeping with this section, there is a balance between evaluation and analysis without being too descriptive.

There are various ways to structure your notes and how you do this will depend on personal choice. The following student response, on a National Theatre production of *Othello*, is an example of how you could use your notes to form an extended written response.

Rory Kinnear as Iago delivering the 'I hate the Moor' speech outlined in the extract on the previous page.

Examples of writing a response

Theatre evaluation – example 1 with a written response

The naturalistic acting style in Nicholas Hytner's production of *Othello* was evident, particularly with Rory Kinnear's interpretation of Iago who used subtle gestures and vocal tonality when manipulating Othello in Act 3 Scene 3. His delivery of 'Beware of Jealousy' was underplayed vocally yet still powerful …' (based on acting style).

John Clark's lighting design often provided the audience with a clear vision of what was happening on stage and where the scene was set but also seemed to underscore what was happening on stage – made clear by the use of darkness and spotlights as Rory Kinnear's Iago schemed in the shadows with Tom Robertson's Roderigo in Act 4 Scene 2 … (based on lighting).

The set designed by Vicky Mortimer really captured successfully the idea that this was a temporary military base with the prefabricated offices and social spaces making the audience believe that this really could be Afghanistan … (based on set/stage).

The use of military weapons and guns in Vicky Mortimer's design added to the naturalistic style of the piece and complemented the costume that clearly set this piece in a modern-day context. Every prop seemed well thought out and this was certainly evident when … (based on costume/props).

Gareth Fry's use of electric guitar music to link the scenes together really added to the dark style of the piece, opening the whole production with a sharp tone, which gave the audience a sense of what was to come … (based on sound/music).

The audience laughed at certain moments, which seemed to go against the convention that this was a tragedy. This was evident during Act 4 Scene 1 where Rory Kinnear (as Iago) took a sip of water while Adrian Lester's Othello lay fainted on the floor. This moment was played quite callously by Kinnear, who seemed to show how Iago had no empathy at all for Othello and yet the audience laughed, perhaps almost in disbelief at … (based on audience). It must be said that this worked effectively, grabbing the attention of those watching as the character developed throughout the performance to become a hateful and hated role, which was in no small part down to the devious portrayal of Iago.

Top tip

You will notice how exact scene numbers and quotes from the text are used to highlight a key moment. This is very important, as both the AS and A level exams ask students to reference key moments in their answers. Using lines or scenes from the text enables you to be specific with your answer.

AS level exam guidance

In order to answer Section A for AS level, you will need to focus on one or two elements in more depth. If the AS paper asks you to look at 'costume' for example, you may use more of your 'costume' notes.

You will notice that in the above response, not all elements were spoken about. Although you will cover all elements in your notes for both AS and A level, the way you answer Section A at both levels will differ slightly.

Another way of structuring notes is as follows.

Theatre evaluation notes – key performance values and key moments – example 2

Othello at the National Theatre in the Olivier Theatre on 4 October 2013

Key Moments

Act 1 Scene 1

Lighting inside and out/use of prop/set with pub sign/sound design uses busy interior of pub/modern stage and costume/Iago and Roderigo in modern-day 'civvies'./Scene opens with sharp guitar sound/underscoring/something sinister about the effect/audience see Iago's early plans to get to Othello through Brabantio/Rory Kinear as Iago/use of very strong southern (London) accent/slight facial tick/masculine interpretation of role/Tom Robertson as Roderigo/plays him as easily led and naïve/almost comic/believes what Iago says/sense of rank suggested/asserts Iago's authority through use of space.

Act 1 Scene 3

Senator's scene with Othello. Boardroom-type design/modern papers/ sandwiches/ Starbucks cup/characters in suits/mainly men though one female actress/suggests modern day high-powered/(suggestions of politics). Lighting natural if a little low/suggests late-night meeting. William Chubb as Brabantio/plays distracted character/lots of pacing up and down/nervous twitches/faces away from Adrian Lester (Othello). Lester's voice is strong/movement committed/passionate delivery/ convincing/audience engrossed. Othello impressive/wins the argument.

Act 2 Scene 1

Othello arrives in Cyprus. Stark overhead lighting/smoke/suggest dock/landing strip/ helicopter sound/dock door opening sound/military clothing and set. Othello embrace with Desdemona/sense of love. Sense of overseas

Act 2 Scene 3

Cassio drunk. In army base, common room/beer cans/loud music/party atmosphere (R and R)/blue wash and spotlight/Iago plans. Noisy/physical. Soldiers sing/chant, rhythmic/shots of alcohol/builds up, believable fight (well choreographed). Moment of comedy (Cassio) with 'this is my left' and audience laugh. Adrian Lester imposes authority/angry vocals and strong physicality.

Act 4 Scene 1

Set in toilets. Othello finally loses it with Desdemona. Literally green with jealousy (sick in the cubicle). Physicality and movement effective/believable faint from Othello. Iago's stillness/use of prop: glass of water moment/audience laugh (seems strange), strong/ emotional commitment throughout.

Act 5 Scene 2

Use of lighting with candle dark. Othello appears from the shadows. Desdemona in white vest and shorts. Othello in stripped down army uniform/very quiet on stage. Adrian Lester psychological dilemma/anxiety of Othello/on the edge. Olivia Vinall as Desdemona/fear through struggling to get free/high-pitched vocals/screaming (too much?)/use of props and blood/audience shocked.

This example uses 327 words so allows space for labelled diagrams of the stage space, for example. It uses key scenes and then (in this case) extended notes to outline what happened at those moments. This makes the transition from notes to prose a little easier, but perhaps doesn't cover as many of the elements that the first structure does. Some examples of how the notes are turned into a response are below.

Theatre evaluation – example 2 with a written response

The naturalistic acting style in Nicholas Hytner's production of *Othello* was evident with the opening of the play, where a 'pub' scene was set up through an imaginative set design from Vicky Mortimer, who managed to convey a sense of the soldiers being 'on leave' through their 'civvie' costume of smart, modern suits. This, coupled with Rory Kinnear's use of a very modern vocal delivery, placing Iago in the modern-day South of England, immediately convinced the audience that this was a modern-day reworking of a classic text … (based on notes for Act 1 Scene 1).

The production took a political turn in Act 1 Scene 3, with Vicky Mortimer's set creating a boardroom environment, with plates of sandwiches and branded coffee cups seeming to suggest that this was a long and important meeting. William Chubb's portrayal of Brabantio in the scene was effective in conveying the character's discomfort and distraction at the news that his daughter had been secretly married. He paced and fidgeted with anxious and tense facial expressions. Nicholas Hytner's direction here, with Chubb (Brabantio) facing away from Adrian Lester (Othello) showed a very effective sense of **proxemics** as … (based on Act 1 Scene 3).

A moment of impressive collaboration between the performers, director and designers was Act 2 Scene 1, where Othello arrives in Cyprus. The use of stark floodlighting in Jon Clarke's design, along with the sounds of helicopters and a large mechanical door opening (through Gareth Fry's sound design), completely set the scene of this being a military base. This was extended by Adrian Lester's facial expressions and body language as Othello, which conveyed complete joy and relief as he embraced Olivia Vinall's Desdemona … (based on Act 2 Scene 1).

In Act 2 Scene 3, the audience were presented with a believable scene of drunken debauchery as Iago's plan to get Cassio drunk unfolded. Jon Clark's lighting design made use of a blue wash and spotlight on Iago outside of the room, which created a shadowy atmosphere and a foreshadowing of what was about to come. The army base and 'mess' room had a 'party' atmosphere as though the soldiers were on R and R, with Vicky Mortimer's design choices cleverly creating the scene with beer cans and a beatbox, which played Gareth Fry's modern, rhythmic music … (based on Act 2 Scene 3).

The scene where Adrian Lester as Othello finally seemed to have been overtaken by jealousy was staged in an interesting way by Nicholas Hytner. The director had Lester and Kinnear discussing Desdemona's supposed adultery in a men's toilet. Vicky Mortimer had created a set that was totally believable, with cubicle doors, mirrors and stainless steel finishes to the space. This allowed Lester to become literally 'green with envy' as he was sick after believing that Cassio 'knew' his wife. The audience response to Lester's faint and Kinnear's relaxed response was very interesting as there was laughter at a very tense point. I am unsure about whether this worked as … (based on Act 4 Scene 1).

Perhaps the pinnacle of tension within *Othello* came in Act 5 Scene 2, where Othello makes plans and then kills Desdemona. The atmosphere created by Jon Clark's blackout and single use of a candle was terrific in building tension and a sense of the unknown within the audience. Adrian Lester managed to convey the psychological turmoil that Othello finds himself in before he commits the deed, with a brilliant delivery of a soliloquy, which was noticeable for the use of dynamic in his voice, which was so quiet that the audience almost leant in to hear more … (based on Act 5 Scene 2).

Glossary

Proxemics
Spatial relationships – that is, how the distances between characters or the distance between characters and set/objects can convey information to the audience.

You will notice from these responses that the answers are fairly general, commenting on a number of production values that contribute to the key moments. Of course, in the real exam you will need to make sure you use your notes as an aid to answering the question. Examiners will be looking for answers that respond to the question at AS level and the statement at A level. Next, we will look at a way of approaching a question at AS level and a statement-based question at A level using writing frames/structures that might help you to make sure you are responding to the statement and **not providing a prepared answer**.

Structuring your response to exam questions

Structuring an answer for AS level

Look at the sample exam question below (you saw this on page 2). Below is a plan of how you might structure an answer to this question. Make sure you remember to look at the key words in the question to help you focus your answer.

AS level exam question

Analyse and evaluate the contribution of the **costume designer** and their use of colour in the performance you have seen.

In your answer you should consider:

- key moments in the performance

- your response as an informed member of the audience.

Your answer must give **balanced consideration** between your analysis **and** your evaluation.

(16 marks)

Introduction
This question asks you to look at the contribution of the costume designer to the play you have seen, focusing particularly on the use of colour. In the introduction you should cover an overall analysis and evaluation of the costume and use of colour as a whole, giving details of the different elements that you will focus on. It is important to give your own view in this opening.
Paragraph 1
Begin to explain your view with supported analysis of one of the elements – perhaps costume colour to emphasise character, for example. You should use a key moment to highlight your analysis. End the paragraph with some evaluation and return to the question. Remember that your response is that of an informed member of the audience.
Paragraph 2
Use a new paragraph to focus on a different element – perhaps the designer's intentions through their use of colour – and whether they were achieved. Again, you should use a key moment to highlight your analysis. As with paragraph 1, tie up the paragraph with evaluative comments and return to the question.
Paragraphs 3, 4 and so on …
Continue using the same structure as for paragraphs 1 and 2, but use each new paragraph to focus on a different element of the costume – for example, the visual effect of the costume, the use of materials or the way the costume helped to set the mood or historical context.
Conclusion
Draw your ideas together and come back to the question, repeating your overall view. Remember to use 'I' in your conclusion, as your answer should be a personal response.

Structuring an answer for A level

Look at the sample exam question below (you saw this on page 2). Below is a plan of how you might structure an answer to this question. Make sure you remember to look at the key words in the question and refer to at least two different theatre makers in your response.

A level exam question

Analyse and evaluate the live performance you have seen in light of the following statement:

'Live performance has nothing to say to a young audience'.

Your answer should:

- include analysis and evaluation of key moments from the performance you have seen and the contribution made by different theatre makers

- offer **balanced consideration** between your analysis and evaluation of the performance and your response to the statement.

(20 marks)

Introduction

The A level question above asks you to respond to the thought-provoking statement, 'Live performance has nothing to say to a young audience'. Therefore, your introduction should engage with the statement as a whole, giving details of the different elements that you will draw on to support your response. It is important to give your own view in this opening. The statement should be at the heart of your answer.

Paragraph 1

You should begin to explain your response to the statement, with supported and balanced analysis and evaluation that draw on your understanding of drama terminology. You should refer to a theatre maker's contribution to the performance and you might use a key moment to highlight your analysis. End the paragraph with some evaluation and return to the statement.

Paragraph 2

Use a new paragraph to focus on a different area from paragraph 1, perhaps a different theatre maker. Analyse another key moment and aim to be as perceptive as possible. As with the first paragraph, tie up the paragraph with evaluative comments and return to the statement.

Paragraphs 3, 4 and so on …

Continue using the same structure as for paragraphs 1 and 2, but use each new paragraph to focus on a different element not already covered – for example, the visual effect of a design element, such as costume or lighting. You might also broaden your answer to comment on the overall aims and intentions of the production, but it is essential that your response to the initial statement is at the heart of your answer.

Conclusion

Draw your ideas together and come back to the statement, repeating your overall response. Remember to use 'I' in your conclusion, as your answer should be a personal response.

Preparing for your exam

Section A: AS level sample answers with commentaries

Analyse and evaluate the contribution of the set designer and their use of different materials in the performance you have seen. In your answer you should consider:

- key moments in the performance
- your response as an informed member of the audience.

Your answer must give balanced consideration between your **analysis** and your **evaluation**.　　　**(16 marks)**

Student A

The set design for the National Theatre production of *Othello* was very effective in showing that this was a foreign country such as Afghanistan, which was a good way of presenting 'Cyprus' to the audience. There were many ways that this was shown and this included the army base, the offices and the bedroom that Desdemona was eventually murdered in. I will look at how the set was used to add to the overall atmosphere of the production.

← *This opening is quite general in style, though it does show some understanding of the play as a whole and how the set fits with the context of this particular production.*

The set worked well in the first scene where Iago is speaking to Roderigo outside of the pub. This is good in showing the audience that this play is set in the modern day and that the characters are typical soldiers having 'off-duty' time in the pub together. I liked the set here as it allowed the audience to see straight away that Iago was planning and scheming as the conversation with Roderigo happened in the dark shadows outside the noisy bar.

← *This section shows that Student A has an understanding of the plot and characters with a sense of how the set design has contributed to this moment in the production. The evaluation and analysis is present but is not fully developed or explored.*

The scene where the set worked very effectively was the moment when Othello arrives in Cyprus. During this moment, there was a huge metal door and lighting shining down on a large area of stage. This looked like an army base, especially with the sound of a large door opening and helicopter landing. This all worked together to make you think you really were in a country like Afghanistan waiting for the army general to arrive.

← *Again, understanding of context is present here as is an attempt to incorporate other elements such as sound design. Student A has made an evaluative comment at the start but this is not followed through in the remainder of the paragraph, which again feels underdeveloped.*

Overall, the set helped the production to work well when the set changed between scenes. The transitions were effective as they allowed the scenes to flow from one moment to the next and this made the production very dramatic in places.

← *As a closing paragraph this lacks detail and depth of analysis and evaluation. Student A shows they have appreciated the contribution the set has made to the production and there is some use of subject-specific terminology.*

Commentary

Student A has given a fairly weak personal response, but does show some sense of how the set has contributed to the production as a whole. Examples from the production are given, which is good practice and shows that the student is responding to a live performance rather than a play text, which is vital for Section A. Evaluation and analysis is quite general in places, lacking the depth and detail to take it to a higher level, with statements made but reasoning and justification lacking to support the points given.

To improve this answer, the student would need to:

- show a more comprehensive understanding of the contribution of the designer in connection with the other elements of the play
- elaborate on evaluative comments, providing examples from the production to support and justify points made
- write in more detail about the set and production, making use of subject-specific terminology to support this.

Student B

Vicky Mortimer's set design in the National Theatre production of *Othello* was evidently well thought out and showed a distinct understanding of the naturalistic approach from director Nicholas Hytner. Each element of the set was well thought out, including the materials used, which were detailed and precise and made the performance more believable. Perhaps the most important contribution made by Mortimer's design was the ability to set the context of the modern Afghan conflict with the British army. This was achieved through a use of materials, style and colour, which I believe worked extremely effectively, particularly in key moments in the performance.

This opening is strong as it immediately offers a sense of the student seeing the contribution of the design in a wider context, connecting it with the style and approach of the director. This introduction shows a balance of analysis and evaluation as well as outlining the points that Student B will use to support their response.

The most striking aspect of the set was the use of a 'prefabricated' army base, most notable in Act 2 Scene 1 when Adrian Lester as Othello arrives in 'Cyprus'. The set immediately made the context believable as this looked like a temporary base similar to those we have seen in the media recently with the Afghan and Iraq conflicts, for example. The set was clever as the use of recognisable 'flat pack' walls and furniture made me realise straight away that this was only a temporary arrangement, as well as setting the play firmly in the modern day.

Student B is making distinct reference to specific scenes as well as making comments on the use of materials, which is important as the question asks for this. Again, there is a comprehensive sense of the context of the play and its modern-day setting.

I felt that the set worked best when reflecting the mood of the scene. In Act 1 Scene 2, for example, Mortimer had created a 'board room' scene with take-away coffee cups, dark maple-wood desks and expensive art work on the wall. This worked effectively as it affected the mood of the scene, which was serious as Adrian Lester as Othello proved his love for Desdemona. In contrast to this, in Act 2 Scene 3, where Rory Kinnear as Iago gets Jonathan Bailey (Cassio) drunk, the set is relaxed, representing the social area for the soldiers. There were revealing calendars on the wall, cheap plastic chairs and cans of lager scattered around the space. The use of set and materials therefore worked well in reflecting the environment and atmosphere in the play.

Student B is able to make detailed and vivid connections with the play, picking out key moments and reflecting an understanding of the themes and issues present in the performance.

I was not always convinced with the quality of the set and whether it was believable. An example for me was during Act 5 Scene 2 where there was an obvious commotion in Desdemona's bedroom. Here, with a murder about to take place, I felt that the design of the very thin walls meant that the delay in help arriving seemed to betray the authenticity of the set, which in most of the production helped to convey the naturalistic style.

There is an effective use of evaluation here with clear justification in the context of this production. Subject-specific vocabulary is also present, with Student B aware of the style of the play and how the set design supports this.

An element that worked particularly well in the set design was the ability of Mortimer to produce a design and use materials that almost symbolised the masculinity present in this particular production. An example of this is the decision to set Act 4 Scene 1 in the men's toilets. This immediately gave the scene a masculine feel as well as making the conversation between Kinnear and Lester (Iago and Othello) seem private. The masculinity was cleverly developed through the use of a hard, cold stainless steel mirror and sink, which Lester leaned on as he punched a hole in the wall in anger as he failed to control his jealousy. The dented metal and hole in the wall seemed to represent the holes in Othello and Desdemona's relationship as well as Othello's character, as Kinnear as Iago taunted 'is again to cope your wife'.

> Student B shows some particularly effective analysis of the set design, again providing scene numbers and exact lines of text to support their analysis. There is an understanding of characterisation and relationships, and a clear outline of how the set connects with the play as a whole.

Commentary

Student B has provided a strong response to the question that goes to the heart of what is being asked. The student places the set design firmly in the context of the play, as well as in the chosen context in this particular production.

There is a strong awareness of the text and there are well-developed and relevant examples provided to support a balance of analysis and evaluation.

The student has recognised the contribution of the designer and her collaboration with the director, and this is illustrated by the use of the names of each theatre maker. Though this isn't a requirement in the criteria, it is good practice and shows an overall awareness of this being an evaluation of a live theatre production rather than a play text.

There is also relevant use of some appropriate terminology to support evaluative comments.

This is a response that shows a detailed understanding of the live production with a clear sense that it is the answer of an informed audience member.

Section A: A level sample answers with commentaries

Analyse and evaluate the live performance you have seen in light of the following statement:

'Live performance today is more concerned with entertaining an audience than it is with making them think.'

Your answer should:

- include analysis and evaluation of key moments from the performance you have seen and the contribution made by different theatre makers
- offer **balanced consideration** between your analysis and evaluation of the performance and your response to the statement.

(20 marks)

Student A

The production of *Othello* at the National Theatre was very entertaining as the army setting really helped the audience to understand what they were watching. This worked well as the audience could see that this was the modern day and not an ancient, typical Shakespearian setting. This means that the live performance we saw did focus very much on entertaining the audience as it chose to bring the performance into the modern day and we could relate to it and therefore enjoy what we were watching.

> This opening does mention the statement, which is good practice. There is also a recognition of the audience response that is relevant to the question. However, the example given regarding the setting is not developed and there is little coverage of the contribution of theatre makers. There is a slight imbalance in the argument in response to the statement, with a lack of reasoning and examples to support this. This does not help to justify Student A's response to the statement.

Another entertaining part of *Othello* was the use of costume design as it was really effective in showing the characters and their place in the play. Othello and Iago wore army costumes, with Othello looking to be a higher rank with the different badges on his costume. They also wore green berets so the audience could see that they were representing the British army. When the characters such as Cassio were not on duty, they wore green khaki t-shirts, which showed that they were relaxed and not actually working on the army base. Desdemona also wore white at the end of the play, which showed that she was innocent and hadn't been unfaithful to Othello, despite his jealous rage in this scene. She also seemed very high status as she was always dressed well, in expensive and modern-looking clothing. This was also shown in the second scene where Brabrantio (Desdemona's father) and his advisers wore smart and expensive-looking costumes.

> There is the sense of a prepared answer here and while Student A starts off by mentioning the 'entertaining' aspect to connect with the statement, this is not followed through. Instead, this becomes a more generalised paragraph about the use of costume in the production rather than the impact of the costume on 'entertaining' the audience or 'making them think'. Characters and scenes are mentioned but are not specific, and using actual scene numbers, for example, would help here.

The acting performances in *Othello* were excellent. Othello was very strong and believable in the way that he used facial expressions and a loud voice, which could be heard by everyone in the theatre. Othello was good in making the audience see his jealousy growing and he became more agitated and angry as the play went on. A moment where this worked well was when he fainted in the toilets with Iago. This was very clever as it looked so real and showed how much the jealousy had got to him. He used his body and gestures really well and you really believed that he was unconscious, which must have been difficult for the actor. Othello also worked really well when he said the line 'Arise dark vengeance' during Act 3 Scene 3 as he was crying at this point, and this was very emotional and moving for the audience who were watching at this point. Othello seemed to have really lost control in this scene and this was because of the good acting used to show the character.

> This is a mixed paragraph as it shows some good practice as well as some areas for development. There is a sense of a personal response here with Student A obviously impressed and moved by the performance. The use of key moments from the production are supported with a quote and scene number, which is useful. This is not consistent though and the 'fainted' example is less developed. As with the previous paragraph, there is a sense that this is a prepared section with no mention of the statement in the answer. There is some basic use of vocabulary (though this could be developed in places), particularly when responding to acting skills used in the performance.

I liked the use of the 'handkerchief' in the performance and this was a key moment in the play as this was how Iago managed to put his plans into practice and really convince Othello that Desdemona was having an affair with Cassio. This was because the handkerchief was really important to Othello as his mother had given it to him and he had then given it to Desdemona. The scene where Othello asked Desdemona for the handkerchief was very good as you could see how important the handkerchief was to Othello as he was so angry when he was asking her where it was. You could also see that Desdemona was confused by how angry he was as she used facial expressions and her voice to show that she was innocent. This made the handkerchief seem more than just a small gift and showed how important the prop was in the story of *Othello*.

> Student A shows knowledge of the play here, but there is a sense of reporting the plot rather than really focusing on how entertaining the live performance was. Examples are given about how the scene was played, but these are very generalised rather than responding to the statement.

Overall I would say that the performance was very entertaining as the audience could relate to and enjoyed many of the scenes that they saw. The acting was very good and the design was also effective in showing the setting of the play of *Othello*. The decision to set the play in a modern-day setting, like a war zone, meant that this was a modern performance that the audience could understand and so they could watch an old play like *Othello* but see how it could work today. This meant that the performance was very entertaining in every part of the play and I really enjoyed watching *Othello* at the National Theatre.

> The final paragraph here does attempt to respond to the statement, though not in any great depth – there is no mention of the performance 'making people think', for example. This is a very personal response and although the paper is looking for a personal response, Student A has given a personal opinion without full justification or support.

Commentary

Student A has offered a very personal response, although it is clear that they enjoyed and were engaged with the performance of *Othello*. However, opinions are offered with a lack of precise examples and a balance in evaluation. Analysis is offered but is too general in responding to the question – exact scene numbers would help here, as would the contribution of different theatre makers. There is a sense of a prepared answer with notes being repeated in the response rather than engaging with the statement, which is mentioned but is not fully discussed. To improve this answer, the student would need to:

- respond to the statement throughout the answer; the statement should be at the heart of each point made
- elaborate on analytical comments, providing examples from the production to support and justify points made as well as reflecting on the contribution of different theatre makers
- make sure that evaluative comments are well supported with examples from the production and a balanced argument that draws on theatrical knowledge.

Student B

Having seen the National Theatre production of *Othello,* I would argue that Nicholas Hytner aimed to create a production that entertained the audience and made them think. This was evident by a setting that the audience would know and understand through the use of a modern-day 'war zone', which would resonate with an audience that is aware of places such as Afghanistan and Iraq. The decision to take a classical text and place it in a setting that could represent modern-day conflict is quite a brave decision by Hytner and the National Theatre and I believe argues against the statement as this was a thought-provoking performance no matter how entertaining it was for the audience.

> This is a very strong opening that immediately responds to the statement. There is a personal feel to the response, which shows that Student B has engaged with the statement and the live performance they have seen. The opinion offered is backed up with examples from the production, which shows a full awareness of the whole context of the production.

Through the use of modern-day media, the audience would have access to images of conflicts today. The Iraq, Afghanistan and Libyan military interventions by the British armed forces would be in the consciousness of the audience watching *Othello*. Today – 'Cyprus' could easily be 'Camp Bastion', for example. This was achieved through a collaboration with designer Vicky Mortimer, who had created a set and costume that the audience would recognise from images on television. The prefabricated army base had a temporary appearance and was in keeping with an overseas base rather than a permanent site. The collaboration of theatre makers with director Nicholas Hytner was very clear in Act 2 Scene 1 when Othello arrives in Cyprus. Hytner had staged the actors in a way that made them seem anxious as they waited for Othello's arrival – the theme here of arrivals in foreign lands certainly made me think about how it must be for British forces in strange and different lands. This allowed me to understand *Othello* in a modern context and not just see it as an ancient play – it made me reflect on the themes of journeys and war, which would clearly indicate that this production made the audience think as well as entertaining them.

> This is a strong paragraph which extends the introduction. There are specific examples used and Student B has covered the contribution of different theatre makers to the overall production. Once again, the wider context of the performance is covered and a key moment is used to exemplify the comments of the student. The extract ends by responding to the statement; again this is very important when responding to Section A in the A level paper.

The performance was very entertaining and I believe that the naturalistic style added to an almost 'filmic' form. This was very clear in Act 2 Scene 3 when Jonathan Bailey as Cassio became drunk. This was a humorous as well as aggressive scene, with excellent fight direction from Kate Waters. This, combined with Gareth Fry's sound design of upbeat music to suggest a party atmosphere, created a sense of chaos on stage and was very entertaining for the audience, particularly as we could see where this might lead as the characters drank cans of beer and became even more inebriated as the scene progressed. I believe that the collaboration here provided a naturalistic setting that was perhaps more about entertaining the audience than making them think.

> This takes a different viewpoint, agreeing with the statement, which offers some balance to the response. The example given is relevant to the argument and draws on the contribution of different theatre makers. There is detail on how the scene worked in performance, showing that Student B has engaged with the production and the statement.

Although I found the performance entertaining, there were a number of scenes that worked particularly well in challenging the audience to think about the themes being presented. Nicholas Hynter made use of a naturalistic style, which meant that the acting style was particularly believable and psychological in the characterisation portrayed. This was certainly shown in Rory Kinnear's delivery of Iago's 'I hate the Moor' speech during Act 1 Scene 3. Kinnear was able to connect with the character's intense jealousy, envy and hatred for Othello in a way that sent shivers down the spine of the audience as Iago became even more venomous at this moment. This intense acting and directorial style was quite brilliant at moving the audience to think about just how far these emotions can push a person and their resulting behaviour. Kinnear's performance was so 'real' that at this moment you couldn't help but think about the production and relationships within.

Following on from the previous paragraph, Student B has provided further balance to the argument in response to the statement. This particular example is specific and makes use of subject-specific vocabulary to support the argument. There is a personal style to this paragraph which shows the student has engaged with the performance seen. This confirms that Student B is responding to a live theatre production rather than a play text.

Commentary

This is a strong answer with the statement at the heart of the response. Student B has engaged with the performance seen and there is a personal style, which works well. The contribution of theatre makers is very present, with key moments used and detailed elaboration to support arguments. The wider context of the production is evident throughout, and it is clear that this candidate has understood and engaged with the question and the live performance seen.

SECTION B Page to stage: Realising a performance text

Overview

This section will explore how you can approach a performance text in order to bring it to life. This means you will need to be thoroughly familiar with the performance text in order to make it work in terms of acting and staging. As you read through the information that follows, you will learn how to search for meaning within a text, and how you can enhance that meaning through performance and design. You will also need to be:

- aware of a range of methods of working both as a performer and a designer
- able to explain how to put these into practice.

The world of the play

Playwrights use the possibilities of live theatre that writers of other forms can't use. The playwright is aware that the play will only come to life when it is performed. And, throughout this section, this will become your task. One approach is to read your performance text in as many ways as you can – alone, in groups, in class. Thoroughly knowing your text will be invaluable in your exam.

Look at the front cover of the performance text. Assuming there is a picture or illustration, what impression does this give you of the play? Now use the following as a checklist as you read the whole text.

- Note the list of characters. In your head, sort out the family relationships and groups, age differences and genders.
- Look out for any information about the setting in time and place. If there are details about the setting, try to visualise it. (It can help to draw a stage plan, giving a bird's-eye view.)
- Take it steadily. Try to hear the dialogue in your head. To get the full impact, it can help to read some parts out loud.
- Read the stage directions carefully. Sometimes reading them two or three times is a good idea. Some playwrights give more information in these than others, but whatever is there will help.
- Look out for details on time gaps between scenes and changes in setting. The time of day can be important. Changes in costume, and the introduction and removal of props can all be significant. Sometimes there are sequences of movement that have dramatic power.
- Visualise the characters as well as the settings.
- Go back and check the text, if you need to. It is easy to lose track of details, or even characters in a large-cast play.
- When you've finished, give yourself a few minutes' reflection. What was the effect on you? Did certain scenes move you? Did you feel sympathy for some characters and not others? You may want to make some notes about your impression of the performance text.
- Look back to the front cover illustration. Now that you know the performance text, does it seem appropriate?

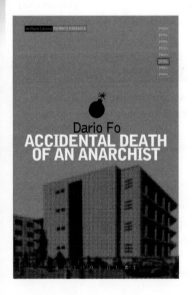

The exam paper

For both AS and A level specifications, Assessment Objective three (**AO3**) is the focus of this section for the examination in Component 2 for AS level and Component 3 for A level.

> **Exam tip**
>
> Your teacher tells the exam board in advance which text you have been studying and you must answer on this text even if you have read or seen one of the other plays on this list.

(AO3) is: Demonstrate knowledge and understanding of how drama and theatre is developed and performed.

In both the AS level and A level exams, you will be answering two questions based on an unseen extract from the performance text you have studied.

- One question will ask you to approach the text as a performer.
- The other question will ask you to approach the text as a designer.

Although these questions are similar in tone and structure, their specific demands are different and the clue to finding the focus of the question will be through the key words used in the question. Below are examples of the sorts of questions you may be asked.

> **AS level exam question (performer)**
>
> As a **performer**, discuss how you might **interpret** and **portray one of the key roles** in the extract. You should use examples from the extract to support your ideas and your answer should make reference to the performance text as a whole. **(16 marks)**

> **AS level exam question (designer)**
>
> As a **designer**, discuss how you would **use theatrical elements** to create **mood and atmosphere** in the extract. You should use examples from the extract to support your ideas and make reference to the performance text as a whole. **(16 marks)**

> **A level exam question (performer)**
>
> As a **performer**, outline how you would use **voice** to create an **impact on the audience** in the **portrayal of one character** in this extract. Your answer should make reference to the performance text as a whole. **(18 marks)**

> **A level exam question (designer)**
>
> As a **designer**, outline how **one theatrical element** could **be developed** to **contribute effectively** to the **impact** of the scene. Your answer should make reference to the performance text as a whole. **(18 marks)**

AS level exam guidance

Component 2 is worth 48 marks and up to 40% of the total AS level mark. Section B carries up to 32 marks in total and is based on how you can take a play from the page to a performance.

A level exam guidance

Component 3 is worth 80 marks and up to 40% of the total A level mark. Section B carries up to 36 marks and is based on how you can take a play from the page to a performance.

The set performance texts

Below is a list of possible set texts for both AS and A level students. You will study one of these texts.

- *Accidental Death of an Anarchist*, Dario Fo (English version by Gavin Richards)
- *Colder Than Here*, Laura Wade
- *Equus*, Peter Shaffer
- *Fences*, August Wilson
- *Machinal*, Sophie Treadwell
- *That Face*, Polly Stenham

Note: You are **not** allowed to take any of these texts into the exam room.

Approaching the text as a performer

This part of the exam doesn't require you to act or perform anything for the assessment. That said, you will need to work on your performance text in similar ways in order to understand fully the dynamics of preparation and performance that result in the finished product. How you work will be up to your teacher, but the following section suggests a variety of approaches and tools, some of which you can use individually and some as part of a group.

The five tools

A performer works with five basic tools, which need to be engaged to produce an appropriate performance:

- intellect (the thought process behind some of the performance decisions you make later)
- imagination
- feelings
- body
- voice.

You will need to work on all these tools consciously in order to let your unconscious work as you get into role. Each area can provide a stimulus that you can then integrate into a performance.

The five tools: Intellect

Individual preparation

Preparing individually using your intellect means being familiar with the text. This involves:

- reading it carefully
- trying to imagine how it will be on stage in performance.

You will also need to consider:

- Stanislavski's ideas of **given circumstances** and **objectives**
- research, and how to do it effectively.

Given circumstances

Exam questions may ask you to focus on the way particular roles are performed. When you start thinking about the characters in your performance text, it helps to be systematic. You could do this by making a full list of any relevant information a text gives you. This relates to Constantin Stanislavski's idea of given circumstances.

Glossary

Given circumstances
The total set of environmental and situational conditions that influence the actions undertaken by a character in a play.

Objectives
What the character wants, expressed as a desire – that is, 'I want …'

Note that what people say about your character, or what you say about yourself, may not be true. Characters say things in anger or frustration, for example, which they don't always mean. But it is important to note these down, as it shows something of the way they feel, even if it's only for a moment.

Top tip

Always read the stage directions carefully. They often contain very useful information. You can also assume that what they say is true, as they will have been written (in almost every case) by the playwright.

Exam tip

As well as being an essential preparation tool, a list like the one opposite can be very useful when revising.

Taking it further

Look at the student notes on Martin Dysart (*Equus*). Now take one of the minor characters in your performance text (if there are any) and copy and complete the sections for their character. You may not find a great deal of information, but it will help you to look for relevant information and familiarise yourself with the text.

ACTIVITY

Go through the script methodically from beginning to end, noting down the following information. Your notes might look like the student's notes below. To help personalise the character information, use 'I'/'my' rather than 'he' or 'she'.

- My character name.
- Facts about my character – age, gender, occupation, appearance, etc. (Do not be tempted to use opinions here. Stick to the facts.)
- What other characters say about me. (Write down the actual words they say.)
- What I say about other characters.
- What I say about myself.

Here's an example of what one student has written. (This is only part of what would be a much longer list.)

Character name: Martin Dysart (*Equus*) – page references to Penguin edition.

Facts about my character:

Age: mid-40s (page 17); smoker (page 17); psychiatrist in a provincial hospital working with young people (page 18).

Shares room with two other psychiatrists (page 19).

Married to Margaret, a Scottish dentist; no children (page 61).

What other characters say about me:

'You're this boy's only chance' (Hesther, page 20).

'You're a dear. You really are' (Hesther, page 21).

'You've done the most superb work with children' (Hesther, page 25).

'You ought to be locked up. Your bloody tricks' (Alan, page 79).

'Nosey Parker! That's all you are' (Alan, page 59).

What I say about other characters:

'She's turned into a Shrink. The familiar domestic monster: the Shrink's Shrink' (about his wife, Margaret, to Hesther, page 61).

'Old-type socialist, I'd say. Relentlessly self-improving' (about Frank Strang, to Hesther, page 28).

'You're really quite splendid' (to Hesther, page 63).

What I say about myself:

'The things is – I'm desperate' (monologue, page 18).

'The doubts have been here for years, piling up steadily in this dreary place' (monologue, page 18).

'I'd like to spend the next ten years wandering slowly around the real Greece' (to Hesther, page 25).

My wife doesn't understand me, Your Honour' (to Hesther, page 60).

'The finicky, critical husband looking through his art books on mythical Greece' (monologue, page 82).

'There's a village I spent one night in, where I'd like to live. It's all white' (to Alan, page 87).

Objectives

'Objectives' is another term from Stanislavski that has been widely adopted in the theatre. A character on stage always wants something. Objectives help the actor to define clearly in words what that 'something' is.

- There can be short-term objectives. For example, in a part of the first scene in *Fences*, Troy might have the objective 'I want to keep my relationship with Alberta a secret from Bono'.

- There can be 'through objectives' (sometimes called 'super objectives'), which last for the entire play. For example, Troy might have the through objective 'I want to have respect from everyone I know'.

Objectives usually meet with obstacles. These may be overcome or they may ultimately defeat the objective. Additionally, objectives should lead to action.

Exam tip

One of your objectives is to be successful in your exam! When preparing yourself for questions on the performance text extracts, it helps to consider the character's 'through objective'. This can be useful in linking the extract to the text as a whole – one of the things you may be required to do in the exam.

ACTIVITY

For the character you are focusing on, write down a clear 'through objective' that will keep them going throughout the performance text. It needs to be as precise as possible. Objectives like 'I want to be happy' are generally not much use to an actor. This is often a challenging exercise that helps you to think about the character more deeply.

Research, and how to do it

What will help you to understand and get a feeling for 'the world of the play'? Rather than start by researching the title on the internet, you could make a list of questions you think would be good to explore. Below are some suggestions, but there could be many more (not least because different plays need different approaches).

- What were the original performance conditions like? When the play was first staged, what kind of theatre was it presented in?

- What issues did the early reviews mention (if there are any)?

- What period does the play belong to?

- Is it associated with any particular style of theatre?

- Is it based on or inspired by any historical incident?

- If so, did the playwright change any details or add completely new ideas and characters?

- Are there contemporary issues or events that influenced the play?

- Does the play deal with any social or political issues directly or make use of them as a background?

- What would the costume, furniture and props have been like in the original performance?

Top tip

It is usually safe to assume that the original performance is close to the date of writing, but there are some exceptions, so make sure you check.

The internet is full of easily accessible information. Much of it is relevant and useful, but it may not always be reliable. So try to look for other sources of research material to stimulate ideas.

- **Books:** There are often books dedicated to playwrights and plays. Check your school or college library and search the database in your local library.
- **Reviews:** Most UK national newspapers that carry extensive reviews have an archive on their websites.
- **Introductions to play-texts:** Some editions have helpful introductions or commentaries.
- **Museums:** The Victoria and Albert Museum in London is an excellent resource, especially as it houses a 'Theatre and Performance' collection. Local museums can also be very useful.
- **The National Theatre:** This has an excellent archive at www.nationaltheatre.org.uk.
- **Databases:** Your school or college may subscribe to useful drama databases or magazines.

Taking it further

As you read your set text you may come across the styles of drama associated with different periods of time – for example, realism, naturalism, expressionism, sentimental comedy and farce (you will find definitions for these throughout this book). Try to read some short articles about these to understand the main principles and conventions of these styles.

Top tip

Plays will often have references to events, objects, places or ideas that you've not come across before. Check these, because the playwright has referred to them for a reason. For example, in Episode 6 of *Machinal*, the Young Woman says, 'I'll never get – below the Rio Grande'. If you don't know that the Rio Grande is a river that separates Mexico from the United States of America, you will miss the point of what she's saying.

Editions of plays that belong to earlier periods often have footnotes or notes at the end. Editions of modern plays don't usually have these, but internet research will often provide the answer. Remember, your teachers are also a useful resource.

ACTIVITY

When you are next reading a text, note down and check any vocabulary you are not familiar with. (If you're studying *Equus*, for example, you may not have come across the word 'abreact'.)

When you have a short list (up to ten words), ask a partner to test you. You could then test them.

Group work

Drama is a collaborative subject. You can achieve things in a group that you can't achieve by yourself. For example, you can divide up areas of research and share your findings in a group, discussing the relevance, importance and implications for performance of what you've discovered.

You can also compare and discuss the character information you have gained from the text, using your notes from the activity in 'Given circumstances' earlier in this section (page 28). In fact, you can agree to put together this information on different characters in your set performance text and then share it. You could also create a timeline.

Creating a timeline

A timeline is a helpful way to approach a text, and involves locating and ordering all the main events referred to. Some of these events may need to be given approximate dates. You could use the date the play was written or first performed to help. Below is a partially filled-in example, using *Fences* by August Wilson.

Date	Event
1904	Troy born in Alabama, one of 11 children
1911	Gabriel born
1912	Troy's mother leaves home
1914	Rose born
1918	Troy leaves home
1923	Lyons born (Troy's son by a previous marriage)
1923–38 (?)	Troy's years in the penitentiary; learns to play baseball
1939	Troy and Rose get married
1940	Cory born
1941–45	Gabriel wounded and brain-damaged in Japan (Second World War)
1957	Act 1 Scene 1
1957	Cory leaves home (after Act 2 Scene 1)
1957–8	(six months after previous scene) Act 2 Scene 2; Raynell born
1959	Cory joins US Marines
1961	Lyons splits up with Bonnie; Troy retires from work
1963	Lyons convicted of fraudulently cashing cheques
1965	Act 2 Scene 5 Troy's funeral

As you can see, this timeline helps to trace the history of the play and its characters. By simply reading through the events that involve Troy, you can begin to think in more detail about his life and the events that have shaped him.

The five tools: Imagination

Individual work

Having created a table of character information from your text (see 'Given circumstances' on pages 27 and 28 as a reminder), you will find there are things that must have happened that can't actually be located in the script. At this point, you can begin to use your imagination to fill in the gaps and develop your sense of the character.

- Your imagination will be working on a solid basis because you have a framework of other facts on which to build. In *Colder Than Here*, we learn quite a lot about Mark (Jenna's boyfriend whom we never see). If you were playing Jenna, you would need to build on this information to imagine Mark and your relationship with him.

In some plays there are off-stage characters who are referred to but never seen.

- In *Fences*, Alberta is a key character for Troy, but is never seen.
- The relationship between Hugh and his new wife in *That Face* is a factor in the play, but she is never seen.

Imagining scenes between characters that are seen with characters that aren't can lead to a fuller understanding of a character. Remember also to imagine the whole world of the play. Try to visualise the settings, the furniture, the props, the social settings and anything else that comes to mind.

ACTIVITY

Using a text you all know, as a group decide on who will work on which character. Individually, research your character and make notes. Then, as a group again, put together a timeline for the text. Your work on the timeline should be punctuated with discussions about the characters and their backgrounds.

ACTIVITY

Look for an important gap in the information in your 'character' table (like the limited information about Dysart's wife, Margaret, in *Equus*). Try to imagine scenes from the past that help to explain the nature of your character's feelings about the missing person/episode.

Try to visualise the setting for a scene from your text. First, try to imagine this as an actual physical scene, keeping the atmosphere of the text. Then try to imagine it on stage, getting a feel for how it might be achieved in production.

Group work

Group work on your text is essential to help build your understanding of a character and their world through the use of imagination. Discussion between group members can open up possibilities that you may not have thought about. Below you will find a range of activities that incorporates:

- improvisation

- imagination

- proxemics

- costumes and props

- set elements

- sound and light.

All of these can be very helpful when the issues that emerge are then discussed as a group.

The activities should be related to the performance text, if possible. All six texts for Section B are modern (late 20th and early 21st centuries), so improvising in language similar to that of the text is fairly straightforward.

As you attempt these practical exercises, keep an open mind and try not to be self-conscious. The more you explore your character and the more you can imagine the gaps in between what you actually know, the better your understanding and performance will be.

ACTIVITIES

IMPROVISATIONS

Try a range of improvisations. These are usually best done when everyone is reasonably familiar with the text and the characters. They can be ways of exploring the characters and their relationships in greater depth.

- **Hot-seating:** Select one person to get into character. Ask them questions about 'themselves'. Try to make the questions relevant to what you know. A discussion afterwards can ascertain which information was most useful for characterisation.

- **Conscience alley (or thought alley):** Choose a moment in the performance text that requires some significant decision. Select one person (in character) to walk down an 'alley' of other people. Those forming the alley give the character advice about the dilemma as he or she passes them.

- **Giving presents:** Imagine it's Christmas and the characters in the performance text are giving each other Christmas presents. You have to think about: a) your character; b) the character who's receiving the present; and c) your relationship with them. (The present is mimed, but the giver explains what it is.) You can then be asked by the group (out of character, while you remain in character) why you have chosen that particular present.

- **Home alone:** Set up a room used in the performance text (or possibly your character's own private room) with furniture and props, some of them personal (for example, books, a hand-mirror, letters). Then spend two minutes in your room being your character. (This needs some thought and preparation.) Discuss with your group what this has revealed to them about your character and what you have discovered.

IMAGINATION

- **Personal props:** Think about a personal prop your character might have, and think how they might use it. (These props are an excellent opportunity for spoken or silent improvisations. For example, in *Equus*, Alan uses a tape recorder.) As a group, discuss these and other props that may not already have been mentioned.

- **Letters and diaries:** Select a moment from the text that seems to you to be important. Write a letter or diary entry revealing your innermost thoughts about the situation and the other characters involved. At key points in your writing, the group should ask probing questions.

- **Prepared monologues:** Prepare a monologue for your character. Monologues give you the opportunity to explore the character's voice, speech characteristics and physical behaviour.

- **Subtext exercises:** Select moments or short scenes from your text. Play the scene, but also incorporate and play the thoughts of the characters before or after their lines.

PROXEMICS

For these exercises, you need to select a few key moments from the performance text and have access to an empty room (a drama studio is ideal).

- One character stands in the centre and the other characters position themselves around them in relation to how 'warm' or 'cold' they feel about them at that point. As you move chronologically through the text, you can chart the change in relationships. You can observe the differences between different scenes, and the way relationships develop and change. Discuss any outcomes. For example, there may be very different perceptions about the relationships.

- It is sometimes possible to substitute a prop or item of costume in the centre of the 'proxemics' circle, if the characters have a particular relationship with it. (The coffin in *Colder Than Here* would be an interesting example.)

> **Exam tip**
>
> Remember **proxemics** as a term and why it refers to something important in performance on stage. When you are responding to the extract from your set text in the exam you will find it useful to consider how the distances between characters convey information to the audience.

COSTUME AND PROPS

Think about how costume and props affect the characters in the text. As a group, make a list of ideas. Sometimes the use of an item of costume or a prop can make a surprising difference when going through the process of exploring the text. The bomb in *Accidental Death of an Anarchist* could be one; the baseball bat in *Fences* could be another.

SET ELEMENTS

Discuss how these could enhance your performance text. Even if you are not able to give a full production, it is useful to explore how your text could benefit from the addition of some elements of the set. Think about other examples you may have come across in other plays. For example, a rostrum could represent the porch in *Fences* or create the bed in *That Face*.

SOUND AND LIGHTS

List ideas on how sound and lighting effects can make a difference to exploring scenes of the performance text. For example, the sound of the footsteps and hospital trolley outside the room in Scene 3 of *That Face*, which makes Mia, Izzy and Henry aware of the possibility of interruption; and the spotlight that isolates etc.

The five tools: Feelings

Your feelings in a scene will be generated by the specifics of the situation and character. You can't force these; they need to arise from your work on the text and with your group.

One way of practising this is to use a technique called **emotion memory**, which derives from Stanislavski.

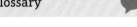
By exploring your own memory bank of feelings (jealousy, anger, embarrassment and so on) you can empathise more effectively with the feelings of a character in a given situation, and therefore play the scene more truthfully.

While this can be applied to any situation where emotions are involved (pretty much the whole of drama!), it can be particularly useful when applied to characters in extreme states – for example, Alan in *Equus*, or Martha in *That Face*. Only you will know if it is working for you, but your group (and any audience) will be able to give you feedback on the result.

Your voice and your body (the next two tools to be explored) can both be used to show your feelings.

The five tools: Voice

Your voice is a central part of you. You can (and should) develop its flexibility and power through exercises, as any good actor does. In order to find the most effective voice for your character, you should:

• study the language of the text

• think about what kind of voice your character has (indeed, all of the characters in your set text)

• be able to describe the voice and its particular qualities.

Studying the language of the play

Recognising the kind of language used in general, or by a particular character, is an important way to start exploring voice. The language will give you a feeling for 'the world of the play'. Here are some basic questions you need to ask yourself.

• Is the language naturalistic or non-naturalistic?

• Is the language formal or informal?

• Is it written in prose or verse?

• Is the language literal or figurative?

ACTIVITY

1. Sit in a circle and take the first scene (or first few pages) of your set text. One person begins to read the text until they come to a punctuation mark. They stop at the punctuation mark, and the person on their left takes over. Continue reading the text in this way. For now, don't try to express meaning or intention; just speak the lines. Try this more than once, with a different person starting each time. Discuss anything you notice about this activity.

2. Using the same scene, take a short speech from a character (not too short, however). Walk around the room, stopping and turning in a different direction each time you reach a new piece of punctuation (other than apostrophes, of course). Try to feel how the energy of the speech works. Discuss any thoughts you've had, including thoughts about the character.

Finding the right voice

Once you understand what kind of language you are dealing with, you can start to work on your text and the characters, thinking about how you can best speak your lines. Some work is intuitive – you get a 'feel' for what a character's voice is like – but remember you still have to be able to find the words to write about this in the exam.

There are several factors that affect how characters in plays (and people in real life) talk. Among the most important are:

- the character's background, education and experience
- the character's status in the scene
- the situation/given circumstances
- the style of the play
- the character's objective/intention.

Once you have completed your work on characterisation (see the sections on 'Intellect' and 'Imagination' earlier) and on the language of the play (see 'Studying the language of the play'), you will be in a strong position to work on the character's voice (and body movement – see 'The five tools: Body' on page 36).

Describing the qualities of the voice

To find the character's voice, you have these elements to work with:

- pitch (the note)
- range (how high and low the voice will go)
- pace
- use of pauses
- tone (which relates to the attitude of the character at this point and the relationship with the person who is listening)
- volume
- articulation (the level of precision with which the words are pronounced).

Take a look at the two extracts below – one from *Machinal* and one from *Colder Than Here* – then read the character notes that follow.

> **Exam tip**
>
> If you are asked to write about how you would perform a character in a particular scene, you will need to consider how they use their voice. You will need a vocabulary for writing about it, which you can link with information about their characters and situations. Words like **emphatic, measured, hesitant** and **fluent** can help to define the character's way of speaking at a particular point.

ACTIVITIES

1. Read the first extract below which comes from *Machinal*. Then walk around, stopping and turning in a different direction each time you reach a new piece of punctuation (other than apostrophes, of course). Don't try initially to 'colour' the speaking of the text too much with your feelings. Try to let the feeling for the text emerge from your reading of it. Try to feel how the energy of the speech works. Discuss any thoughts you've had, including thoughts about the character.

2. Now try the same thing again with the speech from *Colder Than Here* (also below). Discuss as a group how similar or different the exercise became with different texts. Note how this has helped you to find specific voices.

> ### From *Machinal*
>
> Young Woman: (rushing on) I always thought I'd find somebody – somebody young – and – and attractive – with wavy hair – wavy hair – I always think of children with curls – with curls all over their head – somebody young – and attractive – that I'd like – that I'd love – But I haven't found anybody like that yet – I haven't found anybody – I've hardly known anybody – you never let me go with anybody and –
>
> (Scene 2)

> ### From *Colder Than Here*
>
> Alec: … *Tautology*. It means … it doesn't matter. Could you just … Could you *let* me complain at you, I'm afraid I won't feel complete until I've ruined your day too. I mean what is the *point*, what is the blasted point of making a boiler so high-tech there's only two chaps in the country can fix it? What is the bloody point? … So if you agree why can't you do something about it? Somebody somewhere in your company has to take responsibility –
>
> (Scene 8)

Character notes: Young Woman in *Machinal*

The Young Woman works in an office in New York as a typist. She lives with her mother, to whom she is talking. (The play first appeared in 1928.) Have a go at Activity 1 above. When you have completed the activity, notice what you can tell about the Young Woman's character and state of mind at this point.

Character notes: Alec in *Colder Than Here*

Alec is 57, educated, middle class, living in Leamington Spa. His wife has terminal cancer. The central heating boiler has not worked for four months. He is on the phone to a representative of the company (in Glasgow) trying to get them to fix it. Have a go at Activity 2. When you have completed it, notice what you can tell about his character and state of mind at this point.

Having explored the voice, we now turn our attention to the body, including non-verbal communication.

The five tools: Body

Like the voice, your body is also a central part of you. You can (and should) develop ways of moving and being that are appropriate for your character. The body can be used in conjunction with the voice – the way you move in conjunction with the way you speak. However, your body can give many clues, even when you are not speaking. This is known as **non-verbal communication**.

The same list of factors that applies to characters' voices when preparing for a part applies also to character movement:

- the character's background, education and experience
- the character's status in the scene
- the situation/given circumstances
- the style of the play
- the character's objective/intention.

> ### Glossary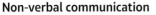
>
> **Non-verbal communication**
> Any form of on-stage action that conveys meaning to an audience. It will include:
>
> - gesture
> - facial expression
> - movement
> - mime
> - tableaux (still images created with actors' bodies)
> - dance
> - mask work.

You are working with a wide range of possibilities here. A character's 'normal' movement may be slow and ponderous, but in a crisis may become swift and surprisingly agile. You may observe a startling difference in character movement during the course of the play. For example, the Young Woman's movement in Episode 3 of *Machinal* (Honeymoon) is likely to be very different from her movement in Episode 6 (Intimate). In Honeymoon, her movement will show tension and anxiety, whereas in Intimate, she moves with more confidence and relaxation.

Taking it further

Rudolf Laban (1879–1958)
Laban is a famous practitioner who established different types of movement that provide a vocabulary for thinking about and identifying characteristic ways of moving. Try to find out more about both Laban and his ideas.

Take a look at the two extracts referred to below – one from *That Face* and one from *Accidental Death of an Anarchist* – then read the character notes that follow.

From *That Face*

Read pages 54–5 from 'Izzy flounces back in' to 'that was harsh, stud muffin'.

Character notes: Izzy in *That Face*

Izzy is 16 and at a private school with Mia, who is 15. She appears confident and brash, a bit of a show-off, but is more vulnerable than she appears. She has spent the night with Henry (Mia's brother, 18) having only just met him and is hoping to continue the relationship. Mia is in serious trouble at school (as is Izzy), and her father is flying over from Hong Kong (where he now lives with his second wife and new child) specifically to sort out the situation. The scene is set in the father's flat at Canary Wharf, which he keeps for business visits. The three young people have got drunk and trashed it on the previous night.

Izzy is initially trying to be seductive and provocative, but has completely misread the situation. She is focused only on what she wants. Henry's blunt dismissal stuns and distresses her.

It is best to play this scene in a group, so that you can work on the changes of movement for Izzy, but also the differences in the non-verbal communication between her and Mia and Henry.

From *Accidental Death of an Anarchist*

Read pages 41–2 from 'I was holidaying in Bergamo' to 'The irony has got through'.

ACTIVITY

Read the extract on pages 41–2 of *Accidental Death of an Anarchist*. Think about how you would direct the actor playing the Maniac and what words you would use to convey the kind of movement appropriate for the character in this situation.

ACTIVITY

Read the extract on pages 54–5 of *That Face*. Think about how you would direct the actor playing Izzy in this scene. What words would you use to describe her movement? What specific movements will help the actor to play particular moments in this scene?

Character notes: The Maniac in *Accidental Death of an Anarchist*

In this extract, the Maniac has disguised himself as a magistrate for the purpose of getting to the truth about the death of a suspect who has 'fallen' from a police station window. He convinces the three policemen to join in his manic miming of arrested suspects being told jokes that lead to screams of laughter (note – probably best not to attempt the somersault!). Only when they are all engaged in this, does he reveal that he's been speaking ironically and has tricked them into showing their real attitudes.

The play is a **farce**, so the physical expression of the characters can be broader and larger than in a realistic play. Start by building up the physical movement of the Maniac – it will need a lot of energy. Then, in a group, involve the other three characters.

The Maniac's body language must try to involve the policemen, trying by his enthusiasm and energy to get them to join in. Their body language must react to this, as they enjoy the fun of it. But the body language of both the Maniac and the policemen changes after he has 'drawn them in' and then gets them to realise what they are doing.

Summary of the five tools

We have now taken a detailed look at the five tools (intellect, imagination, feeling, voice and body) that an actor has at their disposal. Each of these tools is essential for creating character, so it is wise to be familiar with how each one can help you. Through preparing your characterisation, using your imagination to fill in the gaps not supplied by the text, followed by an in-depth study of the text, and the development of a vocabulary to describe voice and non-verbal communication, you can come to a clearer understanding of the nature of the play's characters.

Approaching the text as a designer

What you have to do in the exam

In this section, we look at what you will need to think and write about to prepare you for the design question.

You need to:

- carefully read the performance text several times
- research thoroughly and appropriately
- consider 'the world of the play', including mood and atmosphere
- consider the venue/playing space and stage form
- consider and solve practical problems
- (in an actual production) work closely with the director and be allocated a budget.

In your practical work on the text, you will have time to think about all these aspects. In the exam, you will need to respond to a particular extract while being able to refer to the play as a whole.

The kinds of designers in the theatre

Everything that is seen and heard as part of a performance will be the responsibility of one designer or another. The term 'scenographer' is sometimes used to describe a single, overall designer who integrates all aspects of the design concept with the text and the 'vision' of the director. More commonly there are separate designers for different aspects who work collaboratively. These include:

- set designers (also responsible for props and often for costumes)
- costume designers (but see above)
- lighting designers
- sound designers
- make-up designers
- video projection designers (sometimes these are the lighting designers).

There may also be specialist designers of masks and puppets (and so on) for particular shows.

What different designers have to consider

Set
When you think about a set, you will need to consider the actor/audience relationship and the use of space.

Which stage-form (end-on, thrust, in-the-round etc.) serves the play best?
For example, an in-the round form can provide more intimacy and a greater sense of closeness between actors and audience, but it may create problems if large set elements are needed.

How many different settings are there?
Some plays like *Fences* have a single setting (although this may have changes over time). Some plays (like *Machinal*) have multiple settings.

What period is the play set in?
Some are clearly stated in the text (*Fences* is set in 1957 and 1965). Others, like *Colder Than Here* and *That Face*, seem absolutely up to date for us, so a contemporary setting seems necessary. We know that a play like *Accidental Death of an Anarchist* had a time period when first performed, but it may respond to updating, as may *Equus*. On the other hand, *Machinal*, both because of the style and the references, may respond less readily to updating.

What is the geographical and social setting?
Colder Than Here is set in and around Leamington Spa in Warwickshire, featuring a middle-class family. *Fences* is set in Pittsburgh, Pennsylvania, in the North East of the United States, in a working-class district.

How is the space used in each of the play's scenes? How many exits/entrances are required?
Equus requires space for the horses to enter and for Alan to 'ride' Nugget, and it must be possible for the cast to access the acting area quickly. *Accidental Death of an Anarchist* requires sufficient space in the office for a good deal of vigorous cast movement to take place – and two entrances. Some of the scenes in *Machinal* require ten characters (plus furniture) to be on the stage at the same time.

Are there any large, complicated set elements or props to consider?
The horse masks and hooves in *Equus* are an obvious example. The coffin in *Colder Than Here* has to appear at different stages of being painted (and so needs to be returned to its unpainted state for every performance). The bomb in Act 2 of *Accidental Death of an Anarchist* needs to look appropriately home-made.

Exam tip

In answering this question, you may have the choice of selecting a single aspect of design (for example, the lighting) or a number of different aspects. Bear in mind that you are likely to have about 30 minutes to answer the question, so don't take on more than you can deal with in that time.

Top tip

Research about the original setting is always necessary, even if you are considering changing the time period.

Are levels necessary or potentially helpful?

If the play has multiple settings, levels are often useful for defining different spaces. Even a single-set play like *Fences* benefits from having the raised level of the porch (usually called a 'veranda' in the UK).

Does the setting need to be realistic?

An **expressionist** play like *Machinal* was not written to be played in an entirely realistic style. But it may be that *Accidental Death of an Anarchist* would benefit from a very realistic setting to provide a contrast to the wildly farcical action. This is where you, as set designer, need to respond to 'the world of the play' and create an effective stage environment for it.

There are many more detailed questions that could be asked about any text. You will be involved with thinking about these questions – and supplying your own answers – as you work on your set text.

> **Glossary**
>
> **Expressionist/ expressionism**
> An early 20th-century movement against realism in the theatre, which tried to show on stage the inner motivation and psychological states of the characters. This was reflected in the set design.

> **ACTIVITY**
>
> Go through your set text systematically, listing the number of different locations and where they occur. Note whether there are significant changes in the same location at different times. In a group, discuss what the most appropriate stage form could be, and how the various locations can best be achieved.

Costume

Costume design needs to go hand-in-hand with set design, even at the simple level of colour. Having costumes that clash with the colours of walls or furniture is visually disturbing. Lighting design is also significant here. If a red costume is lit with green light, for example, it will appear brown or black.

You need to consider many of the same areas as a set designer does: period, style, social class, occupation. All these will require research. The idea of 'the world of the play' is also important. You will need to read the play closely for information that is in the text about specific details of the costume.

Finally, you need to think about character, fit, colour, texture and function.

> **ACTIVITY**
>
> Select a character from your set text. Find all the information the text gives you about that character. Note how many costume changes are likely. If the play is set in a defined period, research the costumes of the period appropriate to the character's status. Find as many appropriate images (use magazines, internet sites and so on), as you can and consider how these might help you to create your own costume sketches and notes. Then create these.

Character

Costume can indicate social status and income, but it is a main indicator of character. In *That Face*, one of the markers of Martha's advancing alcoholism is her increasingly disorganised set of clothes. By contrast, her husband, Hugh, is extremely smart, as befits a well-off businessman. In *Fences*, Troy and Bono have their social status signalled for them on their first entrance by the working clothes they wear as garbage collectors.

Fit, colour and texture

Points about character can be made by how well a costume fits, the colour of the items, and whether the texture of the fabric has a high quality or is worn and torn in places.

Function

You should consider how costumes are used. Characters may need loose-fitting garments to move swiftly and athletically, or tight-fitting garments that force them to move in a more restricted way. Some kinds of costumes will be appropriate for certain occupations – the clerks and stenographers in *Machinal*, for example.

Lighting

The aim of the lighting designer will be to create mood and atmosphere to enhance the action. The set will need to be lit, as will the actors, so the design should be created:

- using a close knowledge of the text
- in close co-operation with set designers and sound designers.

Remember that you need to serve the purposes of the play, so part of what you do should help to draw the audience's attention to the significance of a scene.

The basic tools a lighting designer works with are as follows:

- **Intensity/level:** This includes the level of light needed to create an effect, and whether the light is evenly spread over the acting area or in just one area.
- **Direction/angle:** This can affect the way that set elements appear – for example, lighting from the side can bring out the texture of an object in a way that lighting from above does not. Low-level placement of lanterns can create a more sinister effect.
- **Colour:** Colour can affect the appearance of the set and costumes. It is also a powerful tool in creating atmosphere. Lighting designers talk about 'warm' colours (the red/orange yellow end of the spectrum) and 'cold' colours (those towards the blue end of the spectrum).
- **Diffusion:** The more diffuse light is the softer it can appear to be. Some lanterns (like fresnels) produce a softer light, whereas others produce a more hard-edged light. This can have a powerful effect on the mood of a scene.
- **Lighting as scenery:** Lighting can effectively create locations. This is particularly effective in plays where the scenes are short and the locations change swiftly. *Equus* is a good example, as the various swift changes of locations and times of day can be created effectively by lighting changes.

Note that the technology involved in video projection can be complex, although simple technology can often achieve striking effects. It can also play its part in the creation of scenery, by the use of projected images.

ACTIVITY

Take one scene from your set text. Read it closely, making notes about the atmosphere, mood and key events. Then see how you could create a lighting design for that scene, using a minimal set. It will help if you can experiment in a drama studio so that you can see (and adjust) the effect. For more technical detail on lighting, go to 'Types of lighting' on pages 134–5 of Section C.

Glossary

Diegetic sound
These are effects that are called for in the text as part of the performance – for example, ringing phone, chiming bell, gun shot, car engine. These effects are also known as 'spot' cues, as they have to arrive very precisely on cue.

Non-diegetic sound
These are effects that enhance a scene but are not realistically necessary to it. This might be a musical effect to underscore a scene – not part of the reality on stage, but there to send a signal to, or to produce an effect on the audience.

Incidental sound
This is usually introductory pre-show or play-out music or sound effects, there to create a mood or atmosphere before the play's action actually begins, or after it has finished. Interval music comes into this category.

Soundscape
This refers to a sound track that runs continuously throughout a scene. It is designed to suggest and maintain a mood, atmosphere or place – or all of these. It is often not noticed consciously by the audience, although its effect is felt.

Sound

The sound designer can contribute creatively to the overall effect of the production, by creating mood and atmosphere as well as supplying vital effects. There are three types of sound used in live production:

- **diegetic**
- **non-diegetic**
- **incidental**.

The basic tools a sound designer works with are as follows:

- **Volume:** The volume of a sound (loud or soft) is a basic effect. You should consider the effect you want the volume to have on the audience. For instance, the 'Equus' noise referred to might be effective if amplified to a level where it becomes disturbing to the audience.

- **Direction (speaker placement):** This is particularly important for diegetic sound, as it needs to appear to come from the appropriate source. For example, the phone ring for the call that brings news of Raynell's birth and Alberta's death in Act 2 Scene 2 of *Fences* has to come from inside the house.

- **Sound quality:** Sound may be manipulated to create different effects and atmospheres. The stage directions at the beginning of *Machinal* specify that the sound of 'machines' ('typing machines, adding machines, manifold, telephone bells, buzzers') should start before the curtain rises and continues throughout the scene. A sound designer might opt to distort these sounds in order to create a disturbing quality, reflecting the disturbance in the Young Woman's mind.

- **Sound selection and creation:** Sounds (especially music) need to be carefully selected to enhance the play's atmosphere. Music can be very powerful in setting the atmosphere just before the play starts.

ACTIVITY

In a group, discuss what type of music would be most appropriate to set the mood for your text. Don't fall into the trap of suggesting personal favourites. Try to describe the atmosphere you are aiming for and then the type (or specific examples) of music that meets this description.

- **Sound editing and mixing:** Many effects are produced by mixing together different sounds to create a **soundscape**. This is a complex art, but to answer this question (if you are writing about sound) you may wish to describe the various elements of sound you think will work effectively together to produce the effect you want.

ACTIVITY

In a group select a scene (or part of a scene) of about five pages. Look for any examples of diegetic sound and also for the possibilities of non-diegetic sound, including a soundscape. Discuss your ideas and how these might add to the scene.

Introduction to set performance texts

Equus

Basic facts

- First produced in 1973 (National Theatre, directed by John Dexter).

- Film released in 1977 with Richard Burton as Dysart and Peter Firth as Alan.

- Many productions, notably with Daniel Radcliffe as Alan in 2007.

- 'Equus' is the Latin word for 'horse'.

- Play based on actual case of a disturbed young boy who blinded a number of horses for no apparent reason.

- Shaffer apparently only knew the outline of the case, but not the details; the events of the play and the characters came from his imagination.

Playwright: Peter Shaffer (born 1926)

- He was born in Liverpool.

- His first play appeared (on television) in 1954.

- His best-known plays are: *The Royal Hunt of the Sun* (1964), *Black Comedy* (1965) and *Amadeus* (1979).

Reviews and other critical comments

'Peter Shaffer's play is … based on a direct confrontation between reason and instinct … What makes the play so exciting is that it presents this argument in such bold, clear, vivid theatrical terms.' (Michael Billington, *The Guardian*, 27 July 1973)

'[Daniel Radlicffe's] performance also helps to camouflage the fact Peter Shaffer's celebrated ritual drama sometimes betrays its early 1970s origins.' (Michael Billington, *The Guardian*, 28 February 2007)

Structure: As John Simon notes in the review on the previous page, the play has the structure of a 'case history'. The mystery about the motivation of Alan in blinding the horses is gradually revealed in his sessions with Dysart, some of which involve the acting out (in flashback) of relevant scenes. In parallel to this, the emotional and imaginative poverty of Dysart's life is gradually revealed through Dysart's monologues reflecting on the differences between Alan and himself. The action is fluid and continuous, but there are 35 separate 'scenes' – 21 in Act 1 and 14 in Act 2.

Themes: *Equus* raises a number of issues – for example, the nature of normality; the individual quest for meaning in life; the place of worship and the morality of psychiatry. The main way in which these themes are conveyed is through the contrasting of Alan and Dysart, with the more minor characters providing opportunities for these ideas to be expressed and developed.

ACTIVITY

In a group, discuss the methods by which Peter Shaffer creates the characters of Dysart and Alan. (You might consider the use of contrast, monologue, movement and the ways in which other characters are used.) Work practically, trying out and discussing ideas.

Taking it further

Here are some reviewers' comments on the play. It's worth having a look online for others – from papers like the *New York Times* or from magazines like *Time Out*, for example.

Equus

Equus

Style: The underlying style of the acting is realistic. Many of the scenes (for example, those between Hesther and Dysart) can be approached in a realistic way. However, the style also allows for:

- direct address to the audience (by Dysart)
- the use of many non-realistic devices, such as the flashback sequences
- the representation of the horses
- the use of non-realistic sound and lighting effects.

It is interesting to note that the film of the play was notably unsuccessful in trying to find an appropriate style. The director decided to make the blinding of the horses realistic – the metal hoofpick was seen entering the horses' eyes. The non-realistic representation of the blindings in the theatre was far more effective.

Setting: There is a very detailed description of the setting (and of the presentation of the horses and the chorus sound effect) in the text. It is worth drawing the set using the description to get a clear idea of the original setting. Because of the large number of 'scenes' and the different 'locations', any setting has to allow for fluid action.

ACTIVITIES

1. The only character who speaks directly to the audience is Dysart. Find moments in the play when the other characters might speak directly to the audience. As well as considering **what** they would say about their thoughts and feelings at that moment, consider **how** they would express themselves:

   a. the words and phrases they would choose

   b. the ease (or otherwise) with which they would express themselves to the audience

   c. their physical characteristics.

2. Select a character and decide on a treasured possession for them. Describe it in detail and why it is significant for the character. Use this exercise to explore the character imaginatively, building on information in the text.

ACTIVITY

In a group, plan an alternative set that will serve the purposes of the play. Consider which stage form (e.g. in-the-round, thrust) will work well as the first step. Then plan the details. Keep referring back to the text, especially scenes that involve 'flashbacks'.

Both lighting and sound made powerful contributions to the original stage production. When you have agreed on an alternative setting, look at Scene 21. Try to suggest alternative (or more specific) directions for these.

The original production was set 'in the present' – that is, in 1973. Some of the references (the advertising jingles sung by Alan, for example) are of that period. Discuss how you could update the play. Think about how that might affect costume and props design. List alternative ways of presenting the horses.

That Face

Basic facts
- First produced in 2007 at the Royal Court Theatre.
- Directed by Jeremy Herrin.
- Transferred to the West End the following year.
- Received an Olivier Award nomination for Best New Play.
- Opened in the Manhattan Theatre, New York, in 2010.

Playwright: Polly Stenham (born 1986)
- She was born in Bedford.
- She lived with her father (after her parents divorced). He worked in the City and she attended private schools.
- She began (but didn't finish) an English degree.
- She wrote *That Face* when she was 19.
- The play was accepted for production at the Royal Court. (She was a member of the Royal Court Young Writers Programme.)
- She subsequently left university to work on the play.
- Later plays: *Tusk Tusk* (2009) and *No Quarter* (2013), both staged at the Royal Court; *Hotel* (2014) staged at the Royal National Theatre.
- In 2011 she opened an art gallery (with a friend) – the Cob Studios and Gallery in Camden, London.

Reviews and other critical comments
'Not only is *That Face* shatteringly powerful, but it displays a dramatic dexterity and emotional intelligence writers twice her age would envy… I never expected to see a play at this address that began at a girls' boarding school, and went on to portray people with posh accents and loads of money with rueful insight and a complete absence of chippy condemnation. Among much else, the play is a useful reminder that despair and misfortune are no respecters of an individual's bank balance. … there is also a dark wit in Stenham's writing, and a tough, never overstated compassion for her characters.' (Charles Spence, *The Telegraph*, 26 April 2007)

'Stenham strikes me as stronger on the symptoms of moral chaos than its causes. She never makes fully clear what has turned Martha into a psychological wreck. Lurking is an assumption that Hugh, who abandoned Martha for a Chinese mistress, is somehow the guilty party. But

Taking it further

Here are some reviewers' comments on the play. It's worth having a look online for others – from papers like the *New York Times* or from magazines like *Time Out*, for example.

That Face

since the accusations come largely from Martha, at best an unreliable witness, I wasn't sure whether Stenham was attacking the destruction of the nuclear family or a class system that turns women like Martha into victims.' (Michael Billington, *The Guardian*, 12 May 2008)

'What interests me is emotional violence. And that shit goes down irrespective of class and money.' (Polly Stenham, interview in *Time Out*, 7 May 2008)

Structure: There are eight scenes. These alternate between Henry's room in Martha's flat (Scenes, 2, 4, 6, 8) and other locations: Scene 1, the school dormitory; Scene 3, the private hospital room; Scene 5, Hugh's Canary Wharf flat; Scene 7, an expensive restaurant. We see the progression of Martha's decline in the scenes in the flat, contrasted with the life of her children outside – and, in the last two scenes, the relationship between Martha and Hugh, her former husband. The family is only together in the final scene, in which its distressing dysfunctionality is confirmed.

Themes: The play deals with the effects of family break-up in a well-off family. It explores the ways in which individual characters have been affected in different ways and how the course of their lives has been altered. To some extent it also features the way in which a privileged but emotionally deprived lifestyle can affect individuals. For example, Izzy is shown as a brash and amoral 16 year-old who is, in fact, very emotionally vulnerable. Reviewer Michael Billington (in *The Guardian*) commented that it was the first English play he could recall to explore mother–son incest. How far this incest goes is a matter for discussion, but there is certainly an inversion of the normal parent–child dependency.

Style: The dialogue is naturalistic, with clear attempts to catch on the page the intonations and hesitations present in normal speech. All the characters display a facility with language that reflects their education and economically privileged background. This includes a facility with swearing – not shared by Hugh, whose language is more reserved and authoritative. There are occasional moments when public school slang breaks through, as when Mia says 'a lax ball in the face' (Scene 3), by which she means she has been bruised by a ball while playing lacrosse (lax). The acting style required is entirely realistic, with some intense emotional demands made on the actors.

Setting: The play appears to be set at the time it was written (2007). (See 'Structure' for information about location.) The stage directions give useful indications, without providing many specific details. The design challenge is to provide a set that facilitates swift changes of setting between Henry's room and the other four settings, some of which (the dormitory and the restaurant, for example) can be created with minimal furniture, lighting and sound.

ACTIVITY

Improvise a Christmas scenario. You should prepare for this in advance. (If you need to, refer back to your work on 'The five tools: Imagination', where you did a similar improvisation.)

In a group of four, take a character each – all members of a family gathered for Christmas. Note that seven years before this gathering, the family had split up.

Each character will 'give' the others a Christmas present, saying what it is. You have to think carefully about what your character's attitude to the receiver is and what they see as an appropriate gift. In this case, you may also like to think about the social and economic background of the family.

The exercise may help you to feel what the family has lost in the intervening years.

ACTIVITY

In a group, discuss how you can best resolve the design problems so that you achieve both effective settings and a fluent production (the play is usually played without an interval; it lasts about 90 minutes). You will need to consider which stage form will be most appropriate, while remembering that the even-numbered scenes all have the same location (although there are minor adjustments, such as the concealment of Henry's ripped clothing and the addition of an overflowing ashtray in Scene 4). When you reach a good level of agreement, sketch out ground plans of the set. Don't forget to consider the contribution that sound and lighting can make.

ACTIVITY

Choose a character and create (and speak) two monologues: one just before the play starts; and the other after it has finished.

Use this to trace your character's emotional journey. Discuss these as a group.

Taking it further

Several critics have compared the writing of Polly Stenham to that of the great American playwright Tennessee Williams (1911–83). There is a particular similarity between the character of Martha and that of Blanche Dubois in Williams' play *A Streetcar Named Desire*. Either read this play or watch the 1951 film version, with Marlon Brando and Vivien Leigh to see if (and, if so, why) you agree.

Machinal

Basic facts

- First produced in 1928 in New York.

- First performed in the UK in 1931 under its alternative title, *The Life Machine*.

- It has been revived several times in recent years, most notably in a very striking production by Stephen Daldry at the Royal National Theatre in 1993, with Fiona Shaw in the part of the Young Woman.

- 'Machinal' is a French word meaning 'mechanical' or 'automatic'.

- The play is loosely based on the real murder trial of Ruth Snyder, who, together with her lover Henry Judd Gray, murdered her husband after insuring his life heavily. Both were sentenced to death in the electric chair in 1928.

Playwright: Sophie Treadwell (1885–1970)

- She was born in California. Her father had a Mexican mother and spent much of his youth in Mexico.

- Her father deserted her (and her mother) when she was a child.

- She was also a journalist and novelist.

- She wrote several plays and only stopped writing just before her death.

- She directed and appeared as an actor in some of these plays.

- *Machinal*, heavily influenced by the expressionist style, was her most successful play.

Reviews and other critical comments

'By mixing realism with expressionism, Miss Treadwell touched a live nerve in the city she was writing about … Everything that happens in *Machinal* is cruel or contemptible. But Miss Treadwell, being on the side of the damned, made a rueful, touching play out of forbidding materials.' (Amnon Kabatchnik, *Blood on the Stage, 1925–1950: Milestone Plays of Crime, Mystery, and Detection*, Scarecrow Press, 2010)

Taking it further

Here are some reviewers' comments on the play. It's worth having a look online for others – from papers like the *New York Times* or from magazines like *Time Out*, for example.

Machinal

'Ian MacNeil's awesome designs … have to be seen to be believed – from the stunning moments near the start when the revolving cubicles of a packed cacophonous office loom in from the back of the stage, like some bureaucratic circle of hell that Dante had overlooked, all the way through to the stark electric chair scene when the steely intestines of the Lyttleton's nether regions are bleakly exposed.' (Paul Taylor, *The Independent*, 17 October 1993)

Structure: The play is in nine 'episodes' (scenes), each with a different setting. The only character to appear in all the scenes is the Young Woman. There is a very large cast. In the Royal National Theatre production 26 actors played the 48 parts. The narrative reflects the development of the mental state of the main character, the Young Woman, who is seen in relation to the other characters.

Themes: The play has been seen as a pro-feminist work (in New York, Treadwell became an active member of the Lucy Stone League of suffragettes). It has also been seen as a protest against and critique of the mechanisation and materialism of life at the time she was writing. By not providing names or contexts for the characters, Treadwell creates them as representative characters, who themselves are victims of modern society in various ways. But the focus is on the 'tragedy' of the Young Woman, who is seen as a victim of a largely male-dominated and soulless society.

Style and setting: The text is written in an expressionist style, intended to reflect the inner state of mind of the Young Woman. The style also reflects her feelings of increasing isolation and desperation in her mental and physical 'journey' through the wastelands of 1920s USA. This is a challenge for both designers and performers. Set, lighting and sound designers have to create appropriate environments that focus on the way the outside world affects, and is perceived by, the Young Woman. Costume designers need to create costumes that clearly and instantly create a sense of the essential nature of the characters who are deliberately not fully developed. Performers have to create well-defined characters, often with few lines.

ACTIVITY

Read through the monologue by the Young Woman, which concludes the first scene (pages 11–12). Note that the stage direction is 'thinking her thoughts aloud'. The speech has a disjointed quality, with many repetitions. As a result, it is in danger of becoming repetitive and dull. Think about how you can bring a freshness and immediacy to it in performance. Try this as a group and discuss which approaches work effectively.

The stage direction also mentions that it is spoken 'to the subdued accompaniment of the office sounds and voices'. Experiment with the effect of playing it in this way, improvising the background speech and office noises, using the information about characters and office machines you have found in the text of the first scene.

Taking it further

Research the term 'expressionism' in relation to theatre, film and visual art, using both online and reference book sources. Select particular visual resources to share in a group, which seem to you to convey the 'feel' expressionistic techniques are seeking to create.

ACTIVITY

In a group, select any two consecutive scenes. Read them through and discuss how they could be most effectively staged in terms of the set, lighting and sound. (Agree first on the stage form you want to use.) Decide what set elements (furniture, etc.) will be necessary to serve the scenes. When you have agreed on what will work best, consider how you can manage the scene change while maintaining the atmosphere and mood of the play. In doing this, you will need to think about sound and lighting, as well as how the scene change can be accomplished effectively. This is one of the important questions for anyone staging this play.

Fences

Basic facts

- First produced at the Yale Repertory Theatre, Connecticut, USA in 1985, following a staged reading in 1983.

- Play had a long Broadway run, winning a Tony Awards in 1987, as well as the Pulitzer Prize.

- It was revived on Broadway in 2010, with Denzel Washington playing Troy Maxson.

- In 2013 the play was produced by Theatre Royal Bath in the UK, with Lenny Henry as Troy Maxson.

- This production transferred to the West End.

Playwright: August Wilson (1945–2005)

- He was born in Pittsburgh, Pennsylvania and came from a deprived background.

- He lived with his mother and five siblings in a two-room flat.

- His father was largely absent during his childhood.

- At 14 he was the only African American student at his high school, but left following racial abuse.

- His family suffered from racial prejudice when his mother moved to the largely white working-class area of Hazelwood. They were forced to leave.

- He struggled to establish himself as a writer. He had to pawn his typewriter more than once when money was in short supply.

- He conceived the idea of the 'Pittsburgh cycle' of plays (also called the 'Century cycle') to reflect the black experience in the USA through ten consecutive decades, from the 1930s to the 1990s.

- *Fences* is the sixth play in the cycle (they were not written in order of the decades). The most famous play (along with *Fences*) in this cycle is *Ma Rainey's Black Bottom*, revived at the Royal National Theatre in 2016.

Reviews and other critical comments

'It's a far from flawless play. The symbolism of the fence Troy intermittently builds to ward off death is a bit clunky and there is an overlong coda trying to make sense of his life. But Wilson's achievement is to create a towering character full of contradictions: Troy, at different times, is roistering and responsible, debauched and dignified, a victim of history and a domestic tyrant, not least in his relations with his son. He fulfils, however, the first duty of a dramatic hero – he is abundantly alive.' (Michael Billington, *The Guardian*, 27 June 2013)

Taking it further

Machinal is sometimes compared to *Everyman*, a medieval morality play by an unknown author. They share the characteristics of a central character who 'journeys' through the world, and of a set of characters who have only representative names – in the case of *Everyman* names like Beauty, Good Deeds and Knowledge. Read the play (it's quite short) and discuss in groups the similarities and differences.

Fences

Taking it further

Here are some reviewers' comments on the play. It's worth having a look online for others – from papers like the *New York Times* or from magazines like *Time Out*, for example.

ACTIVITY

When you know the play quite well and have done some basic character work (see 'The five tools: Intellect' and 'Imagination'), in a group, read through Act 1 Scene 4.

Each group member should write down character objectives for each character, beginning 'I want …'. Make these as precise as possible. The point of an objective is that it should lead to action on the part of the character.

Compare what you have written and try to agree on what would make the most appropriate objective for each of the characters in this scene.

Structure: The play has one location (the yard of Troy and Rose's house). It starts in 1957, but there are six months between Act 2 Scene 1 and Act 2 Scene 2, and a further two months between Act 2 Scene 2 and Act 2 Scene 3. The final scene after Troy's death takes place in 1965. The play follows the progress of Troy's relationships with his sons and his wife, and to a lesser extent his relationship with his long-standing friend, Bono.

Themes: The themes of the play gather around the complex character of Troy. His desires and disappointments reflect his attitude to manhood – especially in the experience of the black male and the legacy of prejudice in the USA. These are also reflected in the attitudes of his sons: Lyons (with his half-hearted musical ambitions); and Cory (with his ambitions to play professional football). The title of the play, *Fences*, relates to protecting what you have and demonstrates the need to be pro-active in achieving what you want. The fence comes to symbolise Troy's rejection of Cory at the end of Act 2 Scene 4, when he responds to Cory's statement that he'll be back for 'his things': 'They'll be on the other side of that fence.' For Troy, the fence becomes a personal symbol of his need to fend off death. In the monologue he addresses Death at the end of Act 2 Scene 2, when he says: 'I'm going to build me a fence around what belongs to me. And then I want you to stay on the other side.'

Style: The dialogue is naturalistic, using the speech rhythms and vocabulary of black characters of the period. August Wilson had both a well-developed 'ear' for this style of speech and, apparently, a superb memory for it. Although the style of the play is generally realistic, there are non-realistic elements – such as Troy's monologues, and the use of the fence as a clear symbol. Baseball (a symbol of Troy's thwarted ambitions) also becomes the metaphor for Cory's rebellion against his father, when Troy tells him at the end of Act 1: 'You swung and you missed. That's strike one. Don't you strike out!' Gabriel's 'trumpet' and his eerie dance at the end also strike a non-realistic note. The last thing Troy does in the play (at the end of Act 2 Scene 4) is to assume a baseball batter's stance to challenge Death.

Setting: Wilson's text provides a good deal of detail about the set, including the contents of the yard. The set provides the constant factor as the characters experience the changes the play brings about. It represents the social and economic status of the family and, in different ways, the approach to life of both Troy and Rose.

Taking it further

When you have completed the activity on character objectives, try to agree what the through objective for each character is. (You could revisit your earlier work on this in 'The five tools: Intellect' to help.)

ACTIVITY

Troy is the only character who has a soliloquy – that is, a monologue – when no other character is present on stage.

Read through Act 2 Scene 4 again and allocate parts within your group. Then write a monologue for your allocated character, expressing your character's feelings at this point, taking into account all that has happened.

Read your monologues aloud to the group. Discuss what they reveal about the thoughts and feelings of the characters, and how they reflect on the relationships between the various characters at this point.

Colder Than Here

Basic facts

- First produced in 2005 at the Soho Theatre, directed by Abigail Morris.

- There have been numerous productions, both professional and amateur since then, including an off-Broadway production in 2005.

Playwright: Laura Wade (born 1977)

- She was born in Bedford.

- She studied Drama at Bristol University.

- Her first produced play was *Limbo*, 1996.

- Her best-known plays are: *Breathing Corpses* (2005), *Other Hands* (2006), *Alice* (2010), *Posh* (2010), *Tipping the Velvet* (an adaptation of Sarah Waters' novel, 2015).

- *Posh*, widely regarded as being based on the Bullingdon Club (the notorious Oxford student dining club), was adapted into a film, *The Riot Club* (2014).

- In 2005, she won the Critics' Circle Theatre Award for Most Promising Playwright.

Reviews and other critical comments

'Wade has set herself the almost impossible task of writing an anti-sentimental, offbeat comedy about cancer.' (Alfred Hickling, *The Guardian*, 2 August 2012)

'Naomi Wilkinson's set may be a surreal mix of living room and wood with trees growing through the carpet but Myra's typically middle class family are scarily normal in their eccentricities … The development of the family members rings true. Myra remains mentally strong as her body weakens. Her daughters move in opposite directions. As Jenna finally achieves maturity, it is she that has to support her father and sister, having had them thrown on to her by the wonderfully wilful and manipulative mother.' (Philip Fisher, *British Theatre Guide*, February 2005)

'The cast convinced that they were a family, familiar with one another's foibles, as much by their silences and knowing glances as their words. The two sisters sparred convincingly, and there were touching moments of tenderness between the otherwise distant parents … Cross-fades between external and interior scenes were not fully effective … There were also inconsistencies in wardrobe choices, given that the family are living in a house with a broken boiler through autumn and winter.' (Jim Gillespie, *The Reviews Hub*, 18 January 2015)

ACTIVITY

In a group, decide on your approach to set design. Ask yourselves these questions:

- Is the end-stage the only possible form?

- Would any other stage-form work successfully?

Try to find illustrations of similar buildings and see what features you might adopt. The 'porch' (called a 'veranda' in the UK) provides a higher level.

- Are there points in the play when this becomes particularly useful?

After you have decided on the basic features and their relative positons, sketch out a floor plan. Then set this up with objects representing the various features (some rostra would be useful) and act out a scene, seeing how effectively you can use the space.

Colder Than Here

Taking it further

Here are some reviewers' comments on the play. It's worth having a look online for others – from papers like the *New York Times* or from magazines like *Time Out*, for example.

ACTIVITY

After reading the play and completing some basic character work (see 'The five tools: Intellect' and 'Imagination'), create a timeline for the family to give them a shared background. Assume the year at the start of the play is 2005. Begin by entering any dates you know from the text, but then use your imagination to fill out other significant events – for example, when Harriet left home, and when Jenna and Mark got together. Invent dates for events that would have happened but are not mentioned in the text.

Taking it further

Here are some reviewers' comments on the play. It's worth having a look online for others – from papers like the *New York Times* or from magazines like *Time Out*, for example.

Structure: There are nine scenes, which alternate between eco-friendly burial grounds in the West Midlands and the living room of the Bradley family home in Leamington Spa. The time period is between mid-September and late March – seven months. (Myra has been given between six and nine months to live.) The opening and closing scenes feature only Myra and Jenna, thus creating a symmetry. Each of the remaining burial ground scenes features a different combination of characters. Only two scenes (Scenes 2 and 6) feature the whole family.

Themes: Cold and warmth is a central idea. The play moves through late autumn and winter to early spring. The house's boiler is not functioning throughout this period (in the final scene we hear it has been fixed), which means the house is physically cold. This reflects the state of family relationships at the outset, with a coldness (or distance) of different kinds in all the relationships (including off-stage ones, like that of Jenna and Mark). By the end of the play, warmth in the relationships has begun to re-assert itself in various ways. (The title of the play is clearly relevant here.) Death, and the acceptance of death, is a linked theme.

Style: The text is written in a naturalistic style, with a clear attempt to capture the individual speech styles of the characters. Alec's generally precise and ironic mode of speaking (for example, 'Listen, mate – I'm sorry, do you mind if I call you mate, it's not a word I'd normally use, but I feel we've spent a lot of time together' – Scene 8) contrasts with Jenna's more direct and informal mode of expression (for example, 'Bloody hell, mum, this lot don't eat any more, you know' – Scene 1). Use is sometimes made of the forward slash (/) to indicate an overlap in speech, as in normal conversation, for example:

> Jenna: I don't want a / napkin.
>
> Myra: Have a napkin. (The '/' indicates the overlap point.)

Setting: The play appears to be set at the time it was written (2005). (See 'Structure' for information about location.) It is easy to read the play imagining realistic settings, and the stage directions encourage this (look at the set description for Scene 1). However, a realistic approach to design may not be the best solution. Look at the second extract in 'Reviews', for example.

ACTIVITY

The central design problem lies in finding a solution to combining the graveyard scenes with the living room scenes. Any solution should enable the change between scenes to be swift. The text also specifies a 'wall' in Scene 2 on which the audience can read the presentation Myra is displaying to the family on her laptop. The audience needs to be able to see this, as the words are not spoken on stage.

In a group, discuss if a stage-form other than end-on can be made to work. Then discuss how to create a set that enables easy transitions between the various graveyards, and the living room.

Other design features: Note the final review on the previous page, which points to the importance of consistency in choosing costumes that reflect the temperature and atmosphere. Props are also important. The cardboard coffin (which has to appear partially painted in Scene 8) is an obvious example, but the vinyl records and record player that Alec uses in Scene 4 say something significant about his character. It may well be necessary to select music to cover scene changes – so you will need to think about what's appropriate for each change.

ACTIVITY

Select moments in the play, including the very beginning and the very end. Define an area in which you can move. In turn, place one character in the centre and position yourself at a distance that corresponds to how 'warm' or 'cold' you feel towards them at that point in the play. This activity requires a group of four, but you can swap characters between the various 'moments'.

You will need to look closely at the text and understand the sometimes complicated feelings of the characters. For each moment, discuss why each member of the group chose the position they did, looking back to the text as necessary.

Accidental Death of an Anarchist

Basic facts

- The play was originally produced in 1970 in Italy.

- The text evolved during a tour of the play. It was first translated into English in 1979 by Suzanne Cowan.

- Its first production in the UK was at Dartington College in Devon in 1979 in a translation by Gillian Hanna, adapted by Gavin Richards (this version is your set text).

- This later transferred to the West End (with a different cast).

- The play is based on an actual incident – a bombing in Milan in December 1969 in which 16 people were killed. The police immediately arrested a group of anarchists. One of them, Giovanni Pinelli, subsequently fell to his death from the window on the fourth floor of the police station where he was being questioned. It was later discovered that the bombing had been instigated by high-level military and political figures.

Playwright: Dario Fo (born in 1926)

- He was born in Italy.

- As well as being an actor, playwright, director and designer, he is a singer/songwriter and a political activist. He is a socialist and an atheist.

- He is one of the most widely performed playwrights in the world, with his plays having been translated into 30 languages.

- His best-known works (at least in the UK) are: *The Virtuous Burglar* (1958), *Mistero Buffo* (1969), *Can't Pay, Won't Pay* (1974) and *AcciTrumpets and Raspberries* (1981).

- He married the actress Franca Rame in 1954. They worked extensively together in theatre and politics until her death in 2013.

- In 1997, he won the Nobel Prize for Literature.

Taking it further

Here are some reviewers' comments on the play. It's worth having a look online for others – from papers like the *New York Times* or from magazines like *Time Out*, for example.

Glossary

Commedia dell'arte

A popular form of street theatre with improvised scenarios between stock characters (wearing character masks) based on universal types of masters, servants, lovers and so on. It developed in Italy in the 1600s and spread widely across Europe. Movement, gesture and the use of voice to demonstrate the stock character matching the mask were essential features.

Satire

The use of humour, irony and exaggeration to expose and ridicule individuals' stupidity or vices – and through them institutions, such as governments or others in authority.

Taking it further

Look at the National Theatre website for a demonstration of *commedia dell'arte techniques*. See what else you can find out from other sources, too.

Reviews and other critical comments

'The play springs out of a 1960s bombing campaign by neofascists; it is also rooted in the *commedia dell'arte* tradition, in a way that led Joseph Farrell to dub Fo and his wife, Franca Rame, "harlequins of the revolution".' (Michael Billington, *The Guardian*, 27 February 2003)

Note: This production attempted to update Fo's play by introducing current political personalities and events in order to update the **satire**.

Structure: As is usually the case in farce, the plot becomes increasingly complicated through the play's three scenes, with the Maniac's disguise as the judge working to drive the increasing desperation of the police to have their wrongdoing exposed. Unusually, but in keeping with its free approach to comedy, the text provides alternative endings.

Themes: A common theme of farce is the exposure of some form of corruption. Here, Fo uses the power of satirical farce to expose the corruption of the police, but also the institutions of the government and the press for their complicity in the 'accidental' death.

Style: The style is that of a satirical farce. The characters are deliberately one-dimensional, representing types, as in the *commedia dell'arte* tradition. The comedy is broad and often physical. As in *commedia dell'arte*, space is created for improvisation (for example, when Pissani tells jokes and takes applause in Act 2 Scene 1). There is also an acknowledgement of the audience (the Maniac sometimes addresses them directly), and there are in-jokes relating to Dario Fo and to the 'cheapness' of the production itself. In production, the script has regularly been updated to reflect current political personalities and issues.

Setting: There are two sets, both offices in police stations. However, part of the in-joke with the audience about the fact that they are watching a cheap touring production means that the changes between the two are only cosmetic.

ACTIVITY

Look at the section of the play near the beginning of Act 2 Scene 1, which begins with the Maniac's line: 'Did you tell the suspect that one?' and ends with the stage direction: 'They slowly twig that they are in the clear'. By exaggerating the physical and vocal characteristics of the four characters, see if you can create the kind of frenzied, farcical style the scene requires. It may help to put the script down and improvise the dialogue once you have got the shape of the scene. A physical and vocal warm-up before you start on this is essential!

ACTIVITY

DESIGN

In your group, discuss how realistic you think the set should be. Ask yourself these questions:

- Will the farcical comedy work best on a highly realistic set that provides a contrast to the action?
- Or should it be deliberately less realistic and rather 'thrown-together'?

Sketch out ideas and decide what you think is most appropriate. Both approaches have been tried in previous productions.

Responding to the extracts

The following text gives general advice for both AS and A level students about how to approach this section of the exam paper. The important differences between the style of AS and A level questions – and therefore how to respond to them – have been clearly indicated.

You have about **one hour** to answer **two** questions on the extract from your set text. The next few pages will give you some advice on how you might approach answering questions on unseen extracts.

Reading the exam question

You need to be clear about exactly what you have to do, so make sure you read the question *carefully.* Look at the exam questions opposite. The key words in each question are shown in bold. Make sure you know what these words mean and keep those definitions in mind while reading the extract.

> **Exam tip**
>
> As you read through the extract and things occur to you, make pencil notes that you can come back to. Try not to let this process interrupt your reading more than necessary. A read-through in one sitting will give you a good sense of the whole scene. You can revisit and revise your pencil notes at that point.

Reading the extract

The extract will be between 80 and 105 lines long and will include any stage directions. That's roughly between three and five pages of the printed text.

Of course, you will recognise the extract; you know the play well. Be aware, though: however well you know your performance text, when you are reading it with the key words and exam questions in mind, you may see things in a different way.

As a **performer** you should look for:

- what has led up to this point
- development/change throughout the scene
- key points in the scene (for example, decision points/dramatically important actions)
- how things are different by the end of the scene.

As a **designer**, you should look for:

- how your design element contributes to the mood and atmosphere
- how it helps to communicate ideas to an audience (for example about character)
- how it reflects the period and style of performance
- what it contributes to the actor/audience relationship.

Now remind yourself of the question. Read through the extract again, adding to your notes.

- Write down your main aims as a performer or designer for the extract.
- Add (in note form) useful ideas for achieving these aims by preparation and in performance.
- Look for any useful short quotations to support your ideas.

AS exam question (performer)

As a **performer**, discuss how you might **interpret** and **portray one of the key roles** in the extract. You should use examples from the extract to support your ideas and your answer should make reference to the performance text as a whole. **(16 marks)**

AS exam question (designer)

As a **designer**, discuss how you would **use theatrical elements** to create **mood and atmosphere** in the extract. You should use examples from the extract to support your ideas and make reference to the performance text as a whole. **(16 marks)**

A level exam question (performer)

As a **performer**, outline how you would use **voice** to create an **impact on the audience** in the **portrayal of one character** in this extract. Your answer should make reference to the performance text as a whole. **(18 marks)**

A level exam question (designer)

As a **designer**, outline how **one theatrical element** could **be developed** to **contribute effectively** to the **impact** of the scene. Your answer should make reference to the performance text as a whole. **(18 marks)**

Organising and planning your answer

After you have read the extract and made some notes, you need to plan your answer. This will be time well spent and should not take too long.

You will need:

- an introduction (one short paragraph)
- a middle section, where you make most of your points (this can be several paragraphs)
- a conclusion (another short paragraph).

Your introduction will depend on the question. In general, it is a good idea to place the scene in the context of the development of the play.

For the 'performer' question, this might mean mentioning the development of the plot, the characters or the relationships.

For the 'designer' question, this might mean mentioning the set requirements for other scenes and any changes to the set that signal a change in atmosphere for this extract.

Summarise your most important ideas for dealing with the extract. You don't need to worry about the details at this point. Here are two examples for a 'performer' question. Aim for constructing your opening like the first example, which is more effective than the second.

> **First opening:** My main aim would be to show how Jenna is trying hard to keep her grief under control.
>
> **Second opening:** I would make sure Jenna keeps her face hidden as much as possible.

Your middle section is where you will score most of your marks, as this will focus on your ideas about the extract. You should follow on from the main aim or aims you have mentioned in your opening section. So, in the 'performer' question, if your main aim is to show how Jenna is trying to keep her grief under control, you might have the following detailed points to make on how to use:

- her body language
- her vocal range and tone
- pauses and silences
- the space on stage between her and the other characters.

Look at this main aim for a 'designer' question.

> My priority is to ensure that the lighting and sound create the contrast in atmosphere between the two acting areas.

The detailed points might then cover:

- the lighting and sound levels, and the way they change
- the angles of the lighting/the positioning of speakers
- the nature of the light/the choice of functional sound effects
- the colours used in lighting
- the use of atmospheric sound.

You will need to support all these with short quotations from the extract or references to it. You may also find it useful to refer to the play as a whole – for example, showing how X's feelings have developed from a previous scene, or how their reactions in this scene build towards something in a later scene.

> **A level exam tip**
>
> Note that your question will focus on **one** aspect of a performer's or a designer's approach to the extract. It might be just the use of voice (performer), for example, or just the use of a single design element like costume (designer). Your list of detailed points will be different from the list opposite because of this.

Your conclusion helps to tie things together, so that you take an overall view of the extract and draw your ideas together to emphasise the main points.

Examples of responses to 'performer' question: AS level only

The text that follows gives examples of student answers to the AS level 'performer' exam question below:

> **AS exam question**
>
> As a **performer**, discuss how you might **interpret** and **portray** one of the **key roles in the extract**. You should use examples from the extract to support your ideas and your answer should make reference to the performance text as a whole. **(16 marks)**

- Student A's answers are based on an extract from *Colder Than Here* by Laura Wade, from the beginning of Scene 5 to the stage direction *Jenna stands up and puts the coat on over her jacket. She sits down, hugging the coat around her* (pages 54–7 in the set edition).
- Student B's answers are based on an extract from *That Face* by Polly Stenham, Scene 6, from '*Martha:* Excuse me. Who are you?' to the stage direction *He exits to the kitchen* (pages 60–4 in the set edition).

Opening paragraph

Student A

This is the first time in the play when Jenna and Alec (her father) have been alone together. We know that they haven't got on well together in the past. (Jenna says to Myra in the first scene that her dad doesn't like her.) This scene in the unpromising graveyard provides a chance for their relationship to develop. My main aim will be to show how she is trying to develop a closer relationship with her father in this extract.

Commentary

This places the extract in the broader context of the relationship between Jenna and her father in the play as a whole, using a relevant quotation from an earlier scene. It shows an understanding of the purpose of the scene as a whole – to develop the relationship between them. It also states clearly what the student sees as the most important point to develop in the rest of the answer – how Jenna tries to develop a closer relationship with her father. It makes it clear that Jenna is the character selected to write about.

Student B

Henry is Martha's son, but she is pretending not to recognise him because she is cross with him. She is an alcoholic and is difficult to handle. She has made a mess of the room, so Henry has to tidy it up. It looks as though Henry is used to doing this. I will be writing about Martha.

Middle paragraphs

These middle sections continue Students A's and B's opening paragraphs, which you have already read and commented on.

Student A

Jenna is 27 and the younger daughter of Alec and Myra. She has been the 'difficult' daughter in the past, but her mother's terminal illness has disturbed and changed her. I see her objective in this scene as wanting to get emotionally closer to her father. This involves trying to get reactions from him in various ways.

At the opening of the scene I would appear momentarily frozen, my body language expressing surprise (I expected my mother, not my father). Throughout the scene I would express some of my anxiety through small nervous gestures and movements. The stage direction 'Jenna twists the tissue in her hands' indicates one way of doing this, but I would develop some other minor nervous tics, such as fidgeting with my handbag or shuffling my feet.

But she is also very conscious that Alec has difficulty in expressing emotion, so when her focus is on him she becomes more still and leans towards him. Her voice changes from the tense and vocally restricted quality at the beginning of the scene and a more confidential and relaxed tone ('Hello, Dad') as though she is trying to start the scene again on a different basis – an invitation to communicate and confide. As the scene goes on, she becomes more chatty, especially in her story about seeing people fall over. I would play this as an easing-in to the question she really wants to ask: 'Do you miss her?' – a genuine enquiry. Interestingly, she has borrowed the question and the 'missing you already' phrase from her sister, who asked her the same questions in an earlier scene. This gives the clue that she is learning how to explore her own feelings and those of other people.

I would use the actions of eating the chocolate and wearing my father's coat as ways of getting closer to him, by savouring the chocolate and feeling a physical pleasure in the warmth of the coat.

Student B

Martha has a complicated relationship with her son, Henry. In this scene she is drunk. She is cross with him because in an earlier scene he told her that he had sex with a girl. She feels jealous because in an odd way she fancies him. Their relationship is a close one, but a strange one, because Henry (who is 18) is having to look after his mother. One of the reasons is that her husband has divorced her and now he has a new wife and a child in Hong Kong. He turns up in a scene later on.

Martha is very drunk but she does know who Henry is, although she pretends not to. She doesn't really move from the bed, so there isn't much to say about her movement, but her voice changes, depending on how she is feeling about him. At times she treats him like a stranger, so her voice would be formal, even strict. At other times she seems to forget that she's pretending not to know him, so her voice becomes more normal, like when she is talking about the only job she has ever had, which was for a month when she went fruit-picking as a student. Martha is often enjoying herself, having a kind of twisted joke, so her voice expresses that.

Commentary

Student B places this extract in the context of the play as a whole by referring to an earlier scene that helps to explain the relationship between Martha and Henry at this point and also providing another reason for Martha's disturbed state (her treatment by her former husband). There are some suggestions about the tone of voice in which Martha should deliver some of her lines, showing an understanding of her complicated relationship with Henry in this scene. These suggestions are rather vague. More precise comments about the way she uses her voice would be an improvement. The words 'formal' and 'strict' help to indicate tone, but 'normal' tells us very little. Does the pace and fluency of her speech change? Does the pitch of her voice alter? The opportunity to comment on movement is passed over. Even though Martha doesn't move from the bed, her use of body language and gesture could be explored. Does she turn to Henry or away from him at different points? Does she use gesture to dismiss him or encourage him to approach at different points? What kinds of gestures? Identifying exact points in the text, rather than saying generally 'at times' would improve the answer as well.

ACTIVITY

Look again at both student answers. Give Student B's middle section a mark out of 16. Then read through Student A's middle section again. Would you give it a higher or lower mark? What points does Student A make that you think deserve to be rewarded?

Concluding paragraph

Student A

In this scene Jenna has mixed success in reaching Alec, as he finds emotional responses difficult. Later in the scene he flinches slightly when Jenna puts her head on his shoulder. She pushes the boundaries too far when she tells him that she and her boyfriend don't have sex any more. But the point is that she is trying to reach out emotionally to her father and this is what the performer should focus on.

> **Commentary**
>
> This provides an effective, concise summary of the points made in the middle section, adding some useful comments that again place the extract in the context of the play as a whole – this time by showing a knowledge of how the scene develops after this extract.

Student B

This extract shows part of the very strange relationship that Martha and Henry have. Martha needs to show how she depends on Henry in all sorts of ways.

> **ACTIVITY**
>
> Concluding paragraphs should be fairly short – but is Student B's too short? List any other points that you think the paragraph should include.

Examples of responses to 'designer' question: AS level only

The text that follows gives examples of student planning notes and answers to the AS level 'designer' exam question:

> **AS exam question**
>
> As a **designer**, discuss how you would **use theatrical elements** to create **mood and atmosphere** in the extract. You should use examples from the extract to support your ideas and make reference to the performance text as a whole.
>
> **(16 marks)**

> **ACTIVITY HEAD**
>
> **IDENTIFYING THE KEY WORDS**
>
> Read the question carefully and identify the key words that will help you focus your answer.

- Student C's notes and answers are based on an extract from *Accidental Death of an Anarchist* by Dario Fo, Act 1 Scene 2, from the beginning of the scene to '*Pissani*: He blew a raspberry at me' (pages 16–19 in the set edition).
- Student D's answers are based on an extract from *Machinal* by Sophie Treadwell, Episode 3, from the beginning of the scene to '*Husband*: Want me to help you? *Young Woman*: No' (pages 21–4 in the set edition).

Opening paragraph

Student C

I am looking at the way the set in this scene helps to create mood and atmosphere. In the play as a whole there is a good deal of acknowledgement of the presence of the audience. There are a number of **meta-theatrical** jokes which involve the audience in the understanding that they are watching a performance. The set forms a part of this understanding and its design features contribute to the play's atmosphere and impact on the audience, making them feel part of it.

> **Commentary**
>
> Student C immediately identifies the 'theatrical element' the answer will focus on – the set. The paragraph then goes on to show an understanding of the style of the play and how the set should signal this to the audience. There is an understanding of how the audience is involved in the performance in this particular play. The term 'meta-theatrical' is appropriately used.

> **Glossary**
>
> **Meta-theatrical**
> Any device that draws the audience's attention to the fact that what is happening on stage is not real, but a performance. One device could be direct address to the audience, for example.

ACTIVITY

Write a note of advice to Student D, giving suggestions for improvements to this opening paragraph.

Student D

The lighting and the sound can be incredibly important in this scene. I believe they should have a strong impact. They can be used to set the right atmosphere for this scene in which the Young Woman and the Husband appear. They are in a hotel bedroom. It seems like it might be their wedding night. There is a dancing casino opposite their bedroom. I am going to set out some ideas about what the lighting and sound should be like.

Middle paragraphs

Student C's planning notes

Intro: set as part of meta-theatre joke - not realistic/touring set – creates atmosphere

Points:

– small changes from Scene 1

– scene change in audience view

– angular (coat-stand)

– free-standing set (incl. doors)

– window

– update – mini-recording device etc. portrait

Conc: serving purpose of play/farce style

Student C's answer

The mood and atmosphere of the play need to be conveyed by all the elements involved. Although the play makes serious points, it does it through a farcical style and through involving the audience in the running joke that what they are seeing is not an imitation of reality, but a performance. I would make the set indicate that in as many ways as possible. The set should not attempt to be realistic, but consist of free-standing elements – a large pair of flats upstage, with a free-standing window suspended between them (this is the same as Scene 1, but the window is opened in the scene-change).

The stage directions indicate that the set for Scene 2 is very similar to the set for Scene 1. As this is part of the 'meta-theatre' joke, I would make sure that the audience sees the set change being done by the actors, changing just a few things to give it a cosmetic appearance of being a different office. The flats should be angular, as though they have been badly made; the coat-stand should be at an angle as well, looking as though it might fall over. It should look like a cheap set from a bad touring production. (In this extract, the actor playing the Maniac actually says to the Stage Manager (in the wings). 'Remind me not to appear in these cheap touring productions again.') As a part of the scene-change, I would make the two free-standing door-frames identical, but have the cast swap them over in the scene-change, inviting the audience to appreciate their effort to make a 'change'. The view from the window would be changed as well, by turning round a badly painted back cloth, to reveal another slightly different, badly painted backcloth.

I would want to update the production to now, so the portrait (hung at an angle from a flat) would be of the current Italian president and the 'tape-recorder', which the Maniac hides under the desk, would be a modern mini-recording device.

Commentary

Student C has clearly understood the style of the play and how the general atmosphere the production requires can be created through an appropriate set. Student C is aware of the importance of the actor–audience relationship. There is a good deal of detail about specific set elements (the flats, the backcloth, the coat-stand, etc.) and an imaginative idea for how the set could be changed in keeping with the atmosphere of the play. There are appropriate references to the text, both stage directions and actor's lines, and the use of appropriate specialist terminology (flats, backcloth, wings). Updating the text may well be workable, but the idea needs a clearer justification.

Student D's answer

The sound and the lighting need to work closely together. The point of the scene is that the Young Woman feels alone and frightened of her wedding-night. The lighting and sound should try to show this by showing how life outside the window is exciting and lively, but life inside the hotel room is threatening. I think the set should be on a kind of island in the middle of the stage and this island should be lit tightly to define a small area surrounded by darkness. It would be important not to have any light-spill around this area, so lanterns that give a definite cut-off should be used for this. The light should also be cold, so blue gels would be a good colour to use. The Young Woman says at one point, 'It's close', meaning that it's warm and stuffy in the room, but the point is that it isn't. She just says this because she doesn't want to undress. There should be a contrast with the lights outside the window on the dancing casino across the road. These should be created with warm bright colours, reds and yellows, with the lights changing levels constantly and pulsing. The casino lights need to be located at the back of the stage, in the area outside the window, but they could spill out filling a larger space, giving the feeling of an exciting world outside.

The sound should go with this. The script says that there is jazz music coming from the casino. This will be very lively music that people can dance to. This should be mixed with the voices of men and women obviously having a good time – laughing, shouting and shrieking. At one point the Husband opens the window and the sound increases. There is also a stage direction that says the lights fade out part-way through this extract and this must apply to the sound as well. The effect is to make the atmosphere inside the hotel room seem quieter and emptier.

ACTIVITY

For the answers of both Student C and Student D, write a short concluding paragraph. You will need to be aware of the main point(s) made in the middle paragraphs. These should also be identified in the opening paragraphs. Even if you don't know the play, you should be able to base your concluding paragraph on what has gone before.

Examples of responses to 'performer' question: A level only

Because you are dealing with the same texts as AS students, you will find it useful to read through some of the examples of AS student answers on the previous pages. Although your questions will have a different focus, how you approach your answers to the question below will be much the same:

A level exam question

As a **performer**, outline how you would use **voice** to create an **impact on the audience** in the **portrayal of one character** in this extract. Your answer should make reference to the performance text as a whole.

(18 marks)

- Student A's answers are based on an extract from *Equus* by Peter Shaffer, Scene 27, from the beginning of the scene to Alan's line: 'Oooh, I didn't mean that!' (pages 85–8 in the set edition).
- Student B's answers are based on an extract from *Fences* by August Wilson, Act 2 Scene 4, from Cory: 'You don't know what I got. You ain't got to worry about what I got' to the end of the scene (pages 86–9 in the set edition).

ACTIVITY

LOOKING FOR THE POSTIVES AND NEGATIVES

Go through Student D's answer making a list of all the positive points – those an examiner would want to reward. Then go through and look for negatives – for example, points that aren't convincing or not developed. Look also to see if there are any missed opportunities. Then reach a decision about the quality of this answer. Compare it with Student C's answer.

Exam tip

It's always good to introduce a new perspective or make a new link in your conclusion. You may have found this difficult in the previous activity if you don't know the play. Look back to Student A's conclusion and see how the new point about Jenna's 'mixed success' has been introduced, and how it's linked with the main idea of the answer.

ACTIVITY

As you read the question, make sure you understand what you are being asked to do. Start by identifying the key words in the question – that is, the words that will have an effect on what you write and how you construct your answer.

Opening paragraphs

Student A

This scene between Alan and Dysart follows on from previous scenes in which they have had a row (caused by Alan's behaviour to Dysart) and one in which Dysart has received a short written apology from Alan. Both have been disturbed by the row and both are keen to make it up. I am focusing on the way that the actor playing Alan will use his voice.

> #### Commentary
>
> This places the scene in the context of the Alan–Dysart relationship in the play. It provides some information about one of the characters' significant objectives in the scene ('to make it up') and indicates the focus of the answer (Alan's use of voice). It is kept short and to the point, and does its job effectively.

ACTIVITY

Write some notes, giving feedback to Student B about this paragraph. What would you advise the student to take out or to add?

Student B

Cory is Troy's son, aged 17. He is very keen to become a professional football player, but Troy won't let him because of his own experience in suffering racism in his earlier life as a professional baseball player. Cory is full of anger and resentment. There has been a fight between them before. Troy has been drinking and is sitting on the steps in the yard of the house.

Middle paragraphs

Student A

Alan is 17 and comes from a working-class/lower middle-class background (his aspirational working-class father says that his wife thinks that she 'married beneath her'). He doesn't appear to have been successful at school. We don't know exactly where the play is set (Dysart works in a 'provincial' hospital), so there is a choice about the accent he might have. I would choose to give him an Essex countryside accent to contrast his way of speech strongly with the educated **RP** of Dysart.

Alan's use of voice in the scene is affected by both his current state of mind and his objectives in the scene. He often speaks sharply with a pent-up energy, emphasising consonants (for example 'plosives' like 'b' and 'p'). This gives his voice an aggressive edge, seen especially in the early scene in the play when he is at his most disturbed and volatile. When he starts this scene with the single word 'Hallo', however, he is uncertain of his reception from Dysart and delivers it without energy and tonelessly.

He has learned from earlier scenes that he can trust Dysart, but his natural defence mechanisms still come through at times, for example, in the delivery of short, sharp sentences like 'That's the right word. My mum told me.' As the scene proceeds, he becomes more relaxed and confident vocally, adopting a conversational tone. He starts asking questions like 'You got another trick, then?' or 'Can I have a fag, then?' He is still on edge and wary, however, as can be seen when Dysart makes a joke and he responds by shouting at high volume '**I'm serious!**' But as he believes the 'truth drug' is taking hold on him, his voice becomes more natural, less tense, and his interest in Dysart as a human being comes through, so 'How would you Nosey Parker, then?' has a genuinely inquisitive tone. The line 'So are you' in response to Dysart's remark that he is unhappy comes out spontaneously, indicating that his normal way of expressing 'attitude' has been by-passed.

Student B

Troy was born in Alabama, so his accent comes from that part of the USA, in the South, which was the region of slavery. He now lives in Pittsburgh in the North, but he hasn't lost his accent. In this scene he becomes aggressive to Cory because he thinks that Cory is being rude to him and challenging him. Troy's voice will show more aggression as he loses his temper.

Troy is a big and dominant character who needs a loud and powerful voice. In his home he likes to be the boss and to express his views strongly. Recently he has lost status in his

Glossary 💬

RP (received pronunciation)
Standard English pronunciation with no evident accent.

house by getting another woman pregnant and then bringing home the baby for his wife to care for. He feels guilty, although he doesn't admit this. It comes out in his aggression. In his speeches there are a lot of exclamation marks, showing that he is putting a lot of energy into his voice. This doesn't always mean shouting, but there are times when he does, like 'I told you to leave your mama out of this!' Sometimes he uses a lower pitch of his voice to become more threatening and to show that he is more determined to let Cory know that he is boss, like 'Get your black ass out of my yard!' When he realises that Cory won't hit him with the baseball bat he becomes more confident and his voice takes on a tone of authority, for example when he says 'You wanna draw that bat back on me. You're gonna have to kill me.' He then puts on a taunting tone with the next line 'Come on! Come on!'

After Cory has gone and Troy is left alone, his voice shows his depression in 'I can't taste nothing no more.' He then has one of his conversations with Death when he challenges it in the same way he challenged Cory – 'Come on!'

Commentary

Student B provides some relevant information about Troy's background, character and his current situation, rightly pointing out that these will affect his voice and manner of delivery. The student realises there will be variation in Troy's use of his voice, referring to appropriate terminology such as 'pitch' and 'tone'. Several examples are given from the text to support the points being made. These are related to Troy's developing emotions in the extract. All this is on the right lines, although more precise references to other areas of the use of the voice – pace, use of pauses, volume, articulation, for example, and more precise descriptions of how lines might be delivered would have strengthened the answer.

Concluding paragraph

Student A

As with any role, the voice and the character are closely linked and it's possible to see how his changing emotions are shown in his vocal changes. It would only be possible to 'find' Alan's voice after a good deal of preparation by the actor, working on Alan's background and feelings. In performance it will also be closely linked with Alan's repressed feelings, showing marked changes when he is able to feel free of these, as in the scene when he 'abreacts' and rides Nugget.

Commentary

This paragraph offers a brief overview of what has been presented in the middle paragraphs, but goes on to make a valid general point about the close interaction of character, emotion and vocal expression.

Student B

Troy is a complicated character, a mix of pride, guilt and aggression. All these are expressed through his voice, as we see at different points in this scene.

Examples of responses to 'designer' question: A level only

Because you are dealing with the same texts as AS students, you will find it useful to read through some of the examples of AS student answers on the previous pages. Although your questions will have a different focus, how you approach your answers to the question below will be much the same.

> **A level exam question**
>
> As a **designer**, outline how **one theatrical element** could **be developed** to **contribute effectively** to the **impact** of the scene. Your answer should make reference to the performance text as a whole.
>
> **(18 marks)**

> **ACTIVITY**
>
> Read through Student A's answer to the question on *Equus*. Give it a mark out of 18. Would you give this a higher mark than Student B's answer on *Fences*? Write down or discuss the reasons for your view.

> **ACTIVITY**
>
> If you know the play, re-write Student B's concluding paragraph, making improvements. If you don't know the play, make suggestions for what kinds of additions would make it a stronger conclusion.

ACTIVITY

Make sure you read the question carefully before you answer, identifying any key words that will have an effect on what you write.

A level exam guidance

In this question, 18 marks are available:

- **6 marks** for demonstrating knowledge and understanding of how theatre is **performed**
- **12 marks** for demonstrating knowledge and understanding of how theatre is **developed**.

Responses that demonstrate knowledge and understanding of how theatre is performed without discussing how it is developed will only achieve a maximum of **6 marks**.

Responses that demonstrate isolated knowledge without linked understanding will only achieve a maximum of **3 marks**.

This means you have to explain clearly how your design ideas:

- arise out of, and are developed from, the needs of the text
- are presented in performance.

'Isolated knowledge' means information that is not linked to the issues in the play. See Student I's answer on *Machinal* (in 'Preparing for your exam') for an example.

For the following two students, the full answer is given. Note that they are still structured with an opening paragraph, a middle section (comprising several paragraphs) and a concluding paragraph.

- Student C's answer is based on an extract from *Colder Than Here* by Laura Wade, Scene 7, from the beginning of the scene to the stage direction *Jenna pulls a box of Tic-Tacs out of her bag* (pages 75–8 in set edition).
- Student D's answer is based on an extract from *That Face* by Polly Stenham, Scene 7, from pages 67–9 in set edition).

Student C

I am going to focus on the set as the design element to be developed. The play alternates between the odd-numbered scenes set in various 'greenfield' graveyards and the even-numbered scenes set in the family home. This is the fourth graveyard visited by members of the family, and the second time the sisters, Jenna and Harriet, have been seen together on a visit. They were previously seen in Scene 3 in a different graveyard.

Because this is an intimate play, I would see it taking place in a studio, with the audience close to the action. It's important for them to feel involved with the characters and their relationships. The play is written naturalistically, but an entirely naturalistic set is difficult to achieve because of the necessity to keep the play flowing without time-consuming set changes. There is no interval given in the text and the play would be more effective if played without breaks, so the action is maintained. It's important to create the different atmospheres of the graveyards. I would create swift changes by using a large projection screen completely covering the upstage area and back-project images on to it. This can have an immediate visual impact on the audience.

This graveyard is the one chosen by the family, so it must feel peaceful and look pleasant. As the text says that it is a 'surprisingly warm March day' the image should suggest a warm light in the sky, shining on the trees, grass and flowers. Internet research on greenfield burial sites shows that there are many appropriate images available. The sisters sit on the ground, so it will be important to provide a floor cloth of artificial moss, into which the crocuses can be woven. This will have to be temporarily fixed in place during the scene change.

The scene also shows a growing warmth and understanding between the two sisters, who have sometimes had an awkward relationship. Harriet talks about her feelings and problems with eczema and Harriet offers her advice (E45 cream), Tic-Tacs and makes the occasional joke ('croci/croaky'). So the audience should feel that the warm atmosphere created by the set reflects that growing warmth.

In terms of the set, these are the important elements to suggest the setting, without providing a full naturalistic environment. I would want to work closely with the lighting and sound designers, of course, to make sure the lighting is also warm and that there are pleasant 'summer-day' background sounds.

Commentary

Student C states clearly what the chosen design element is and places the design in the context of the structure of the play, with its alternating settings. There is an evident awareness of the practicalities involved as well as the importance of creating the right atmosphere for the scene. This involves not just the creation of the pleasant nature of the place, but an appreciation that this must serve the scene by providing an appropriate setting for the development of the relationship between the sisters. Student C refers to research undertaken to support choices and also uses short quotations from the text to support points. There is reference to the broader context of the play. Although no reference to lighting and sound is required, the final paragraph shows an understanding of the necessity of how these could serve the set. A more detailed description of the image and the floor cloth would have improved the answer.

Student D

In this scene the costumes worn by the characters will be important in helping the audience to realise who they are and their states of mind, as well as the relationship between them. They are father (Hugh) and his 15-year-old daughter, Mia. She has been suspended from her boarding school and he has flown over from Hong Kong to sort out the problem. They are eating a meal in a posh restaurant.

Hugh is a broker and obviously well-off. He can afford to live in Hong Kong and keep a flat in Canary Wharf in London. He also pays for his children to go to private schools. His costume should reflect this. He should have a very well-cut, expensive, three-piece suit which fits him very well. It should also be made out of a light material, which will go with the fact that he lives in Hong Kong, in a much warmer climate. He needs to look formal, to go with being a businessman, so he should have a shirt with a well-knotted tie. The overall effect should be of a smart, conventional well-off businessman.

Mia is in term-time at school, but has been suspended. It looks as though she has had to go to an interview at the school with her father about her suspension, because Hugh says 'I thought that went well' before talking about how he has arranged to give the school some new digital cameras as part of a deal to let Mia stay. She would have to dress up to go to this interview, so she should look smart as well. She would be wearing a white blouse to look more formal than usual, and a smart pencil skirt, in a navy blue, just above the knee. She would also have blue tights and black court shoes. She should also be wearing large earrings, just as a mark of defiance, as the school would not normally let her do this.

The scene between them is very awkward, because they don't really know what to say to each other. Because they are both dressed quite formally, it means that it feels harder for them to have a normal conversation. In that way, the costumes help them in performing the scene and the audience will realise the tension in the situation.

Because the scene is set in an expensive restaurant, they would have had to dress up anyway, but Hugh is certainly used to doing this. Mia may feel a bit more awkward in her costume.

ACTIVITY

Read this answer closely. Then jot down, as a bullet list, the main points of the answer. Create a plan containing three sections: opening paragraph, middle section, concluding paragraph. Allocate points for each of these. Then answer the following questions.

- Is your order of points the same as Student D's?

- Are there any sentences or short sections you would cut completely?

Preparing for your exam

Section B: AS level sample answers with commentaries

As a **performer**, discuss how you might interpret and portray one of the key roles in the extract.

You should use examples from the extract to support your ideas and your answer should make reference to the performance text as a whole. **(16 marks)**

These answers are based on an extract from *Fences* by August Wilson, Act 2 Scene 2, from the beginning of the scene to Rose's exit after Troy's speech: '*I ain't pushing nobody away. Just give me some space. Just give me some time to breathe.*'

Student A

In this scene Rose is angry at Troy because he has made another woman pregnant and she is just about to have his baby. She hasn't talked to him for months, but tonight she has decided to. She wants to challenge him about spending time with Alberta (the woman he has made pregnant). She knows that the next day is Friday, which is pay-day, and that Troy is likely to spend time with Alberta. She has decided that it is time to have it out with him.

> This shows some understanding of the scene in the context of the play as a whole and of Rose's state of mind at this point.

I would show my determination by entering positively and standing with my arms folded. I would stand my ground and let Troy be the one who moves. In this way I would be grounded and feel in charge of the scene. She knows Troy well as they have been married for 18 years, so she knows that she has to pin him down, as he will try to wriggle out of things.

> This makes some basic suggestions about how Rose's intentions might be portrayed physically.

I think Rose has planned what she is going to say and knows how Troy will react. She keeps her sentences short and sharp. She knows about Troy signing the papers to get his hands on some of Gabriel's money and plans when to bring this up. I would not let Troy off the hook.

> Student A realises that Rose has a plan for the conversation and is prepared for Troy's opposition, which shows in the delivery of her lines.

When the phone call comes, I would soften my voice telling Troy about the death of Alberta to show some sympathy for his loss, but not really comforting him. I feel a bit sorry for him, but I still know that he has done me wrong.

> There is an understanding of Rose's underlying attitude to Troy and how her voice can convey this.

Commentary

Student A has shown enough knowledge of Rose's feelings and intentions as this scene develops, and there is also evidence of a more general understanding of her relationship with Troy in the broader context of the play as a whole. There are only a few suggestions as to how this will affect her playing of the scene in vocal and physical expression.

Overall, this is a rather varied response, lacking sufficient specific points. To improve this answer, Student A would need to:

- show a more comprehensive understanding of the context of the scene in the development of the text as a whole
- make more specific suggestions as to how the performer could prepare herself for the demands of the scene
- make more detailed suggestions as to how the character could be portrayed on stage to bring out the conflicting elements that exist in her.

More use of appropriate specialist terminology is also needed.

Student B

I am focusing on the role of Rose. This scene occurs six months after Troy has told her that another woman, Alberta, is carrying his child. In playing this scene it will be important to imagine what that six months has been like, with Troy increasingly spending time with Alberta in the evenings after work. In preparation I would spend time imaginatively creating scenes from Rose's life in those six months and improvising wordless scenes with the actor playing Troy, in which the atmosphere between them is tense, while the emotions remain unspoken.

This places the scene firmly in context for the development of Rose's character and makes perceptive suggestions about how a performer would prepare to play this scene.

Rose's bearing and movement will be important in this scene; they need to convey the way in which she has begun to separate herself emotionally from Troy. I would play her as moving more slowly and with less ease than in previous scenes. Her movement and gestures should remain controlled and tight, conveying the way her life has become more constrained. In terms of proxemics, the distance she maintains from Troy will also be significant, especially as in the previous scene Troy has physically hurt her by grabbing her arm. She should feel that she no longer wants to be close to him, perhaps by remaining on the raised level of the porch, while he stands in the yard.

This shows appropriate use of terminology: proxemics and level, for example. Again, there is evidence of a comprehensive grasp of the context of the whole play.

As the birth of the child becomes imminent, Rose feels pressure to speak out and assert herself. Her objective now is to have a showdown. She should show this assertiveness in the way she delivers her lines, putting emphasis on the repeated 'I want' and 'I won't live like this' – not angry, but assertive and deliberate.

Student B makes appropriate use of short quotations and shows a sophisticated understanding of Rose's feelings at this point.

In the play's final scene, Rose speaks about how she made the mistake in her marriage of not making Troy 'leave some room for me'. In this scene, she needs to show how she has become more self-contained and is capable of seeing Troy clearly and judging him. When talking about the way in which Troy has signed the papers for Gabriel, even though Troy denies this, she remains clear-sighted, accusing him evenly and without anger: 'You went back on yourself, Troy. You gonna have to answer for that.' I would play her as being vocally clear and confident, with a crisp, positive delivery, while standing still and upright, showing her settled determination.

Rose's development is again seen in the context of the whole play, and appropriate suggestions are made for how this can be portrayed physically and vocally.

The lines when Rose delivers the bad news to Troy need to be played with an understanding of the impact that the news will have on him, so I would play them more gently, while maintaining my physical distance from him, leaving a pause before beginning as a way of easing into the subject and helping to soften the blow. She never loses some of the love she has for him. Even when he reacts with anger, I would show these feelings of remaining love and support through the gentle delivery of the line, 'I am your wife. Don't push me away.' This is consistent with her behaviour in the following scene, that evening, when she agrees to take in and look after the child.

There is a relevant reference to another scene (the following one) to provide evidence of an interpretation of Rose's character. There are further positive suggestions for the portrayal of this in performance.

Commentary

Student B has approached the response to the question in an organised way. The student places the scene firmly in the context of the play, but also in the context of the development of Rose. The student shows a comprehensive awareness of the text, and makes intelligent and relevant suggestions about how the actor can achieve the desired effect through the delivery of lines and through movement and stillness. Student B notes that there is a subtle change in her attitude towards Troy, which nevertheless doesn't entirely compromise her motivation in the scene. There is relevant reference to the text, with short and apt quotations being selected to demonstrate points of both attitude and delivery. There is also relevant use of some appropriate terminology.

This is a strong response that shows a detailed and perceptive understanding of the text and the process of preparation and delivery from the point of view of the performer.

This answer is based on an extract from *Colder Than Here* by Laura Wade, Scene 8, from Myra's words: *'When I'm gone'* to the end of the scene.

Student C

Alec finds it difficult to express his feelings and to talk about Myra's approaching death. In this scene he begins to accept the inevitable, so my main aim would be to show him beginning to open up emotionally to Myra and to recognise his own feelings and to tell her about them. Apart from a few moments at the end of Scene 4, this is the only time so far in the play that we have seen them alone together. Previously in the play he has used 'displacement' activities to avoid having to express his feelings – finding things to do or to say that mean he doesn't run the risk of breaking down. I would show him doing this when he says 'Nice bath' using a forced, rather bright tone, trying to have a normal conversation. His body language is usually tight and restricted, keeping himself in control. I would start the extract physically in this way.

> Student C shows relevant knowledge of other parts of the text. There is good awareness of the interpretation of Alec's character and good use of the extract to illustrate a point.

I would play the line 'Do you think I should move house?' in a rather pre-occupied way, because he doesn't realise that it shows that he's thinking about her death and what happens after. I would then try desperately to talk quickly and row back until Myra stops me. He doesn't usually swear or curse, so 'Christ, Myra' is said with strong feelings of shock. He shifts in his chair, showing how difficult and uncomfortable he is finding the topic of remarriage, but I would then use the long pause to gather myself physically and vocally to begin to express my feelings to Myra.

> Student C shows a positive use of the text to demonstrate how physical and vocal means can be used to portray the character's feelings in this extract.

When he changes his mind about where to sit to read his book, I would show in my face the feeling that I am deliberately moving closer to Myra. And even though I would tense up at the first physical contact she makes, I would gradually relax, giving up the pretence of reading and eventually kissing her head. Telling Myra that he does cry and will cry more is like a gift, the closest he comes to telling her he loves her. I would express this physically through the stage direction 'He holds her tight', as he expresses all his suppressed feelings of love and affection.

> Student C makes a sound interpretation of the character's emotional journey in the scene, again with appropriate examples from the extract to demonstrate points.

Commentary

Student C has approached the question in an organised way, offering an interpretation of Alec's character and tracking his emotional progress through the scene, using the text to supply suggestions for appropriate physical and vocal expression. This is quite a strong answer, which could be improved by more detailed suggestions for portrayal of the character, together with a greater use of specialist vocabulary to describe the use of physical and vocal qualities.

As a **designer**, discuss how you would use theatrical elements to create an appropriate impact on the audience in the extract.

You should use examples from the extract to support your ideas and make reference to the performance text as a whole.

(16 marks)

Exam tip

Remember that at AS level you can choose whether you wish to concentrate on one theatrical element (e.g. sound), or on more than one (e.g. set and costume) or to deal with the whole range of relevant theatrical elements.

This answer is based on an extract from *Equus* by Peter Shaffer; the whole of Scene 15.

Student D

I am going to deal with sound, lighting and set in answering this question. *Equus* is a play that has a powerful impact on the audience, so my job as a designer is to help that impact to be as strong as possible.

The main dramatic effect in this scene is the entry of Jill and her effect on Alan. The audience need to be made very aware of her impact on him because of how important the relationship between her and Alan will be in the rest of the play. I would make as much as possible of the build-up to her entrance. I would set the play in the round, with three entrances between the audience seats. The audience seats will be on a steep rake, so the entrances will be like tunnels (like in a football stadium). The acting area should be quite small. (This is similar to the touring Roundabout theatre, which has influenced me.) The reason for this is that I think there needs to be a close relationship between the actors and the audience. The audience need to be 'grabbed' and involved in the play. They need to be close to the action, so the in-the-round stage form is the best for this purpose.

> Student D provides a clear consideration of what stage form would be appropriate for the extract with equally clear justifications.

The only furniture on stage should be three wooden benches. These should be made of the same light wood as the circular stage floor and not decorated in any way. I would use LED lighting, so that the intensity and colour can change quickly to show any change in atmosphere. The speakers would be placed on the walls high up behind the audience to give a 'surround-sound' effect, except when any effects have to be directional.

> Various areas of design have been considered. Colour and material have been recognised as significant elements of set design, and some basic technical knowledge of lighting and sound has been demonstrated.

Dysart should be sitting in the front row of the audience, on one of the audience seats (several seats in the front row will be reserved for the use of the cast). Other members of the cast are scattered around the auditorium. When Alan enters he sits on a bench on stage. The stage would be generally lit, but at a low level. When the scene changes to the shop (when the other actors start calling out, there should be a single, bright spot on Alan in the middle of the stage. The sound of the actual actors should be reinforced by other voices coming through the speakers so that the audience has the feeling of the same impact as it has on Alan – an overwhelming effect as he is feeling exposed and drowning in sound. (Some of the names of equipment might have to be updated.) When Jill enters through a tunnel, she has her own spotlight, so both she and Alan are in pools of light. The actors' voices and the soundtrack stop immediately to give the audience the same shock effect that her entry has on Alan.

◄— Attention is paid to specific moments in the extract, giving clear ideas as to how impact on the audience can be created through the use of design elements. There are some bold choices, but again justifications are offered for these.

My aim with the design is to make the audience feel part of the action, as though they are sharing Alan's experience in the scene.

◄— Short final paragraph that introduces a new thought, drawing together some of the ideas introduced earlier in the answer.

Commentary

Student D has clearly stated the theatrical elements to be dealt with in the answer (set, lighting and sound). There are clear ideas about how the extract should be staged, with the design ideas being applied to the broader context of the play, as required by the question. The student mentions an influence on the venue design and is clear about the stage form (in-the-round) and the ways in which lighting and sound integrate with this design. The question is about creating 'appropriate impact' on the audience, and Student D shows an awareness of this, demonstrating an understanding of how the meaning of the scene is to be communicated. The student has demonstrated some understanding of a number of design-related areas: set, lighting, sound, use of space, proxemics, levels, entrances and exits, the actor/audience relationship and the use of the theatrical venue. There is good use of subject-specific terminology in a number of areas of design.

- The answer could be improved by covering aspects of the scene not mentioned. The first section of the scene is dealt with in a limited way, with no mention of Alan's entrance or whether the scene remains static. There is no mention of whether Dysart (sitting in the audience) should be lit, or of the final stage direction, which involves a change of setting.
- This answer demonstrates a good deal of assurance, however, with very sound ideas about the impact of design of the extract, and an awareness of the play as a whole.
- Most play-texts give a fairly clear indication of the set and other design features. A designer does not have to follow these instructions, although it is sensible to take note of them. For example, a set that will work for an end-stage production will not work for an in-the-round production. The play-text of *Equus* gives an extremely specific description of the text – but it can be staged effectively in different ways.

This answer is based on an extract from *That Face* by Polly Stenham, from Scene 3, *They both hear the sudden sound of someone knocking on the door* to the end of the scene.

Student E

I would make it clear that the scene is set in an expensive, private hospital. The bed will be of a high spec, with a mechanism for raising and lowering sections. The sheets will be spotlessly clean and the drip which Alice is attached to will have gleaming metal. It will look clean and organised. Izzy looks round the room and says, 'Not bad, eh? She must have had insurance', which shows that she is impressed by the quality of the room. It should also be larger than necessary, with a very large television screen on the wall and with a carpet. There should be a large bedside table, with a vase where Izzy's flowers get placed, and the floor should be carpeted.

> Student E begins with a good, clear idea here, with support from the text. The detail is well described and gives a good impression of the student's intent.

The one thing that should stand out is the large bruise on Alice's face. This should be carefully created by make-up to look raw and unpleasant. It should stand out against the whiteness of Izzy's bandages and the sheets. The impression that the room should give is of high-level equipment, comfort, with the sense that it's the best that money can buy. There should be some tasteful paintings on the wall to add to this impression.

> This is a good description of contrast – the visible rawness and discomfort of the bruise set against the cleanliness of the bandages and sheets.

I would make the lighting quite soft to give a sense that the room is peaceful and also not provide any sound except for the one time that the stage directions say that there is a sound of footsteps and a passing trolley outside the door, as this is necessary to create tension among Mia, Izzy and Henry. There could be a difference between the costumes that these three are wearing, because Izzy has planned her visit and would have come looking smart, but Mia and Henry have just thrown clothes on and come on impulse.

> There is an opportunity here to expand on this detail. The student could have given more detail about staging, for example. They could also have made broader links to the play as a whole.

Commentary

Student E has a strong central idea – that the setting of the private hospital room should convey to the audience an impression of a high-quality and expensive environment. Various details are gradually assembled about the set to reinforce this impression – the whiteness of the sheets, the carpet, the large television screen, the carpet, the gleaming metal of the 'drip' equipment. These are all helpful visual statements that support the central design idea. There is support from the text for this idea in the quotation from Izzy. The suggestion that make-up should provide a visually striking bruise for Alice in order to strike a discordant note is also sound. However, the point could have been reinforced by mentioning the earlier effect of Alice's appearance on Henry. He had not seen her before and realises only at this point the severity of the damage inflicted on her by Izzy and Mia.

The answer seems to assume an end-stage form, but doesn't address this specifically. It assumes walls and a door, so a realistic approach to the design is implied. The suggestion is that it is played on a 'box set'. Given that this is only one of the five settings required for the play, attention needs to be paid to overall requirements of the design for the play and the logistics of scene changes.

While the answer has a relevant main point, less consideration is given to some of the elements mentioned – sound, lighting and costume. It could have been improved by a clearer awareness of the performance text as a whole, by a more careful and less general consideration of some of the design features, and by greater use of appropriate specialist terminology.

Section B: A level sample answers with commentaries

As a **performer**, how would you use non-verbal communication to create an impact on the audience in the portrayal of one character in this extract?

You should use examples from the extract to support your ideas and your answer should make reference to the performance text as a whole.

(18 marks)

These answers are based on an extract from *Accidental Death of an Anarchist* by Dario Fo, Act 1 Scene 2, from the Maniac's line *'Talking of schools … if you don't mind my saying'* to the Maniac's line *'Brilliant'*.

Student A

I have chosen to write about the role of the Superintendent in this extract. In this scene he is being treated like a puppet by the Maniac, who is definitely in charge of the proceedings.

> This paragraph is very short. It contains basic detail, but has missed the opportunity to give useful background to the scene.

The Superintendent doesn't know the Maniac, who is pretending to be a judge. When the Superintendent enters earlier in this scene, he throws his weight around, but changes completely when he thinks that the judge has come to check up on him. I would make sure that his non-verbal communication shows that he is frightened of the judge at first, because he stiffens with fear. But this changes when he thinks that the judge is on his side and they start singing a song together. He clicks his heels in a way that a fascist would do and joins in with the saluting rather like a schoolboy having a game.

> The student could expand this paragraph by explaining how a performer could demonstrate the various methods of non-verbal communication.

His body language shows that he thinks of the judge as a superior and his facial expressions show that he is worried when the judge starts asking him questions about the death of the anarchist. He still thinks the judge is on his side, though, because he thinks the judge is a secret fascist and that he can trust him. When the judge stops him after his entrance when they are reconstructing the scene with the anarchist and he goes back and enters again, his body language is aggressive until he is stopped again by the judge. After that the judge keeps interrupting him and his body language shows that he is losing confidence.

> Although the facts are in place here, once again the student has missed the opportunity to link their ideas with how they could be achieved through performance.

In this scene the Superintendent goes through some changes of attitude. All these are shown in the way he uses non-verbal communication.

> Once again, some examples would be useful. The student could add here how the non-verbal communication in this scene has created meaning for the audience.

Commentary

Student A shows a basic understanding of the scene in its context of the play as a whole but does not comment on the aim of the Maniac in impersonating the judge. It is important to an understanding of the scene to be aware of this. The opening paragraph, which is weak, could be expanded to include this information. The student correctly identifies some of the changes that would affect the non-verbal communication required in the scene, but offers no clear suggestions on how a performer might achieve these in performance. If the 'body language is aggressive', for example, what does the performer actually do to achieve this? The suggestions for non-verbal communication are taken from the stage directions, but not developed (for example, the clicking of the heels and the

saluting). The conclusion is a vague summing-up of what has gone before, failing to show any new insight or perspective. Crucially, there is no evident understanding of the farcical style of the play, which will have a powerful influence on the style of non-verbal communication. Little attention is paid to the part of the question that refers to 'impact on the audience'.

Student A has shown at least some awareness of the interpretation of intentions, of characterisation and of the relationship between other characters in the extract. The student also shows some awareness of the use of entrances and exits. However, overall the awareness is not at a high level and the answer focuses too heavily on plot elements at the expense of more relevant points.

Student B

I shall discuss the way in which the Maniac uses non-verbal communication in this extract. The actor playing the Maniac (originally Dario Fo himself) has to be very versatile and physically agile. A background in traditional *commedia dell'arte* (which Dario Fo knew well) is a distinct advantage in creating the larger-than-life character types required by the farcical nature of this play.

> There is some good background detail in this opening, along with a clear definition of the style of theatre adopted by the playwright.

I would base the physical elements of performance on the *commedia* 'Dottore' character – the doctor, who is academic, authoritative and also has some malicious qualities (there is no 'lawyer' figure on *commedia*, so this is the closest character). As the judge, the Maniac assumes authority in a pedantic way, just as the Dottore does. Placing the weight on the back of the heels enables the character to look down his nose at other characters which will support the delivery of such 'authority' lines as 'And who asked your opinion?' and 'Speak when you're spoken to'. Traditionally, the Dottore remains quite still, another demonstration of authority. While the others are moving around at his command, the Maniac can dominate the stage physically. When there are head movements, these should be sharp and defined, for example, when he says 'That's not what I've got here. This is a documentary reconstruction. I want the exact words in the exact manner.' The precision of movement should reflect the pedantic nature of the character. Any gestures should also be precise and authoritative, as when the Maniac 'gets the Superintendent up' – that is, he gives a signal with an arm gesture and a facial expression opening his eyes wide and pursing his lips, daring the Superintendent to defy him. His sitting position is held with his body taut and alert, making himself the focus of attention. Just like the Dottore, when the Maniac engages in academic and legal talk, he strokes his chin, signalling careful thought (as in 'What is a raptus? Bandieu, in his authoritative work on the subject …'). All this is made up, of course. Lines like those about the 'raptus' indicate that the Maniac is playing for two audiences – the characters on stage and the real audience. I would look for moments when the Maniac plays for the real audience, colluding with them. A good point to do this is when he has tricked the Superintendent into revealing his Fascist past and he 'winks at him knowingly'. I would add another wink to the audience, to indicate to them that my plans are working.

> This is a very long paragraph. It could be broken into two or three clearly themed paragraphs. That said, the student makes good use of supporting text and descriptive language. The student gives a range of ideas, along with how and why they would work.

In this way, through physical means, the actor playing the Maniac can fulfil the role he is playing in the storyline of the play, while also staying in line with the 'meta-theatrical' style of the play. The Maniac is therefore having an impact on the audience in two distinct ways, both intended by Dario Fo as the playwright.

> There is a lot of detail in this answer. The student has given a clear opening and conclusion, and covered a range of information in the middle section of the essay.

Commentary

Student B's response goes into much more depth than Student A's answer. Student B has evidently undertaken some research into *commedia dell'arte*, but is also able to use this research effectively and relevantly by applying it to both the character of the magistrate, which is his current disguise, and to the detail of the scene. Good use is made of short quotations that illustrate the various body movements and gestures needed in the scene, as well as a competent understanding of the role the Maniac is playing. There are specific relevant suggestions, such as placing the weight on the heels to demonstrate how the actor can achieve the intended effect through non-verbal communication. Words used to describe the physical actions are well chosen – for example, 'sharp', 'defined', 'precise' and 'authoritative'. This student also displays good knowledge of the play as a whole, by acknowledging its 'meta-theatrical' as well as farcical nature, and by showing an understanding that it is important for the Maniac to be aware of the two audiences.

As a **performer**, outline how you would use space to create impact on the audience in the portrayal of one character in this extract. You should use examples from the extract to support your ideas and your answer should make reference to the performance text as a whole.

(18 marks)

This answer is based on an extract from *Colder Than Here* by Polly Stenham, Scene 6, from '*They look at the coffin, then at each other*' to the end of the scene. Only the main part of the essay is printed here (not the introduction and conclusion). The student has selected the character of Jenna to write about.

Student C

This is the only scene when all four members of the family are together. This extract occurs about two-thirds of the way through the play. Jenna is the most 'distant' of the family. She is sensitive, but has difficulty fitting in. Her use of proxemics in this scene indicates a lot about her relationships and feelings towards the other characters at this point and this would have an impact visually on the audience.

> A promising start, giving a good demonstration of theoretical understanding through the use of the term 'proxemics'.

The presence of the coffin in the scene makes the coming death of Myra more real to everyone. Jenna and her older sister, Harriet, have agreed to paint it. They are inevitably close together on the floor when doing this, but I would make Jenna take a decision to work on the opposite side from Harriet when they start painting, to indicate that she is not entirely comfortable with the joint effort. This means that she can be critical of Harriet's section of drawing. The theory of proxemics is based on the signals sent out by different distances, so that 'intimate' space is the closest, followed by 'personal', 'social' and 'public', all getting more distant. Jenna is uncomfortable with 'intimate space' and even 'personal space' (within about a metre), so tends to keep her distance, generally maintaining 'social' space – more like 2 or 3 metres – when she can. After she has got into the coffin, she feels a sense of guilt – when she says 'This didn't happen. We didn't do this.' and distances herself from Harriet and the coffin by moving away from the door to the other side of the room. This use of space would immediately register with an audience. When Alec comes in with the news that Myra is coming (and will therefore see the coffin for the first time) he is worried that Jenna may behave inappropriately. Jenna senses this as she 'shivers', but moves towards him, challenging him, when he warns her about it. When Myra comes in, I would make Jenna move towards her sister and father because she shares their worries about her mother's reaction. Although she doesn't feel that close to them emotionally, she feels a kind of solidarity at this point. The audience would become aware of the effect of this group of characters being close together in the larger space of the room. After Myra comes in, Jenna only has one line, but that places a stronger emphasis on her physical position and presence. I would make her gradually fade further upstage from the others, as she feels more isolated and unable to cope. When Harriet is the only one to embrace her mother at the moment of crisis at the end of the extract, I would make Jenna take a tentative step forward as though she would like to be able to comfort her mother, but then a relieved step back in line with her difficulty in coping with her feelings.

> A good understanding here of space and how it is used to demonstrate both isolation and connectedness between characters.

In the final scene, Jenna shows she has come to terms with her feelings and is much more relaxed in her mother's presence.

> Perhaps the student could have improved this paragraph with a more detailed explanation and extracts.

Commentary

Student C correctly uses the term 'proxemics' to discuss the use of space; the response demonstrates an understanding of the basic principles of proxemics, together with some understanding of the details of the theory. There are several examples of how Jenna's use of space in the scene can signal both her feelings and her relationships with the members of her family at this point. Detailed points in the scene are referred to with corresponding details of Jenna's position in relation to the others. There is an awareness of the wider context of Jenna's position in the play as a whole, demonstrating how her 'journey' may be shown through the use of space. At several points in the answer Student C points out the impact on the audience of the positioning of characters on the stage space, as required by the question. The answer could be improved by rather more references to the impact on the audience and also to more subtle uses of space (i.e. smaller movements and adjustments of position).

As a **designer**, outline how **one theatrical element** could be developed to create meaning for an audience in this extract.

You should use examples from the extract to support your ideas and your answer should make reference to the performance text as a whole. **(18 marks)**

This answer is based on *Machinal* by Sophie Treadwell, Episode 7, from the beginning of the scene to the Young Woman's line: 'I try not to be.'

Student D

I am going to write about how the set could be developed to create meaning for an audience in this extract. It is important to note that the play was heavily influenced by the expressionist style. I would want to keep it in this style because it is an essential part of the play.

> A clear outline of intent and a demonstration of theoretical understanding of the style chosen. The student knows what they want to do and why.

Sophie Treadwell, the playwright, wrote this play in 1931, when the theatre in the United States was being influenced by the expressionist movement, which had started in Germany with the playwrights Ernst Toller and Georg Kaiser being very prominent in the movement. She was a journalist and had been involved with covering a real murder case and attended the trial. The murder was committed by a woman called Ruth Snyder. She and her lover killed her husband and were sentenced to death in the electric chair. Sophie Treadwell decided that a play written in the expressionist style would be a suitable way of dealing with this story.

> There is a lot of background detail here. Although it is interesting and well written, it doesn't help to answer the question.

The aim of expressionism is to try to present the sense of the inner state of mind of a character in the way it is staged, so all the theatrical elements including the set have to be part of this. I would want to have this play performed in a large end-on theatre where there can be a distance between the audience and the actors. The audience should feel that the Young Woman is part of a much larger world that is ruled by machines and routine, and that it all works against her and her chances of being happy in life. Each scene has to be simply set, as there are nine scenes, each with different requirements. I think this is an advantage, as a large, bare stage with only a few items on set can create a sense of isolation and this is important in conveying meaning to the audience – the meaning being the atmosphere of isolation for a woman living her life in a lonely way in an unfriendly world.

> There are clear links here between theoretical understanding, the student's own ideas and impact on the audience.

The stage direction mentions only three set elements – a divan, a telephone and a window – in this scene so it's possible to create a kind of island in the centre of the stage in a pool of light, creating a sense of a threatening space outside it. There are newspapers as props as well, and I would have these made much larger than normal to convey a sense of strangeness. This would apply to the telephone as well, which would be similarly oversized, but the window, which I would suspend from a bar, would be tiny, creating a sense of confinement even within the general atmosphere of isolation. This helps as a statement that the set is deliberately non-naturalistic.

> A good understanding of how the three set elements can create impact and give meaning. The student could improve it by mentioning colour and possibly the size of the divan.

Overall, the audience would be able to have the meaning of the scene established visually, even before hearing the dialogue, which shows clearly that the Young Woman feels alone and unhappy in her marriage and is isolated from her husband.

The student has shown a good understanding of the play-text, the genre and the staging. It could be improved by more detail about the set elements.

Commentary

Student D opens with a clear statement about the meaning to be conveyed by the set and a confirmation that the expressionistic style of the original text will be used in its design. The second paragraph is an example of what examiners call 'isolated knowledge' (see page 64 in 'Responding to the extracts' for a comment on this). It is knowledge that it is not relevant to this answer – the paragraph should be cut. The point about expressionist style is competent and well made in the following paragraph, so the background to it is not necessary. From that point, the answer proceeds in an assured way. It makes good points about the atmosphere, and how the style is realised in the creation of the set and in performance. There is good reference to how meaning is created for an audience by the visual element of the set. Thought has been given to the type of venue, stage form and the use of space. The conclusion provides a confirmation of the intention and the way in which the set serves the extract as a whole.

Student D has shown at least some awareness of how their chosen theatrical element can be developed to create mood. The student has recognised how atmosphere creates meaning and impact for an audience. The student has also shown how their chosen theatrical element can be developed to communicate ideas to an audience, along with a consideration of alternative ideas. Mention has been made of: the actor/audience relationship; the use of the theatrical venue, space, levels and proxemics; the effect of specific technical and creative choices; and designing to reflect the style and atmosphere of the performance text. There is evidence of research relating to the context of the text, such as time period, social, political, cultural aspects that develop and communicate ideas through their chosen theatrical element, and of intended audience impact.

This answer could be improved by the removal of paragraph 2 and by more detail about the set elements. However, there is no mention of the use of colour, for example, or the size of the divan (although other set elements are given sizes).

This answer is based on an extract from *Fences* by August Wilson, Act 1 Scene 1, from the stage direction *'It is Friday night …'* to Troy's line *'It's the truth! Like you riding on Goodyears!'*

Student E

I have chosen to write about sound as the theatrical element to develop in this scene. On the surface there is little requirement for sound in this scene – there are no sound cues referred to in the text. But this is only integral sound – that is, realistic sound cues that are necessary in the play, like the phone that rings later in the play. I shall be concentrating on the two other kinds of sound, atmospheric and incidental, which could have an important effect on the audience in this extract.

> The student has made a brave choice here to pick the element of sound when the play-text gives no real detail. That said, there is a clear explanation of how the student intends to make this work.

Because this scene is the opening scene of the play, it is important for an atmosphere to be set, so that the audience can have a feeling for the play and its mood. The play is set in Pittsburgh, in the Hill district that is the area of the city where the African American population lived. Most had moved up from the South, looking for jobs. As a result, the area was known as a centre for jazz and the blues, so it is appropriate to start the play with music of this kind. As well as the setting in time, it would be good to establish a sense of the time-period, as this isn't referred to in the text of the play. So a blues number by one of the blues singers of the period like John Lee Hooker or Muddy Waters (who was based in Chicago) would work well. This would be played through the auditorium speakers and would fade out under the beginning of the dialogue between Bono and Troy. (I would also use similar music between all the scenes of the play and in the interval.) There is a link with the play because Troy's son, Lyons, is a 'wannabe' musician who talks about how he wants to get involved with the music scene in the city.

> There has been some good research here about the area and the music linked with it. The student could have gone further and named some specific tracks.

Atmospheric sound can also have an effect on the audience, giving them a sense of the district that Troy lives in. I would establish this as a follow-on from the introductory blues music, but using on-stage speakers, specifically from the side of the stage that has the entrance to the yard. As usual, this would be established at an audible level for the audience, but then faded down to a 'sub-liminal' level – that is so that the audience no longer consciously hears it, but is aware of when it stops. The sound would try to convey the sense of the place, so it would need to be a mixture of the sounds that would be heard on the streets of a residential area like the Hill District. I would produce a mix of occasional cars passing – we know from the text that Troy is fighting the case for black workers to become drivers of the garbage trucks, and in the last line of the extract Troy makes a rather crude joke about 'Goodyears' referring to high-quality tyres, so cars must have been a feature of the area. Other sounds would be passing footsteps and voices, as it's Friday night and it's likely that people would be passing to go out drinking or socialising. I'd also mix in (at a very low level) some sounds of music – perhaps someone practising a trumpet, or the distant sound of jazz music coming from a club.

> This paragraph contains good linked detail. The student has clearly thought about what kinds of incidental and other sounds to use, and why. This is tied in with theoretical understanding of the use of sound to give added detail.

The important thing is that the sound supports the whole scene, rather than specific points in the text, although there are some possibilities. For example, when Alberta is mentioned I would like to bring in, at a slightly increased level, part of a blues number that deals specifically with love. Just the nature of the melody might hint to an audience that there is more to Troy's relationship with Alberta than he is saying, preparing the audience in a small way for the revelations that come later in the play.

> The student shows here how sound – another song in this instance – can provide subtle hints for the audience.

Commentary

Student E has made a choice that, initially, wouldn't appear to be promising because of the apparent lack of sound required in the text. The student has realised, however, that there are ways of using this design element to support the text even though there is no mention of it. The student is aware of the three basic categories of sound and competently identifies them, focusing on the two categories that can be utilised to enhance the extract: incidental and atmospheric. The identification of jazz and blues with the Hill District provides evidence of useful background research. The link with Lyons' ambitions helps to justify the choice.

There is also justification for the soundscape that Student E identifies, although the word itself is not used in the answer. Its function is correctly identified, along with some basic technical detail about the use of onstage and auditorium speakers as sound sources. Thought has been given to the direction from which the sound will come, as well as the level at which it will be set. There is evidence of competent understanding of the 'sub-liminal' nature of a soundscape and the effect it can have on an audience without their conscious realisation that sound is being used. All the elements that will go into the sound mix have also been considered, and these are consistent with the area in which Troy's house stands. The idea that a particular melody might be associated with the mention of Alberta may have come as an afterthought, but it provides further evidence that Student E has read the extract closely – as does the mention of 'Goodyears' in the context of the traffic sounds.

This answer shows a good grasp of the possible contribution of sound as a theatrical element. It focuses well on examples of how sound can create meaning for an audience. It could have been improved by the identification of specific jazz/blues numbers that would create exactly the atmosphere Student E wants to suggest. It could also have been improved by more specific identification of the kinds of sound to be used on the soundscape – for example, whether the voices are aggressive, drunken, happy and so on. These sounds would all also affect the nature of the atmosphere. On the whole, this is a well-considered response.

Theatre makers in practice

Top tips

You should develop an understanding of the performance style, genre (see definition on page 82), historical period and setting. However, your interpretation will always be aimed at a 21st-century audience.

You can, if you wish, change the performance style, historical period or setting. You can also change and edit the structure of the text. However, you are *not* allowed to cut the language or alter the meaning of the original text.

Top tip

Make sure you have the correct translation and version of your text for the exam.

Overview

You will only study Section C for the A level exam. You will practically explore one performance text in light of one practitioner. This exploration will inform your response in the written examination. You will write from the perspective of a director developing an interpretation of the text for a 21st-century audience. Your ideas for the production, including the acting and the design elements, will draw inspiration from your chosen practitioner. You will be given an extract from the text in the written exam to focus your response, but you should also make reference to your overall production concept. You will be allowed to take in a clean copy of your chosen text.

Interpreting a performance text

Your practical exploration of the performance text should give you an appreciation of the original aims and intentions of the playwright.

Performance text	Edition
Antigone, Sophocles (adapted by Don Taylor)	Methuen: ISBN 9780413776044
Lysistrata, Aristophanes (translated by Alan H. Sommerstein)	Penguin Classics: ISBN 9780140448146
Doctor Faustus, Christopher Marlowe (A Text)	Norton & Company: ISBN 9780393977547
The Tempest, William Shakespeare	Cambridge Schools: ISBN 9780521618786
The School for Scandal, Richard Brinsley Sheridan	Dover Thrift: ISBN 9780486266879
Hedda Gabler, Henrik Ibsen (adapted by Richard Eyre)	Nick Hern Books: ISBN 9781854598424
Woyzeck, Georg Büchner (translated by John Mackendrick)	Berg Publishing: ISBN 9780413388209
The Maids, Jean Genet (translated by Bernard Frechtman)	Grove Press: ISBN 9780802150561
Waiting for Godot, Samuel Beckett	Faber & Faber: ISBN 9780571229116

Responding to a practitioner

You must be able to show that you can apply the key theories, methodologies and concepts of your chosen practitioner to your own production concept. You should focus on directing a production with an emphasis on the final performance rather than the preparation and development with the company. Remember that you must use the practitioner's ideas as a foundation for your own original concept that appeals to a 21st-century audience.

Practitioner	Vision for theatre
Constantin Stanislavski (1863–1938)	Theatre should entertain the audience and make them think about humanity. There should be a highly charged atmosphere that causes infectious emotion.
Antonin Artaud (1896–1948)	Theatre should remove the security of language and abolish established ideas of the performer/audience divide. Ritualistic performance should infect its audience like a plague.
Bertolt Brecht (1898–1956)	Theatre should change the world through entertainment and education. Opposites should be highlighted in plays and productions to create a debate among audience members.
Joan Littlewood (1914–2002)	Theatre should both present community and be a community where all participants are equal. It should be playfully disciplined and structured anarchy. The theatre is live interaction.
Steven Berkoff (1937–)	Theatre should fuse together opposites and celebrate contradictions: mime must collide with the spoken word; performance must be energetic and exaggerated but capture subtlety and detail; strict choreography must allow for moments of improvisation. The actor and the ensemble are central to the theatre.
Kneehigh (1980–)	Theatre should be a memorable, community event that takes place in a charged space where stories are shared with a spirit of joyful anarchy.
Complicite (1983–)	Theatre should be a collaboration between performers, audience, director and designers. It should stimulate the senses. Theatre must always evolve and never be the same.
Punchdrunk (2000–)	Theatre should focus as much on the spectators (audience members) and the performance space as on the performers and narrative. Each spectator must be immersed in the world of the play so they discover their own meaning and narrative through an imaginative journey.

Your practical work and research on these practitioners should give you knowledge and understanding of:

- the social, historical, political and cultural contexts that shaped their theatre practice
- their vision for theatre and how this was translated into practical, theatrical ideas and methodologies
- their use of theatrical style and conventions
- their collaboration with and influence on other practitioners
- how the relationship with audiences is defined in theory and then carried out in practice.

The exam paper

Component 3 is worth 80 marks and up to 40% of the total A level mark. Section C carries up to 24 marks.

(AO3) is: Demonstrate knowledge and understanding of how drama and theatre is developed and performed.

To fulfil AO3 you will have to demonstrate how your re-imagined production concept will communicate ideas to a contemporary audience. You will also need to outline how the work of your chosen practitioner has influenced your overall production concept, and demonstrate an awareness of the performance text in its original performance conditions.

A level exam question

You are the director of a new production concept of the performance text you have studied.

EITHER

5 As a director, discuss how you would apply the methodologies of your chosen theatre practitioner to the acting styles used in your production concept. Your answer must focus on the named section listed above for your chosen performance text. Your answer must make reference to: the overall aims of your production concept in response to the play as a whole; how your practical ideas will work in performance; the original performance conditions of your chosen performance text. **(24)**

OR

6 As a director, discuss how you would apply the methodologies of your chosen theatre practitioner to the lighting design used in your production concept.

Your answer must focus on the named section listed above for your chosen performance text.

Your answer must make reference to:
- the overall aims of your production concept in response to the play as a whole;
- how your practical ideas will work in performance;
- the original performance conditions of your chosen performance text.

(24)

Exam tip

You must keep the specified element of your chosen question as central to your response, but you should make reference to how it interacts with other elements of the production.

Performance texts

Antigone

Playwright: Sophocles

First performance: c442 BC, The Acropolis, Athens, Greece

Synopsis

The city of Thebes has just survived an invasion from the army of Argos, but there are many left dead. Eteocles and Polynices were brothers killed in combat but they fought on opposite sides. Creon, now King of Thebes, is angry that his nephew Polynices was a traitor and refuses to allow his body to be buried. He declares that anyone caught burying the body of a traitor will be punished by death. Antigone, Polynices' sister, defies her uncle Creon and gives her brother the burial that is the unwritten law of the gods. She is caught by her uncle, Creon, and he sentences Antigone to death, despite the pleas of his niece, Ismene, and his son, Haemon, who is engaged to Antigone. Creon ignores them and has Antigone sealed in a tomb, alive. The blind prophet Tiresias tells Creon he has made a mistake and says that his child will die if Antigone is put to death and Polynices is not buried. Creon decides to release Antigone but it is too late; Haemon had already gone to the tomb and found that she has hanged herself. When Creon arrives, Haemon threatens him with a sword, before killing himself. Creon arrives back at the palace carrying his dead son and a messenger tells him Eurydice, his wife, has killed herself after hearing the news. Creon is left grieving the tragedy that has enveloped his family.

Genre

Tragedy was a popular **genre** that was mastered by the ancient Greeks. The philosopher, Aristotle's (384–322 BC) description of tragedy in Poetics (c350 BC) still influences playwrights and screenwriters to this day. Tragedy, according to Aristotle, presents serious stories of great importance that make the audience feel both pity and fear. The main character is of a high status and suffers a downfall because of a sequence of logical and unstoppable events.

Structure

Aristotle emphasises the importance of a tightly structured plot in a tragedy. Sophocles' Antigone follows the structural conventions of a tragedy. There is a series of escalating but logical confrontations that builds towards the deaths and Creon's downfall. Antigone has a sequence of seven main scenes, including a prologue, an exodus (final departure) and five episodes with six **chorus** scenes in between.

Key roles and relationships

Characters in Greek tragedy did not have the psychological depth and individuality of later eras. The characters have qualities that fit their heroic role or their social status. The tragic hero role in *Antigone* is split between two characters – Creon and Antigone. They are both courageous to the point of stubbornness in their desire to stand by their decisions.

Creon: Has just been made King of Thebes and wants to assert his authority. He begins the play as the traditional tragic hero, but he does not maintain his heroic stubbornness and instead changes his mind about Antigone. At the end of the play he is left alive with the guilt and pain caused by his family's deaths. Creon's strong political language is not followed with any conviction and this weakness reduces his heroic status.

Antigone: Remains defiant throughout the play and stubbornly has the conviction to see her decision through to her own death. She refuses to change her mind in the face of her sister's pleas, Creon's threats and the disapproval of society presented through the chorus. This strength and determination reinforces her position as the true heroic figure of the play.

Glossary

Genre
A category of literary or dramatic composition. Examples are tragedy, comedy, farce and melodrama.

Glossary

Chorus
A group of performers who sing, dance, or recite in unison. In Greek drama, the chorus was the group of performers who sang and danced between episodes, narrated off-stage action and commented on events.

Antigone

Key moments

Prologue: Antigone and Ismene mourn the deaths of their brothers and discover Creon has denied Polynices a burial.

- How will you direct the actors to establish the contrast between the cautious Ismene and the courageous Antigone?
- How will you control the build-up to the first moment of **climax** where Antigone ignores her sister's caution and leaves to bury her brother?

First chorus: The elders of Thebes make up the chorus and represent the whole of society.

- How will your casting and costume choices establish the chorus as the voice of society?
- How will you support their descriptions of the war visually?
- How will you use the grouping of the chorus and their position on the stage to communicate with the audience?

Second episode: Antigone is brought before Creon after she was caught burying her brother.

- How will you reinforce the opposing ideas of Creon and Antigone?
- How will you show that Creon is trying to assert his status as King?
- How will you direct the actor playing Antigone to react to her death sentence?

Fourth episode: Antigone sees her tomb and is led into it to die a slow death.

- How will you capture the intensity of Antigone's emotions?
- How will you use sound and lighting to reinforce these emotions?
- How will you direct the actor playing Creon to enter before telling the guards to hurry up?

Fifth episode: The blind prophet Tiresias warns Creon.

- How will you ask your actor to physicalise Tiresias?
- How will you emphasise Creon's arrogance and denial?

It is the chorus' support of Tiresias that eventually persuades Creon to change his mind.

- How will you group and position the chorus to show they side with Tiresias?

Glossary

Climax
The point of greatest intensity in a series or progression of events in a play, often forming the turning point of the plot and leading to some kind of resolution.

Original performance conditions

Antigone was presented at the annual Theatre of Dionysus festival around 442 BC as part of a drama competition. The theatre space was an open-air amphitheatre that was built out of the natural shape of the Acropolis hill. The audience sat on the slope of the hill looking down on the stage circle. There was a wooden building at the back of the space that was known as the skene. This area was the main entrance and exit, and was decorated to reinforce the plot. There were two further side entrances that held significance for the audience, as the right represented civilisation and the left represented the wilderness. Women usually used the central entrance, whereas the men used the side entrances. These established rules of the space meant that deviations held significance – for example, Antigone would have used a side door when exiting. Plays would have been performed by three actors. They wore long robes and masks that signified character. The use of masks led to an acting style that was characterised by stylised movements and gestures to support the spoken word. The position and grouping of the chorus also created meaning for the spectators.

Antigone

Top tip

You will have to be able to communicate a production concept that is relevant for a 21st-century audience. Try to find parallels between today and the context in which the play was written. This is a good way to justify your ideas for a modern production.

Glossary

Hubris
From Greek tragedy, whereby the downfall of a character comes about due to their great arrogance and excessive pride.

Social, political, cultural and historical context

Below is a selection of original context points that have been linked with some of the key themes of *Antigone*.

Family vs state

Antigone was written between the Persian and Spartan wars. It was a time of great political change as power shifted away from aristocratic family lines to the citizens themselves. There was a shift away from the family unit to more localised tribes and people's names changed to reflect this. The confrontations in *Antigone* reflect the shifting political environment of the time.

Battle of the sexes

Political changes and the power of the citizens did not include women. They, along with slaves, were not allowed to vote and their central function was continuing the line of pure Athenian citizens. Women were in service to the men in their lives, and this included the performing of burial rites for the males in their family. On the one hand Antigone is a feminist heroine as she stands up to her uncle, but on the other she is driven to fulfil her service to her brother.

Justice and religion

The development of democracy and man's mastery of nature was seen by some philosophers as proof that the gods were no longer relevant. There was an emphasis on man-made laws over the laws of the gods. *Antigone* reinforces the power of the gods' laws over man's and is seen as a warning against man's foolish arrogance – **hubris**.

Doctor Faustus

Playwright: Christopher Marlowe (1564–93)
Written: c1588 or 1592; published 1604
First recorded performance: 1594 at the Rose Theatre by the Lord Admiral's Men. It is believed that the play would have been performed at least two years earlier.

Synopsis

Doctor Faustus is desperate for more knowledge, but he turns his back on logic and learning in favour of magic. He uses magic to summon a devil, Mephistopheles, who acts as a messenger for Lucifer. He agrees to give Lucifer his soul in return for 24 years on Earth with Mephistopheles as his servant. Doctor Faustus begins to have doubts about the deal after acquiring some of the knowledge he desired. Mephistopheles uses all kinds of delights and mischief to stop him repenting and distract him from his inevitable plunge into hell.

Genre

Doctor Faustus was inspired by the medieval morality play and follows many of the same conventions: an innocent man, who represents all humanity, is tempted by vices in human form. This man eventually succumbs to temptation and falls from innocence but is redeemed by God's grace. The plays carried a serious message of Christian forgiveness, but appealed to the masses through their coarse comic style. Instead of broad archetypes, Marlowe created two complex psychological characters: Mephistopheles, the miserable, bitter and tortured antihero; and Doctor Faustus, whose ambition, despite an internal struggle, leads to eternal damnation. Marlowe used the popularity of the morality play to present the tragedy of a complex and human individual.

Structure

The A Text of *Doctor Faustus* is in three sections. The beginning section shows Faustus making his pact with Lucifer. The middle section shows different experiences during the 24 years with Mephistopheles as his servant. The end section shows the final parts of Faustus's life and his final plunge into hell. The Chorus commentates on the action of the main plot, much like in an ancient Greek tragedy. There are also comic interludes that mirror the main plot with Robin and Rafe using magic with far bawdier intentions. The main body of the play begins and ends with soliloquies delivered by Faustus, making his psychological journey the very heart of the play.

Key roles and relationships

Doctor Faustus: An eloquent and intelligent man who encapsulates the Renaissance desire to acquire knowledge. The Renaissance was a period of great learning between the 14th and 17th centuries that moved Western civilisation from the Middle Ages to the Modern Age. This desire to acquire knowledge is combined with a foolish arrogance that the ancient Greeks would have referred to as hubris. The first and last sections show Faustus at his eloquent best, but the middle section reveals the lack of substance beneath his words as he fails to use his power and knowledge for anything worthwhile.

Mephistopheles: A complex, ambiguous and contradictory character. He relishes the opportunity to be Faustus's servant for 24 years and encourages him to take the blood oath with Lucifer. But Mephistopheles remains miserable in hell and has many regrets about his own damnation. He states that misery needs company and continues to manipulate Faustus so that he does not repent.

Key moments

Act 1 Scene 3: Mephistopheles appears to Faustus after a magic ritual observed by Lucifer.

- How will your production present the magic in this scene?
- How will the actor playing Mephistopheles establish the complexity of this character?
- Will the characters from hell move differently to Faustus?

Act 2 Scene 1: Faustus cuts his arm and writes the agreement with Lucifer in his own blood. The Good and Evil Angels appear as Faustus's conscience at the start of this scene.

- How will you manage this morality play convention while avoiding clichés and making it relevant for a 21st-century audience?
- How will you present the stage illusion of a character cutting his own arm?
- How will Mephistopheles react to this moment? Will you give emphasis to Mephistopheles' warnings at the end of this scene?

Act 2 Scene 3: Lucifer, Beelzebub and Seven Deadly Sins appear to prevent Faustus from repenting.

- How will your production present the power and theatricality of their appearance?
- How will Faustus interact with the Sins in the space?

There is a shift away from **blank verse** to prose in this scene.

- Will you support the contrast in language with specific visual and movement choices?

The Chorus scenes before Act 3 and Act 4: The Chorus appears midway through the play to help the sense of time passing swiftly.

- How will your production concept reinforce the sense of time passing at these moments?
- Will the Chorus be cast as a particular group of characters or will they remain neutral?

Doctor Faustus

Glossary

Blank verse
This is unrhymed iambic pentameter, which means the underlying rhythm in each line has five repeated units of an unstressed and a stressed syllable. However, constantly repeating this pattern would become very dull, so Shakespeare varies the number of stresses a great deal.

Act 5 Scene 2: Lucifer, Mephistopheles and devils return to Faustus and drag him to hell.

• How will you present hell in this moment?

• Will your production become gradually more hellish as time passes?

Mephistopheles does say hell is more of a state of mind than a particular place.

Original performance conditions

Plays were a popular form of entertainment at the time,, but the first purpose-built playhouse was only built in 1576. The Theatre in Shoreditch was an outdoor playhouse designed to resemble the inn courtyards, which had held performances up until that time. The Lord Admiral's men performed *Doctor Faustus* at the Rose Theatre in 1594; the famous Globe Theatre was not built until 1599. Most of what we know about outdoor theatres of the time comes from a sketch of the Swan Theatre by Johannes de Witt in 1595. This sketch was used when designing the current, fully functioning replica Globe Theatre that is in Southwark, London. Plays had to compete with other popular entertainments, such as bear-baiting, bare-knuckle boxing and cock-fighting. There was a strong appetite for violence and Doctor Faustus's graphic scenes would have appealed to the masses.

Doctor Faustus is an important play as it is one of the first recorded to be written in blank verse. This is a type of verse that has no regular rhyme scheme, and while it has the rhythmic pattern of the iambic pentameter, this is often broken to give emphasis. Blank verse gave *Doctor Faustus* a sense of psychological realism that had not been seen on the London stage before.

Social, political, cultural and historical context

Below is a selection of original context points that have been linked with some of the key themes of *Doctor Faustus*.

Knowledge and power
The Renaissance signalled a great progression in knowledge and an emphasis on the individual man rather than an external power. A huge variety of methods was used to further man's understanding, from magic to alchemy. This explosion of thought led to confusion and misunderstandings that only began to be ordered when Francis Bacon presented a scientific method that resembled what we have today in *The Advancement of Learning* (1605).

Fate vs free will
Doctor Faustus was written during a time of great change in Western philosophy, and specifically Christian thinking, known as the Reformation (1517–1648). This is the time when people started to question the perceived indulgences of the Catholic Church. Marlowe is not afraid to mock the Pope and the Catholic Church in *Doctor Faustus*. The Reformation had two key figures: Martin Luther (1483–1546) and John Calvin (1509–64). Luther thought of man as having free will and control of his life. In contrast, Calvin believed God had ultimate control. This debate between fate and free will is played out in *Doctor Faustus*.

Top tip

Remember that most plays presented were written in a combination of 'verse', which is rhymed lines with set rhythms, and 'prose', which has no regular rhythm or rhyme scheme.

Top tip

You will have to be able to communicate a production concept that is relevant for a 21st-century audience. Try to find parallels between today and the context in which the play was written. This is a good way to justify your ideas for a modern production.

Doctor Faustus

Hedda Gabler

Playwright: Henrik Ibsen (1828–1906)
Written 1890; first performance 1891 (German, Norwegian and English)

Synopsis

George Tesman, an academic, and Hedda Gabler, the daughter of an aristocratic general, return from their sixth-month honeymoon. Hedda's beauty and social status make her a great catch for George. But the marriage is simply convenient for Hedda as it offers security and stability. George is hoping to be made a professor soon and the promotion would further secure their future. However, Hedda clearly feels trapped and rebels against her situation by being rude to George's maid, Bertha, and belittling his aunt, Juliana. George remains oblivious to Hedda's behaviour and remains optimistic about their future together.

Their world is disrupted by the arrival of George's academic rival, Eilert Loevborg. No longer the weak alcoholic that George once knew, Loevborg has turned his life around and written a successful book in the same academic field as George. Loevborg's reversal of fortunes is down to the help he received from Hedda's old school friend, Thea Elvsted, who left her husband for him. Loevborg visits George and explains how he is focusing on a groundbreaking sequel to his first book. While Loevborg is at the house, it transpires that he had a relationship with Hedda in the past. She is jealous of how Thea has been such a positive influence and endeavours to spoil it all by encouraging Loevborg to drink again before Judge Brack's party that evening.

The next day George tells Hedda that Loevborg dropped the draft of his new book while drunk, but he has kept it safe. Loevborg visits the house later, upset at having lost his groundbreaking work, and says he wants to commit suicide. Hedda doesn't tell Loevborg about the draft and encourages his suicide by giving him a gun. She burns the manuscript before telling George she did it to support his career and secure a future with the baby she is expecting. Judge Brack arrives and announces Loevborg's suicide. Thea is distraught and George pledges to help her re-write Loevborg's book from his notes. Judge Brack takes Hedda away from the others and tells her Loevborg was most likely murdered at a local brothel and that he knew the gun was hers. Hedda can't stand the idea that Brack will be able to control her, so she retreats to the rear room and shoots herself in the head.

Style

Hedda Gabler is an example of both naturalism and **realism** because it is a realistic portrayal of life. The **dialogue** is fast-paced, fragmentary and it is not broken by unnecessarily long speeches. Hedda's psychological frustration and instability is central to the plot. Ibsen was an innovator of realism, showing a shift away from actions determined by environment as featured in naturalism to ones determined by individual choice.

Structure

Hedda Gabler is divided into four acts. The events of the play take place in one location during a 36-hour period. Ibsen adheres to the unity of time and place described by Aristotle (384–322 BC) in *Poetics* (c350 BC) as a way of enhancing the intensity of the tragedy. This is then combined with quick-fire, witty dialogue that is a feature of **comedy**. The combination of the two creates an unease and uncertainty within the audience.

Key roles and relationships

Hedda and George Tesman: Hedda is from an aristocratic family and has all the ruthlessness of someone who holds authority as a birthright. Tesman is an orphan raised by his aunts and has had to work for everything to remain a part of the middle class. Hedda continually goads

Glossary

Realism
This is almost the same as naturalism (see definition on page 4), with the exception that characters' actions and motivations are rooted in their individual choices rather than the environment.

Dialogue
Spoken conversation used by two or more characters to express thoughts, feelings and actions.

Comedy
A play that treats characters and situations in a humorous way.

Hedda Gabler

Tesman as part of her rebellion. George does not have the social awareness to offer any reply beyond asserting the fact that, as his wife, she is his property.

Hedda and Eilert Loevborg: Their past relationship had been mutually beneficial as Loevborg's stories of his antics were therapeutic for him and allowed her to escape her mundane life. Their meeting during the play is mutually toxic, as Hedda drives Loevborg to drink while her fantasies become destructive.

Hedda and Judge Brack: Hedda respects Brack's position as it shows an understanding of social roles and an authority that she finds attractive. Their relationship is one of flirtation as Hedda is able to tease and manipulate Brack. The power shifts towards the end as Brack threatens to control her life.

Key moments

Act 1: Hedda is trapped and angry.

- How will you direct the non-verbal communication of the actor playing Hedda to emphasise her feeling trapped?
- How will you manage the spatial relationships of all four characters when Hedda gets angry at Bertha (a servant of the Tesmans)?

Act 2: Hedda and Loevborg discuss their past.

- How will you direct the vocal delivery of the dialogue to communicate the connection between Hedda and Loevborg?
- How will you get the actors to move in the space as the status and authority shifts in the scene?
- How will you direct the actor playing Loevborg to show he is gradually letting Hedda get under his skin?

Act 3: Hedda encourages Loevborg to commit suicide.

- How will you create a contrast between the two characters as the power is now clearly with Hedda?
- How will you direct the actor playing Loevborg to use gesture and posture to reveal his pain and anguish?

Act 4: Hedda's suicide.

- How will you direct the actor playing Hedda to react to Brack's revelation and control over her?
- Will you show the suicide in some way?
- How will you design the set so that Hedda can take herself away from the others?

Original performance conditions

The first performance at the Residenztheater in Munich in January 1891 and the first performance in Norway a month later were failures. The declamatory style of line delivery failed to capture the nuance and dynamism of Hedda Gabler. The most successful early performance happened in April 1891 at the Vaudeville Theatre in London. Elizabeth Robins gave a virtuoso performance developed through the careful study of Hedda's responses to other characters and how they revealed conflicting character traits. All three of these early productions would have used similar staging techniques within a **proscenium** arch theatre. The set would have been painted backdrops taken from the theatre's existing stock, while costumes would have been contemporary and accurate. Lighting would have emphasised the natural light and the passing of the day.

Top tip

Realistic and naturalistic writers like Ibsen created dialogue that audiences believed to be true to real life. To support the illusion of reality created by the dialogue, directors like Stanislavski created a visual illusion of a complete and realistic world behind the fourth wall of the proscenium arch.

Glossary

Proscenium
A frame or arch separating the stage from the auditorium.

Social, political, cultural and historical context

Below is a selection of original context points that have been linked with some of the key themes of *Hedda Gabler*.

Women

Society held that a woman was a man's possession and a footnote to his success; women helped the aspirational middle-class capture the power of the old aristocracy by creating new family lines. However, Ibsen did not believe all women were made for motherhood. He challenges the stereotype with the confrontational Hedda character, and the intellectual and influential character of Thea Elvsted.

Control

The aristocracy was abolished in Norway in 1821, but the leading military and judicial families continued to see themselves as the 'elite' class. Authority and control were only maintained through reputation and convention. But this was lost as the old military leaders and judges died and their children continued some semblance of status by joining the middle class.

The self vs society

Reputation was of vital importance to the middle class as it led to opportunity and wealth. There was a conflict between the need for recognition from peers and the desire to be free and independent. The amount of leisure time enjoyed by women in particular led people to question their position in society.

Top tip ☑

You will have to be able to communicate a production concept that is relevant for a 21st-century audience. Try to find parallels between today and the context in which the play was written. This is a good way to justify your ideas for a modern production.

Lysistrata

Playwright: Aristophanes

First performance: 411 BC

Synopsis

In the middle of the Peloponnesian War between Athens and Sparta, Lysistrata persuades the wives of the soldiers on both sides to withhold sex until the war is brought to an end. The women strengthen their position by taking control of the Acropolis where the state's money is held. A chorus of old men arrive at the gates of the Acropolis ready to burn down the gates. But before they can, they are stopped by a chorus of old women carrying buckets of water. They defend the younger women by soaking the older men. A magistrate makes an effort to break into the Acropolis and recover funds for the war effort after criticising the women's promiscuity and the men's weakness. He is caught by the women and taken to Lysistrata. She allows him to question her rebellion and she **articulates** why she is against this war of masculine arrogance. To prove her point, the women dress the magistrate as a woman and then as a corpse before letting him go. Some of the women become desperate for sex and start leaving the cause. Lysistrata manages to galvanise them again and continue their protest. One husband appears and pleads for sex from his wife; he is teased with an inviting bed and oils, only to be turned away. Lysistrata brings the Athenians and the Spartans to ask them to agree to the women's terms. A beautiful, naked woman named Reconciliation is paraded in front of the sex-starved men and so they agree to the terms and stop the war. They all exit dancing and celebrating.

Genre

Ancient Greek comedy was set in contemporary Athens and had special license to comment on the individuals of the audience and the gods. Insults in comedy were a celebration of the freedom of speech allowed by a civilised democracy. Comedy induced a knowing laughter as it presented utopian ideals that contrasted the social and political reality of the time. The unconventional political solutions were supported by the baseness of the physical comedy. The long, limp penis sewn to the tights of the male characters was the centre of much of the comic business. Aristophanes gave all the male characters (apart from the chorus) a large erect penis sewn to their tights to emphasise the themes and the comedy.

Glossary

Articulate/articulates/ articulation
The clarity or distinction of speech – emphasis on consonants or words.

Top tip

Remember that, in ancient Greece, comedies dealt almost exclusively with contemporary figures and problems. Low comedy is physical rather than intellectual; high comedy is more sophisticated, with a verbal emphasis.

Structure

Comedy does not have the rigid structure of tragedy. The events of the play are ordered to emphasise the increase in comic tension. Aristophanes draws parallels between the sexual tension and the comic tension. Physical and visual comic set pieces complement the comic contrasts between onstage ideals and the reality of the audience's world. The chorus in Aristophanes' *Lysistrata* is divided in two to reinforce the division of the sexes.

Key roles and relationships

Lysistrata: She orchestrates the action of the play but remains distanced from the rebellion, observing and directing others. Lysistrata is more controlled and commanding than the other women in the play. She advises them on how to assert themselves with their husbands but does not have a husband herself. Lysistrata's removed position is similar to that of an omniscient goddess.

Cinesias and Myrrhine: Myrrhine's actions are directed by Lysistrata, whereas Cinesias' actions are led by his uncontrollable sexual desire, manifested in his huge, painful erection. This leads to a comic scene as neither character is truly in control of themselves.

The two choruses: The old men and old women of the two choruses mirror the battle of the sexes in the main plot. They provide comical confrontations that emphasise the battle of the sexes. The physicality and movement of these groups' attempts to assert their power would have caused much hilarity.

Key moments

Lysistrata's sex strike: Lysistrata persuades the women of Athens and Sparta to withhold sex and seals the agreement with a ritual.

- How will you show the division between the Athenians and the Spartans?

- How will you make Lysistrata's speech persuasive?

- How will you create a comical reluctance in the women?

- How will you present the ritualistic drinking of wine?

The occupation of the Acropolis: The male chorus confronts the female chorus but is repelled with buckets of water.

- How will you characterise and physicalise these two groups?

- How will you use space to support the comic power struggle?

The women weaken: Lysistrata is anxious that the women's will is weakening. As she speaks, women begin to leave the Acropolis.

- How will you contrast Lysistrata's sincerity with the sexual desire of the women?

- How will you draw the comedy out of the women's attempted escape and their movement across the stage?

Myrrhine teases Cinesias: Lysistrata directs Myrrhine to tease her husband Cinesias with a welcoming bed, only to reject him.

- How will the actor playing Myrrhine use non-verbal communication with Lysistrata to emphasise the idea she does not quite know what to do?

- How will the actor playing Cinesias move in response to his erect penis?

Reconciliation: A naked woman named 'Reconciliation' is paraded in front of the Athenian and Spartan soldiers.

- How will you show the climax of the men's frustrations?
- How will the vocal choices of Lysistrata further torment the men during her long, final speech?
- How will your production create the revelry of the final celebrations?

Original performance conditions

Lysistrata would have been performed as part of the Theatre of Dionysus festival. A large audience would gather on the raked seating in the natural hill of the Acropolis. The closeness of the play's setting and the location of the theatre reinforced ideas of audience interaction. The actors in a comedy would have addressed the audience directly and there was probably physical interaction as well. It is believed that the spectators at the theatres were all men, and they would have been targeted for the sexual humour. The conventions of performance, such as mask wearing, would have been referred to and mocked in comedies. The presence of the large penises as part of the costume would have been essential to the comedy. The vocal delivery in comedy would have been more realistic than tragedy, with the use of local dialects and accents increasing the comedy for the audience. Gestures would also have been more realistic, allowing for moments that parodied the more stylised tragic gestures to be highlighted for comic effect.

Social, political, cultural and historical context

Below is a selection of original context points that have been linked with some of the key themes of *Lysistrata*.

Women

Women had no democratic rights in the Athens of ancient Greece, but they did hold positions of authority within the traditional religious order. Athena Polias was an important religious group in Athens, celebrating Athena as the protector of the city. The high priestess of the group was one of the most influential women in Athens because her authority came from the gods rather than the state. The high priestess in 415 BC was a woman name Lysmache. It is unclear whether Aristophanes is mocking this powerful woman of the time or simply using her as a point of reference for the audience.

Men

Philosophers of the time were beginning to assert the authority of man over the gods and nature because of the civilisation they had created. The men in the play represent democracy and its ongoing struggle with nature and the gods. Dialogue is at the heart of democracy and the play mocks this as it contrasts it with the action of the women.

Sex

The ancient Greeks had a far more open attitude towards sex. It can be argued that Aristophanes simplifies sex in such a way that it would itself have been a source of humour. The idea that men would suffer without women would have been hilarious because of the popularity of homosexual intercourse. Again this can be seen to reinforce the idea that civilised man has conquered nature and the gods.

Peace

Athens was constantly at war at the time the play was written. After many failed military actions, the citizens genuinely feared for their continued existence. Many of its enemies wanted Athens to abolish its democracy in favour of religious order. *Lysistrata* mocks this ongoing debate, and mocks both the simplicity of bowing to a natural order and the foolishness of democracy.

> **Top tip**
>
> You will have to be able to communicate a production concept that is relevant for a 21st-century audience. Try to find parallels between today and the context in which the play was written. This is a good way to justify your ideas for a modern production.

Lysistrata

The Maids

Playwright: Jean Genet (1910–86)

Published: 1947 (French); first performance: 1947 (France), 1952 (Britain – French), 1954 (Britain – English).

Synopsis

Two maids plan and rehearse different ways of murdering their mistress. They repeat the ritualistic role-playing in an attempt to achieve perfection. Gradually, they involve more imaginary characters in their brutal fantasies.

Style

Theatre of the Absurd shared the characteristics of staging anxiety and disillusionment. Genet's work, and particularly *The Maids*, is characterised by its use of never-ending plays within plays. He compared the experience of his theatre to being in a hall of mirrors. The desired result of the plays within plays, fantasies within fantasies, was to remove characters and replace them with symbols. Therefore, characters became metaphors for what they represented.

Structure

The Maids is a one-act play that features characters repeatedly rehearsing and performing within the play. The play-within-a-play structure is established immediately when one of the maids is dressing their mistress. The mistress kicks her maid in the head with her heel. The maid comes to and slaps her mistress in the face. Only then is it revealed that the mistress was being performed by the other maid and it was all a role-play. The real mistress only appears in the middle of the play. This structural device allows the audience to see the maids performing for their mistress as they fail to fulfil their fantasies. A long speech concludes the final role-play and the play, with one of the maids describing how she murdered the mistress offstage.

Key roles and relationships

Claire: The younger of the two sisters, but she is the more domineering of the pair and always plays 'Madame' in the fantasies. Beneath the loathing of her mistress, she has some affection for her and defends her, but it is never clear what is 'performance'. She enjoys dressing in Madame's clothes and wearing her make-up. Claire enjoys violently abusing her sister during the role-plays. She also likes writing fantastical stories and wrote the letter that got her master put in prison.

Solange: The elder of the two sisters, but she is happy to be dominated by her sister and always plays the maid. She enjoys the violent abuse she receives from her sister during the role-plays, but does lash out in return. Solange has a maternal instinct towards her sister and describes the violent abortions she has performed on herself so that she can stay with her sister. She reads Claire's stories and criticises fantastical escapism.

Madame: A wealthy woman who is more conscientious than the maids portrays. She feels guilty that she can enjoy the finer things in life while her husband is in prison. She starts to give away her furs to Solange and declares she takes pleasure in making other people happy. When she finds out her husband is out on bail she takes back the fur. She repeatedly says that the maids are trying to kill her with flowers or tea.

Top tip

Remember that, the Theatre of the Absurd was a definition created by Martin Esslin to retrospectively categorise Beckett's work alongside the writing of Eugene Ionesco, Antoine Artaud, Samuel Beckett and Jean-Paul Sartre.

The Maids

Key moments

The first fantasy: Claire plays Madame, while Solange plays the maid.

- How will you integrate the mirror into your set?
- Will you choose to conceal the performance from the audience or would you like them to realise it is Claire performing as 'Madame'?
- How will you choreograph the violence?
- How will the vocal delivery differ for the fantasies compared to reality?

Phone call: Claire answers the phone and hears that Monsieur has been bailed.

- How will you lay out the set to include the phone?
- How will you direct the actors playing the maids to be both defensive about their approach and aggressive about the failings of the others?

Run the world: Claire speaks as if she will master the world with murder and describes famous murders.

- How will you direct the actor playing Claire to be *exalted* in her voice and movement?
- How will you use the **pace** of speech to build towards a ritualistic climax?
- How will you direct the actor playing Solange to react to her sister's speech?

Madame returns: Madame returns for tea while her husband is in prison.

- How will you capture the status of Madame within the space?
- How will Claire and Solange perform as the maids?
- Will you get the actors playing Claire and Solange to communicate non-verbally as their 'real' selves during this scene?

The white dress fantasy: Claire puts on a white dress of Madame's and begins a role-play.

- How will the frustrations of the missed opportunity inform the maids' latest performance?
- How will you direct the performed strangulation that seems to go too far?

The final speech: Solange describes how she murdered Madame offstage.

- How will you reinforce the explicit theatricality of this final speech?
- Will you use production elements to reinforce the idea that the audience are watching a play or will you keep them as pure imagination?

Glossary

Pace
Rate of movement or speed of action – continuum of fast to slow delivery.

Original performance conditions

The Maids was first performed at the Athénée Theatre in Paris in 1947. The play was directed by renowned French actor Louis Jouvet and the set was designed by Christian Bérard. The production featured a majestic and accurate set of great detail. The illusion of the set was important as it allowed the action and words of the play to teeter on the edge of fantasy and reality. Jouvet was a long-time collaborator of Jacques Copeau and shared his emphasis on the importance of the text. He wanted a theatre that was a communion between actors and audience. Genet would have been attracted to his loyalty to the text, and his emphasis on actors and audiences engaging in a shared performance. Genet initially wanted men to play all the parts in the original production, no doubt to increase the layers of fantasy and reality, but Jouvet changed his mind.

Top tip

You will have to be able to communicate a production concept that is relevant for a 21st-century audience. Try to find parallels between today and the context in which the play was written. This is a good way to justify your ideas for a modern production.

Social, political, cultural and historical context

Below is a selection of original context points that have been linked with some of the key themes of *The Maids*.

Otherness
Genet always felt that he was an outsider as he was abandoned by his mother and bought up by a peasant family. Aged 10, he was wrongly accused of being a thief, so he decided to become a thief. He felt the world rejected him, so he rejected it. He spent much of his 20s as a criminal roaming Europe, feeling comfortable on the outside of normal social hierarchies and order.

Fantasy and illusion
When Genet returned to France in his 30s he spent much of his time in prison. It was the forced entrapment that led him first to poetry, then prose and then plays. His confinement caused him to explore fantasy and illusion. He felt that the dramatic form allowed him to construct objective reality but infuse it with the subjectivity and illusions of poetry.

Failure
Genet's experience led him to believe that life was a failure. He wanted to capture the idea that humans spend their lives striving and failing. He believed that the human desire for more always led to feeling unfulfilled, the ultimate failure being death. The theatrical form and its emphasis on action allowed him to expose failure.

The School for Scandal

Playwright: Richard Brinsley Sheridan (1751–1816)

First performance: 1777, Drury Lane, London

Synopsis

The play is set in the world of high society gossip and scandal. The comedy comes from confusion and hearsay as the action shifts between three houses. The audience are introduced to the turbulent relationship between Sir Peter Teazle and his wife Lady Teazle. Sir Peter has arranged for his ward, Maria, to marry Joseph, but she is opposed to the idea. Back in Lady Sneerwell's house, Joseph declares his love to Maria, but he is interrupted by Lady Teazle who thought Joseph liked her. He insists that he was only saying this to Maria to stop her telling Sir Peter about his true love for Lady Teazle. Sir Oliver Surface, the uncle of Charles and Joseph, returns from India and decides to test the true character of his nephews. He disguises himself as a moneylender and visits Charles, who is enjoying partying with his friends. Charles offers to sell the disguised Sir Oliver all the family's paintings. Sir Oliver is angry at his nephew's disregard for family history, but is pleased when Charles refuses to sell the portrait of his uncle. The action moves to Joseph's library where he is seducing Lady Teazle, but they are interrupted by Sir Peter Teazle. Lady Teazle avoids her husband and hides behind a screen. Sir Peter tells Joseph that he is happy to divorce his wife and give her a generous settlement. Charles then enters and Sir Peter hides. Both Lady Teazle and Sir Peter are uncovered in their hiding places. Lady Teazle is delighted with her husband's generous offer and decides to confess her affair. Sir Oliver arrives in a new disguise and tests Joseph, but he fails to impress his father who decides that Charles will be his heir. The play concludes at Sir Peter's, where he angrily chases away a group of gossipers and goes to make up with his wife. Sir Oliver reveals himself to his nephews and criticises Joseph. All the characters finish on stage with Charles and Maria declaring they will marry tomorrow.

Style

Sheridan revived the 'comedy of manners' style for *The School for Scandal* that was popular 100 years earlier during the Restoration era. A comedy of manners is a witty and highbrow style of comedy that mirrors the behaviour of people attempting to meet the social standard of the upper classes. It is a satirical style because it holds up the behaviour of high society for ridicule. The satirical comment, witty dialogue and the fragile atmosphere is more important than the plot in this style of theatre. The audience are drawn into the 'conversation' of the play when the characters address them as an aside.

Structure

Sheridan follows the convention of the time and presents *The School for Scandal* in a five-act structure. This allowed for the balanced presentation of plot that the audience would have been accustomed to. The witty dialogue and flair of the writer was the main attraction for the audience. The structure of the scenes emphasised this as shifts in location allowed for the different houses to comment on and gossip about each other. Sheridan keeps the scenes fresh and lively by carefully controlling the number of people engaging in dialogue: scenes of two characters are quickly followed by scenes of multiple characters.

Key roles and relationships

Sir Peter Teazle and Lady Teazle: An ageing husband who struggles to cope with his younger wife. They are fiery opponents. Lady Teazle is a country girl with the shrewdness of her city friends. She teases and torments her gullible husband.

Joseph and Charles Surface: The brothers are comic opposites – Joseph, despite attempts to be moral, is villainous and deceptive, whereas Charles, despite his partying and spending, is generous. Neither is what they appear on the surface.

Sir Oliver Surface: A wise older man who is able to place himself outside of the social conventions to observe the other characters for who they really are.

Lady Sneerswell and the Scandal School: Lady Sneerswell and her group of gossipers are more complex and individual versions of a chorus. They give the other characters a social context, while their names give clues to their individual characterisation.

Key moments

Act 2 Scene 1: Sir Peter and Lady Teazle argue about her extravagance.

- How will you direct the shifting status between these two characters?

- How will you direct the actor playing Sir Peter to capture the contrast between his fiery temper and his powerlessness with his young wife?

- How will you show Lady Teazle to be ambitious to fit in with city fashion despite her country background?

Act 3 Scene 1: Sir Oliver plans his disguise. Sir Peter tries to get Maria to agree to marry Joseph and Lady Teazle charms money out of Sir Peter before starting an argument again.

- How will you position Sir Oliver and Sir Peter in the space as they plot?

- How will you capture the fragile atmosphere and shifting moods between Sir Peter and the women in his life?

Act 3 Scene 3: Charles is partying with his friends when his uncle enters disguised as a moneylender.

- How will you capture the party atmosphere and the frivolous attitude of Charles?

- How will you direct the actor playing Sir Oliver to physicalise the moneylender?

- How will you direct Sir Oliver's asides to the audience?

The School for Scandal

Act 4 Scene 3: The climax of the deception takes place in Joseph's library. Characters hide and are discovered. The truth begins to come out.

- How will you manage the actors in the space to maximise the comedy?

- How will you engage the audience with the action on stage?

Original performance conditions

Drury Lane Theatre was a place to be seen and the auditorium would have been well-lit with chandeliers throughout the performance. Drury Lane had an actor-manager system and Sheridan took on the role from the most famous actor-manager, David Garrick (1717–79). Sheridan would have written *The School for Scandal* with a specific cast in mind. Costumes would have mirrored the fashions of the day and deviances would have been a comment on the character. For example, a male character wearing a wig despite it no longer being fashionable would have revealed his lack of status. The front of the stage protruded out from the proscenium arch and the most expensive boxes were next to the stage. The set was a mixture of painted backdrops taken from the theatre's stock and brand new designs by renowned theatre painter Philip James de Loutherbourg. Each act would be divided by the lowering of a screen at the proscenium arch, while all other changes took place in full view of the audience. Live orchestral music would have complemented the action. The audience were unruly and far more audible in their responses to plays. Drury Lane was wrecked five times between 1743 and 1776 because of audience riots.

Social, political, cultural and historical context

Below is a selection of original context points that have been linked with some of the key themes of *The School for Scandal*.

Scandal and reputation

The School for Scandal was written at a time when the middle classes were growing. Wealth was no longer kept for the landowners. The trade within an expanding British Empire and the Industrial Revolution led to more substantial private incomes that allowed many people to live very comfortable lives. There was an increase in leisure time, especially for young women, who were supported by the wealth of their fathers and husbands. As wealth distributed itself across the middle classes, a great emphasis was put on fashion, social standing and reputation, especially amongst women. This led to the culture of gossip and scandal that is satirised in Sheridan's play.

Money, women and marriage

Property and possession were an important part of achieving social recognition. Women were the possessions of men, with fathers marrying their daughters to the most suitable husbands. Marriage was a commodity, like those traded across the British Empire, as women would have come with a substantial amount of money and property known as a dowry. The collision between this sense of ownership and the independence that women found during their increased leisure time was a great source of comedy.

> **Top tip**
>
> You will have to be able to communicate a production concept that is relevant for a 21st-century audience. Try to find parallels between today and the context in which the play was written. This is a good way to justify your ideas for a modern production.

The Tempest

Playwright: William Shakespeare (1564–1616)
Written 1610/11; published 1623; first performance 1611

Synopsis
Prospero, the former Duke of Milan, and his daughter, Miranda, watch a storm from an island that they inhabit with the savage, Caliban, and the spirit, Ariel. Prospero rules the island with magic after being banished by his brother, Antonio. A ship is wrecked in the storm and all

the passengers, including Antonio, are thrown into the sea. Prospero rescues the passengers with his magic and they end up separated on the island. Miranda meets Ferdinand, one of the passengers, and they instantly fall in love. Magic-induced confusion takes hold of the survivors as they try to find each other on the island. Meanwhile, Caliban gets drunk and plots to overthrow Prospero with the help of the jester Trinculo and Stephano, a drunken butler. Their plot fails as everyone arrives at the same place on the island. Prospero gives up his magic and reveals himself as the Duke of Milan. He forgives his brother, Ariel is set free, Caliban and the other plotters are forgiven, and Miranda and Ferdinand get married. Sailors arrive to say that the ship was not wrecked and they all celebrate.

Genre

The Tempest is considered to be a 'romance' play. These feature natural events as a dramatic device, a long-held conflict that is eventually resolved, the need for repentance in order to avoid unhappiness, and a happy ending that is tinged with the guilt and sadness of the past events. Shakespeare also took elements of pastoral drama, where an idyllic, natural world is created to reflect the real world, and elements from epic drama with its sense of fractured time. He also used conventions of the newly popular 'tragicomedy', with the reversal of Prospero's fortunes leading to a happy ending rather than death.

Structure

The Tempest is written in five acts. **Act 1** explains everything and triggers the action of the play. **Acts 2** and **3** show all the strands of the plot building towards the climax of the play at the end of **Act 3**. **Act 4** shows the characters resolving the crisis caused at the climax of the plot. Finally, **Act 5** presents the conclusion with all strands of the story neatly tied together. Shakespeare's transition between Acts 4 and 5 diverts from his established convention of acts running one into another smoothly. Here Shakespeare harks back to the more overtly theatrical convention of making a clear break between the final two acts and filling it with music. The break is obvious because Prospero is the last to exit in Act 4 and the first to enter in Act 5. This device was most likely included as another way of reminding the audience of the theatricality of *The Tempest*.

Key roles and relationships

Prospero: He begins the play by trying to keep his power and authority. He has mastered magic but not human emotions, and he punishes those around him in an attempt to remain in control: he refuses to admit that Miranda is becoming a woman; he causes the storm; he enslaves Ferdinand; and he threatens both Ariel and Caliban. The play presents him gradually softening, triggered by the love he sees Miranda has for Ferdinand. He relinquishes his anger and need for power in favour of a more kind, accepting authority.

Miranda and Ferdinand: Miranda has spent all 15 years of her life on the island and has only seen two men before: her father, Prospero, and Caliban. Ferdinand is an honest and good man who represents the virtues of humanity. The love they have for each other is innocent, pure and natural. The force of their love is the cause of change in the play and not Prospero's magic.

Ariel: The son of the witch who ran the island before Prospero's arrival. He has been in Prospero's service ever since, but he is desperate for his own freedom. Despite being an invisible spirit, he experiences human emotions and, as he orchestrates Prospero's manipulation of the island, he pities his human victims. This compassion contributes to Prospero's change and leads Ariel to obtain his freedom.

Caliban: On the surface Caliban is predominantly a comic character. However, he is the 'native' of the island, imprisoned by his conqueror and his presence has serious undertones.

The Tempest

Key moments

Act 1 Scenes 1 and 2: The ship caught in the storm is followed by Prospero explaining everything to Miranda before the entrance of Caliban, Ariel and Ferdinand.

- How will you capture the audience's attention with the storm?

- How will you sustain the audience's attention during Prospero's long speeches?

- How will you capture the essence of Caliban, Ariel and Ferdinand through movement and costume?

Act 2 Scene 2: Caliban meets Trinculo and Stephano.

- Will you try to illicit any sympathy for Caliban during this comic scene?

- How will you create the scene of drunkenness and confusion in the characters' actions?

- How will you create the set-piece joke of the four-legged monster?

Act 3 Scene 1: Ferdinand and Miranda declare their love for each other. This is a delicate scene rooted in dialogue and contrasts with the knock-about comedy of the previous scene.

- How will you capture the gentleness of the love between this couple?

Act 3 Scenes 2 and 3: Pivotal scenes in the play as Ariel doles out Prospero's punishments on his brother and Caliban. There is a lot of stage action mixed with magical music and a banquet.

- How will you maintain a sense of pace in transitions?

- How will you create Ariel's magical music?

Act 4 Scene 1: The masque.

- How will you create the magical masque that Prospero presents?

- Will you contrast the movements of the spirits with the movements of Ferdinand and Miranda?

Act 5 Scene 1: All the strands of the story are drawn together.

- How will the finale to your production capture the 'brave new world' that Miranda observes?

- How will you present the epilogue with the actor playing Prospero coming out of role to address the audience?

Top tip

You will have to be able to communicate a production concept that is relevant for a 21st-century audience. Try to find parallels between today and the context in which the play was written. This is a good way to justify your ideas for a modern production.

Original performance conditions

The Tempest is considered to be Shakespeare's farewell to the theatre as he retired shortly after it was performed. Prospero is believed to represent Shakespeare himself, with parallels made between magic and theatre. The original production would have used the Globe's theatricality to its fullest, with Shakespeare tuned into the possibilities of the space. The gallery, the trapdoor and the discovery space at the back of the stage would all have been used. The conventions that he had mastered would have all been highlights of the production: capturing nature at its harshest with sound-effects created under the stage; long speeches confidently delivered by the accomplished Richard Burbage to keep the audience's attention; blank verse used to capture realistic human emotion and interaction; and comic interludes that are more complex and challenging for an audience than they first appear.

Social, political, cultural and historical context

Below is a selection of original context points that have been linked with some of the key themes of *The Tempest*.

Power and control

People began to question and debate established power structures during the Renaissance because of a new focus on man as an individual as well as a move away from the idea of an all-powerful God. Philosophical thinkers like Thomas More (1478–1535) began to consider what would make a 'utopia', a perfect society, in 1516. This change in thinking, combined with a spirit of adventure, led to the discovery of the Americas, 'the New World', in the 1570s.

Betrayal, revenge and forgiveness

Betrayal and revenge characterise many of Shakespeare's tragedies and histories. It is as though betrayal and revenge were at the heart of the greatest social changes in Shakespeare's day. Monarch's were conspired against and overthrown with violence, while their offspring would plot their revenge and the cycle of betrayal and revenge would go on. The spirit of forgiveness is rooted in Christian theology, but is perhaps how Shakespeare believed real change could be possible.

Waiting for Godot

Playwright: Samuel Beckett (1906–89)

Written 1949; published: 1952 (French), 1954 (English); first performance: 1953 (France), 1955 (Britain)

Synopsis

Two men, Estragon and Vladimir, sit under a tree on a country road, waiting for a meeting with Mr Godot. A small boy arrives to tell them that Mr Godot will not be coming. The two men return, sit under the same tree and wait for a meeting with Mr Godot. The small boy returns to tell them that Mr Godot will not be coming.

Style

Theatre of the Absurd shares the characteristics of staging anxiety and disillusionment. Beckett himself was averse to the categorisation of his plays. They are so different that some refer to the style as simply 'Beckettian'. His work is characterised by its minimal language, plot and production.

Structure

Beckett splits *Waiting for Godot* into two acts. The second act mirrors the first. Nothing happens in either of them. Beckett creates a structure out of the balance of opposing characters.

Key roles and relationships

Estragon 'Gogo': A tramp who is reserved, but perceptive and resourceful. He has more of a 'masculine' personality, as well as being abrupt and volatile. Having been together for half a century, Estragon needs Vladimir as a distraction from the tedious wait. Estragon repeatedly plays with his boots. He feels a kinship with Pozzo.

Vladimir 'Didi': A tramp who is talkative, but intelligent and logical. He has more of a 'feminine' personality, as well as being sympathetic and passionate. Having been together for half a century, Vladimir needs Estragon as a distraction from the tedious wait. Vladimir repeatedly plays with his hat. He feels a kinship with Lucky.

Top tip

Remember that the philosopher Michel de Montaigne (1533–92) wrote *Essays* (1580) that suggested Europeans could learn from the natives living in the Americas, as their society was pure and untarnished.

Top tip

Remember that 39 years after *The Tempest* was written, England went through a major social and political change when the people, led by Oliver Cromwell, tried King Charles I for treason and executed him in 1649. There was no replacement monarch and a new government of the people was established.

Pozzo: The master of Lucky whom he literally keeps on a long leash. He carries a whip.

Lucky: The servant of Pozzo who is literally kept on a long leash. He carries a heavy bag, a folding stool, a picnic basket and a great coat.

Key moments

Hurts! He wants to know if it hurts: Estragon tries to take off his boots but it hurts. Vladimir needs to wee but it hurts.

- How will you ask the actors to physicalise their pain?

- How will you establish the relationship between to the two of them?

- How will you have them interact non-verbally to reinforce the comedy?

To treat a man … (gesture towards Lucky) … like that: Pozzo has Lucky on a leash and beats him with a whip.

- How will you direct the actor playing Lucky to capture his animal qualities?

- How will you create connections between the characters to show sympathy?

- How will Pozzo's physicality reinforce his power?

Estragon approaches Lucky and makes to wipe his eyes. Lucky kicks him violently in the shins.

- How will you direct the physical comedy?

- How will you direct the actors to portray the more tragic emotions?

- How will you control the sudden shifts in tone?

Shall we have him dance, or sing, or recite, or think, or: Lucky thinks at the command of Pozzo.

- How will you capture the comedy and the tragedy of this moment?

- How will you direct the actor playing Lucky to vocally deliver his long speech?

- How will the other characters respond to Lucky's thinking?

We have to come back tomorrow: The pair are told again that Godot won't be coming.

- How will you reinforce the cyclical repetition of the end to each act?

- How will you use lighting to capture the end of the day, literally, or will you give it a symbolic quality?

Original performance conditions

Waiting for Godot was first performed at the Théâtre de Babylone, a 75-seat theatre in Paris, 1953. It was directed by Roger Blin, who also played the part of Pozzo. The well-made play with its clear plot and structure was popular, as was the increase in 'political' theatre. Beckett's play doesn't give an audience the security of a plot or even ask them to act on what they have seen; instead it forces a contemplation of the futility of life. The play was performed on an empty stage. It was Blin's choice to have Estragon and Vladimir dressed as tramps. Pozzo wore a top hat and long coat of the aristocracy, and Lucky had long, messy white hair. Beckett's theatre was very much a writer's rather than a director's theatre, and he dictated precise action to accompany the words. But Beckett also professed to not knowing a lot about the theatre when he wrote *Waiting for Godot*. He made changes to his play in response to early productions as he learned more about the theatre. He began directing his own plays in the 1960s and formulated many of his staging ideas for *Waiting for Godot* when directing it at the Schiller Theatre in Berlin.

Waiting for Godot

Social, political, cultural and historical context

Below is a selection of original context points that have been linked with some of the key themes of *Waiting for Godot*.

Time and repetition

Beckett was a part of the Resistance movement in Nazi-occupied Paris during the Second World War. He was forced to leave occupied Paris and fled for Vichy, France. His experience in the Resistance would have involved long waits, confusion and poverty. This experience of the war would have been within the broader context of a turbulent period in history. The destruction of the First World War was quickly repeated in the destruction of the Second World War and the uncertainty of the Cold War years followed.

Humanity and suffering

Beckett was an intellectual and an academic who studied literature and read the great philosophers of the time. He lived in Ireland from 1906 to 1932, and experienced the poverty and deprivation caused by the civil war and the trade war with Britain. He engaged with broader questions about humanity and suffering, and travelled across Europe. The context of the wars and the atrocities of the Holocaust raised questions about how humans treat each other.

Performance

Beckett enjoyed the music hall and comic cinema of Laurel and Hardy, and Charlie Chaplin. These greats of early Hollywood captured a sense of tragic tears alongside slapstick humour. The films were set during the Great Depression and depicted the struggles of tramps. They showed the characters looking for work, food and companionship, but they also showed them simply existing, filling time.

Top tip

You will have to be able to communicate a production concept that is relevant for a 21st-century audience. Try to find parallels between today and the context in which the play was written. This is a good way to justify your ideas for a modern production.

Woyzeck

Playwright: Georg Büchner (1813–37)

Written: 1836; first published: 1878; first performances – November (Munich) and December (Berlin) 1913

Synopsis

Woyzeck is a batman in the military who serves the Captain. He is also part of the Doctor's medical trials and is forced to only eat peas. He has a child and a common-law wife (Marie), but she has an affair with a visiting Drum Major. Woyzeck has visions potentially caused by the experiment. He is bullied and mistreated by the Captain, the Doctor and the Drum Major. He resorts to murdering Marie and drowning himself. The play ends with Woyzeck's friend Andres appearing to have visions, implying the same fate is in store for him.

Style

Woyzeck is believed to be the first 'modern' play as it foreshadows realism/naturalism, expressionism and the Theatre of Cruelty. Stanislavski, Brecht and Artaud all claim the play as appropriate for their contrasting styles. It is easy to forget that these styles and practitioners did not exist when the play was written.

Melodrama was the popular form of theatre when Büchner wrote the play in 1836. Characters in melodrama were heavily influenced by Italy's *commedia dell'arte* tradition – characters were caricature types to simplify and exaggerate emotions and social contrasts. Büchner places the unnamed character types alongside named characters to highlight complex and conflicting human emotion.

Top tip

It will be useful to remember that this play was inspired by a true story that Büchner read about in a scientific journal. It was the account of a man named Woyzeck who murdered his wife.

Woyzeck

Taking it further

Find out more about *commedia dell'arte* by watching the National Theatre *commedia dell'arte* videos on YouTube.

Structure

Woyzeck is a condensed and compact play. Episodic scenes are short and jump from moment to moment. They are interchangeable and work when reorganised. The structure goes against the Aristotelian idea of tragedy, with one moment logically leading to the next. Instead the episodic scenes emphasise the random nature of events. The randomness of the structure reinforces the theme of cruelty and hopelessness. The tragic experience is not cushioned by logic, but enhanced by the fragmentary nature of human experience. This makes for a stark and challenging experience for the audience.

Key roles and relationships

Woyzeck: Lack of education and vocabulary don't allow him to communicate his thoughts. His intellect struggles to compute the emotional turmoil that he endures. There are parallels between Woyzeck and Shakespeare's King Lear and Hamlet, but he has none of their education or status. He is also the same age as Jesus Christ when he was crucified. The diet of peas could be seen as a physiological justification for his behaviour. Woyzeck's closest 'ally' in the play is Andres, but their scenes are full of broken dialogue as they are unable to communicate with one another.

Marie: She is a complex and contradictory character. The fragmentary structure of the play makes her confusing for the audience, placing them in the same position as Woyzeck. Her flirtatious behaviour and active courting of the Drum Major makes their aggressive sexual encounter difficult to comprehend. Any performance of Marie must capture the conflicting and contrasting elements of her character.

Doctor and Captain: These two character types are taken from the *commedia dell'arte* tradition and their scenes are meant to be comical and funny. They provide a contrast to the emotional intensity of Woyzeck, but also mirror his weaknesses in comical ways. The Doctor has moments of rage and violence, while the Captain lacks the vocabulary to explain himself. But they hold the higher status and this should fuel both the comedy and the tragedy.

Key moments

Scene 3, the fairground: As a director, you have to be able to manage this large-scale scene.

- How will you manage such a large-scale scene that does not fit with the intimacy of the other scenes?
- How you will present the 'unstageable' stage directions?

Scene 8, Doctor lecturing students: The stage directions cast the audience as the assembled students.

- How will you indicate this in the space?
- Does this scene lead you to include more audience participation?

Scene 9, Doctor and Captain in street: The Captain taunts Woyzeck.

- How will you capture the pace and comedy of this exchange as well as the darkness of the bullying?

Scene 10, Woyzeck confronts Marie: This is the moment of Woyzeck's most realistic expression of himself.

- How will you direct your actor to show his anger is tipping over into madness? Pace, proxemics and **pauses** will hold particular significance.

Glossary

Pause
Choice of breaks in speech and their length.

Scene 20, Grandmother's fable: This is a dream-like interlude that has a dark, depressing moral.

- How will your production create an appropriate atmosphere?

Scene 25, Andres cutting sticks: This final scene highlights the cyclical nature of the play.

- How will you capture this with the different elements of production?

Original performance conditions

First performed 1913: The first performances of the play actually happened within a month of each other but neither can be considered 'true' representations of Büchner's *Woyzeck* because a corrupted text was used.

8 November 1913: Eugen Kilian directed the play in the Residenztheater, Munich. Despite following the corrupted version of the text, the production was a success. A revolving stage was used to enable the swift scene changes that created a moving experience for the audience. The production was praised for its surface comedy while maintaining the underlying tragedy.

1 December 1913: Victor Barnowsky, a leading expressionist, directed the play in Berlin. He used elaborate, expressionist sets that resulted in a frustrating experience for the audience, as they were left looking at a curtain during long scene changes.

Social, political, cultural and historical context

Below is a selection of original context points that have been linked with some of the key themes of *Woyzeck*.

Power and status

The Napoleonic Wars ended in 1815, leaving two million dead and a depression across Germany. Peasants (like Woyzeck) were forced to take roles in the military. At this time, Germany had a hierarchical system with aristocrats at the top. Towards the end of the 1800s, the aristocrats were replaced by industrialists due to the Industrial Revolution. There was a growing unrest among the common people, along with a failed revolution in 1830. Woyzeck, the common man, is a failure who is stuck in the lowest position of the military, social, religious and medical hierarchy.

Trapped/oppressed

Germany was made up of 39 states and travel between states was restricted by a passport system. Mobility and the financial rewards of a network were not available to the poor, uneducated peasantry. Büchner's additional characters all had the benefits of mobility, plus a network of colleagues and family across Germany – Freemasons, soldiers of rank, journeymen and a Jew. Their presence in the play would have been a clear representation of freedom in the 1830s. The uneducated, inarticulate and poor Woyzeck contrasts with these other characters because he is trapped by his circumstances.

Hopelessness and eternity

Büchner turned his back on the socialist revolutionary movements that he once leafleted for. Instead he was determined to show that the idealistic belief in man's capacity for enlightenment and justice was a false one. The tragic events that are depicted and the way they are presented in a brief, episodic structure reinforce a sense of eternal hopelessness. The humanity of Woyzeck's character is the thing that stops the play from presenting life as meaningless.

> **Top tip**
>
> You will have to be able to communicate a production concept that is relevant for a 21st-century audience. Try to find parallels between today and the context in which the play was written. This is a good way to justify your ideas for a modern production.

Practitioner texts

Practitioner: Antonin Artaud

Born: Marseille, France – 4 September 1896.

Died: Rodez, France – 4 March 1948.

Occupation: Playwright, Poet, Theatre practitioner, Actor, Director, Designer, Film theorist, Screenwriter, Radio broadcaster.

Vision for theatre: Theatre should remove the security of language and abolish established ideas of the performer/audience divide. Ritualistic performance should infect its audience like a plague.

Style: Theatre of Cruelty – a performance that was strict, persistent, unrelentingly definite, irreversible and absolutely emphatic. Note that Artaud did not mean 'cruelty' in the sense of merciless bloodshed, pointless pain or gratuitous violence.

A productive madness

Artaud had both mental health problems and a drug addiction. Despite these problems he wrote his first manifesto for a Theatre of Cruelty in 1932 and returned to his ideas in a second manifesto in 1933. He also managed to act in the theatre and on film until 1935. His influence for his theatre ideas came from:

- living in Mexico for one month with the Tarahumara Indians

- encounters with two Eastern theatre traditions – a Cambodian theatre, and a Balinese dance group.

In 1924 he joined the Surrealist movement, but he was expelled in 1926. He founded the Théâtre Alfred Jarry in 1926, but this only lasted four years after several projects came to nothing. Many of his ideas were planned and then aborted, including a production of Büchner's *Woyzeck* in 1932. The only major play he adapted and managed to produce was Shelley's *The Cenci* in 1935. It was meant to be a practical realisation of his Theatre of Cruelty, but the critical response was mixed and it only lasted 17 performances. This was to be his last practical involvement in the theatre. He would spend the rest of his life in 'mental institutions', continuing to write about the theatre. His book *The Theatre and its Double* was published in 1938.

Key ideas

Artaud wrote about theatre in an often poetic and philosophical style. He wanted a theatre that recovered a language of movement and spatial relationships rather than realistic speech and text. His uncompromising thinking and philosophical style of writing were major reasons why his ideas were never properly realised in his lifetime.

- **Ritual**: Artaud believed the theatre was similar to ancient religious ritual. His ideas were formed by his experience of Balinese dance and the Tarahumara Indians. Movement and gesture were the primary forms of communication. Rhythm and repetition flowed in the performers and created a trance-like state. The physicality of the ritual would result in vocalised sounds that were beyond language. This ritualistic theatre would present mythical and historic themes. His idea was that these mass concerns would be more disturbing than any personal ones.

- **The plague**: Artaud used the idea of a plague to express the power the theatre should have over its audience. He believed performers should be in a state of delirium, as if suffering from a plague. This, in turn, would infect the audience like an epidemic. In his style, silence and sudden stops are followed by abrupt rushes of feverish movement. Gestures are taken to the limit and the body is pushed to extremes. In this state, both performer and audience are forced to rebel against the infection with one last heroic gasp for a cure.

- **The encircled audience**: Artaud wanted to abolish the actor/audience divide. He preferred to establish an area where every participant in the theatre co-existed. This single, undivided location should be the scene of the action, with direct contact between actor and audience. To achieve his style, he believed barns or large spaces should be used and organised like a religious temple. The audience should sit in the centre on swivelling chairs and the action should take place all around them. There should also be overhead galleries for the actors, to allow them to explore the limits of height and depth.

- **Satisfying the senses**: Artaud believed the theatre should bring back the idea of **total theatre** and satisfy the senses. He wanted to reduce the importance of intellectual understanding and replace it with instinctive feeling. Physical and spatial communication, along with rhythm and sound, were to be targeted at the whole anatomy rather than just the eyes and ears.

- **The actor's body**: Theatre should not use one object to represent another. Artaud did not want a dust cloth to be used as a mountain. He believed the theatre should not try to represent what cannot be represented. He wanted the actor to use real-life objects if they were available, with the rest being created with their body. Artaud felt the set could be created with the body and the face.

> **Glossary**
>
> **Total theatre**
> A theatre that combines acting, dance, music, lighting and film to create a larger-than-life illusion for its audience.

An Artaud production concept

If you choose Artaud as your practitioner, you must be able to refer to his theories in your own production concept. You should make reference to how you would use Artaud's key ideas to develop a production concept that is rooted in ritual and satisfies the senses with the power of a plague. Below is an overview of the theoretical conventions of an Artaud production concept that you can adopt and adapt for your written exam.

- **Acting**: Actors must be muscular, like athletes. This physical fitness will allow them to manipulate their bodies in a vast number of ways and take the body to its limits. Artaud believed the actor should be in an active state on the stage similar to a boxer, a sprinter or a high-jumper. Breathing would allow for the exploration of the extremes of the body and the voice. The rhythms that the actor presents with their breath, body and voice should infect the audience and allow them to identify with the performance.

- **Venue**: A barn or similarly large building. There should be galleries around the edges that give the space height and depth. The walls are whitewashed to absorb the lighting.

- **Lighting**: This can be used to create monsters of objects through the manipulation of angles. Moving and flashing lights as well as a full range of colours must be used to stimulate the minds of audience members. Artaud felt the lighting equipment of his day was not adequate. He described technical ideas that have been designed and used since his death.

- **Set and props**: Real-life objects can be used, but everything else is created by the actor's body.

- **Sound and music**: The sounds and musical rhythms of a ritual should be created by the actor. In addition, Artaud described a vision for 'surround-sound' that would allow sound to have a physical impact on an audience. Technological advancements since his death mean that the use of sound in this way is now achievable.

- **Costume**: Artaud wanted to avoid modern dress as much as possible because he preferred ritualistic costumes that reveal the spiritual beauty of the human body.

Berkoff

Taking it further

Artaud wanted the Theatre of Cruelty to take ideas from the paintings of Grunewald or Hieronymus Bosch. Explore these art works and use them to inspire your own production concepts.

Legacy

Artaud's ideas about the theatre have influenced a huge number of theatre makers. Many of these were more successful than Artaud himself at realising his ideas in actual productions. It is worth researching his legacy to find ideas for your production that are rooted in his theories but are actually workable. Jacques Lecoq (1921–99), originally a physical education teacher, shared Artaud's view of the athletic performer who is able to fully manipulate their body. This attitude towards the actor's body is shared by theatre practitioner Jerzy Grotowski (1933–99). His idea of 'via negativa' proposed stripping the actor back to their physical essence. Grotowski's performances were also ritualistic, and each production investigated different spectator–actor relationships. The Living Theatre company (1947–) experimented with creating theatre in different spaces that immersed the audience in the action. It also experimented with ritualistic 'happenings' that captured a sense of trance-like performance. Peter Brook (1925–) directed *Marat/Sade* (1964) at the Royal Shakespeare Company as an experimentation of the Theatre of Cruelty. Contemporary examples of Artaud's legacy are often captured by dance-trained performers because they have the awareness of their body that he demanded. Dance theatre practitioners such as Pina Bausch (1940–2009), Jasmin Vardimon (1971–) and Hofesh Schecter (1975–) explore the limitations of the human body and the ritualistic form.

Practitioner: Steven Berkoff

Born: London, UK – 3 August 1937.

Occupation: Playwright, Director, Theatre practitioner, Actor.

Vision for theatre: Theatre must fuse together opposites and celebrate contradictions: mime must collide with the spoken word; performance must be energetic and exaggerated but capture subtlety and detail; strict choreography must allow for moments of improvisation. The actor and the ensemble are central to the theatre.

Style: Expressionism presents everything on the stage from the perspective of an individual character. Voice, movement and production elements are heightened and distorted to reflect this perspective. There is an emphasis on chorus and ensemble, with moods and ideas more important than plot. Berkoff's work has also been described as 'in-yer-face theatre'.

From outcast to individual

Berkoff's ideas for the theatre were developed in response to his feelings of being an outsider. He is proud of his Jewish heritage and performs/works under the name Berkoff, even though his father changed the family name to Berks on arrival in the UK.

Berkoff grew up in East London but was uprooted several times by his parents. This added to his already difficult relationship with his father. He trained at the Webber Douglas Academy of Dramatic Art, but he never felt fully stimulated by the experience. He grew disillusioned with the theatre establishment and left the UK in 1965 to train with Jacques Lecoq at his school in Paris. There he met Jean-Louis Barrault, who (along with Lecoq) taught Berkoff the idea of 'total theatre'. Lecoq's teaching was rooted in mime, but focused on developing individual theatre makers with their own style. Berkoff's education in Paris motivated him to return to the UK and create his own style of theatre that contrasted with the theatre 'establishment' (for example, the more conservative West End). He wrote, produced, directed and starred in many of his own plays. He found fame with his successful adaptations and interpretations of the writers Franz Kafka, William Shakespeare and Sophocles.

Key ideas

Berkoff's ideas are very similar to those of Lecoq. The French teacher can take a lot of credit for Berkoff's use of mime and stylised movement. Berkoff's originality is not necessarily in the elements of performance but rather their combination in an aggressive and uncompromising style. This is rooted in his admiration for Antonin Artaud's writing, but also in his own life experiences. He has always positioned himself as an outsider, working against the 'norm'. This can be seen through his experimentation with contradictions within form and content in the theatre.

- **Mime**: This is usually action without words or objects, but Berkoff often combines it with speech. The gestures, facial expressions and body posture that make up the mimes are extremely precise. The mime is often exaggerated and grotesque. The use of mime emphasises the character's personal reaction to their environment rather than the environment itself.

- **Stylised movement**: This is an elaborate and exaggerated way of moving that captures the essence of a character. An example of this is the slow, high-knee, long-stride walking used by authority figures in Berkoff's production of Kafka's *The Trial*. Stylised movement is used as an expressionistic tool to portray secondary characters as moving in a way that reinforces the central character's perspective. The main character in *The Trial*, Josef K, perceived the authority figures as powerful and dominant, and their walk reflected this perception.

- **Irregular voice**: Vocal characterisation creates the environment through the use of purposeful over-articulation, wild variations in **pitch**, extended vowel sounds and strange rhythms. Speech is not only a method of communicating content, but also a tool that communicates the atmosphere and mood through its musicality.

- **Chorus**: This is an element of performance heavily emphasised in Lecoq's teaching. Berkoff believes the chorus should comment, illustrate and clarify the action. He considers the chorus to be a separate production element that could create mood and atmosphere as much as sound and lighting. This atmosphere would be created through a combination of strange and distorted voices that serve as sound effects. The chorus could also be a role similar to that of narrator, describing action that is mimed by the other performers.

- **Ensemble**: Berkoff places great emphasis on the collective group – the ensemble. This is in contradiction to his perceived arrogance and domineering style of directing. He prefers to work with groups of actors where the emphasis is on trust and experimentation. He demands precise synchronisation when choreographing the ensemble, but also encourages improvisation. The contradictory use of synchronisation and improvisation came together to highlight the disjointed and strange worlds that his productions presented.

Glossary

Pitch
The particular level of voice, instrument or tune – continuum of high to low quality.

Berkoff

A Berkoff production concept

If you choose Berkoff as your practitioner you must be able to refer to his theories in your own production concept. You should make reference to how you would use Berkoff's key ideas to develop a production concept that captures contradictions and reinforces the main character's view of their world. Below is an overview of the conventions of a Berkoff production concept that you can adopt and adapt for your written exam. It is important to remember that the elements combine and integrate in the 'total theatre' style.

- **Acting**: Actors are central to a Berkoff production. They are the first element the director uses to create character, environments, objects, atmosphere and mood. The work of an actor in a Berkoff production is precise and physically demanding, while the vocal range is stretched to its limit. The actors use caricature and melodrama to create grotesque, exaggerated characters that fit the perspective of the main character.

- **Venue**: Berkoff toured with most of his productions so they had to be flexible enough to adapt to any venue. Technical elements are important to his productions, but more emphasis should be placed on the actor and their relationship with the audience.

- **Set**: Berkoff follows the constructivist tradition of scenic art. This is the idea of minimal sets that rely on one or two simple structures. The structures used as a set should be stripped-down versions of the world of the play. An example is the cube structure made of metal bars in *Metamorphosis*, or the multiple movable doorframes used in *The Trial*.

- **Lighting**: The lighting design is important in a Berkoff production as it creates a sense of location not realised in a minimal set. Simple techniques should be executed with precision, as shape of light can distinguish between different parts of the stage. The harsh-edge quality of the lights, brightness and angle should be used to create atmosphere and mood.

- **Sound**: Sound effects should primarily be created by the actors. Recorded sound and music is integrated with the soundscapes created by the ensemble. The pace, pitch and rhythm of the sound and music are often distorted to reinforce the atmosphere and themes.

- **Costume, make-up and masks**: Berkoff repeatedly uses a black-and-white palette for his costumes and make-up. This has its roots in German expressionist cinema and art. He would always start with black and white and only add colour if it served a purpose. Costumes are detailed and often the most expensive part of his designs, as they serve as the main scenic device. Although rooted in realism, costumes should be taken to extremes to reinforce character and themes. Masks can occasionally be used as they dehumanise the actor, but heavy make-up often has the same effect.

Legacy

Berkoff's legacy is incomparable to the breadth of influence held by his teacher Lecoq. But it is their connection that gives Berkoff his position as a trailblazer of the British theatre. Lecoq taught Berkoff not simply to look for work but to create work himself. Berkoff's legacy is his independent approach to theatre making, rather than his distinctive style. His model of simple, actor-centric, fringe theatre that finds a larger audience is one that many have followed.

Practitioner: Bertolt Brecht

Born: Augsberg, German Empire – 10 February 1898.

Died: East Berlin, East Germany – 14 August 1956.

Occupation: Playwright, Director, Theatre practitioner, Poet.

Company: Berliner Ensemble.

Vision for theatre: Theatre should change the world through entertainment and education. Opposites should be highlighted in plays and productions to create a debate among audience members.

Style: Epic theatre used realistic acting to make the audience identify with the characters and themes. But the production elements of bright lights, songs and placards were used to detach the audience from this reality and make them examine it critically.

Early career, exile and the Berliner Ensemble

Brecht developed his ideas on theatre through practice. He wrote plays from 1923 while working on productions with Erwin Piscator (1893–1966) and Max Reinhardt (1873–1943). These directors influenced his own work as a theatre maker, but he also drew ideas from the playwrights William Shakespeare (1564–1616) and Georg Büchner (1813–37) – the latter's play *Woyzeck* was discovered during Brecht's lifetime. Additionally, from 1926 Brecht found inspiration in Marxist theory, and this led him to flee Hitler's Germany in 1933 to find exile in Switzerland and

Brecht

then the USA. His 15 years of exile in the USA saw the growing popularity of Lee Strasberg's psychologically realistic 'Method', leaving Brecht's Epic theatre in its shadow. But these years did allow him to re-evaluate his own plays and develop his theories for the theatre.

Brecht returned to East Berlin in 1948. He founded the Berliner Ensemble in 1949, with his long-time collaborator Helene Weigel (1900–72). Brecht lived for eight more years, which were extremely productive. An established company of actors, along with Caspar Neher (his set designer) and a venue, meant he could continue to experiment with his Epic theatre ideas.

Key ideas

Brecht is often misunderstood as a director whose theatre was moralistic rather than fun and entertaining. This misunderstanding has led to some very dry, dull productions labelled as 'Brechtian'. In fact, Brecht understood that theatre had to be fun and entertaining in order to cause moral and social change. He encouraged a scientific approach to theatre where ideas were tested. His theoretical ideas, recorded by him in note form, led to occasional contradictions and misinterpretation. His ideas are further complicated by the German wording he applied to them – wording that is often difficult to translate with accuracy.

- **Verfremdungseffekt (V-effect)**: This is the process of moving an audience from identification to detachment. They are presented with a reality and then distanced from it. All elements of a production had to work together to achieve verfremdungseffekt. An example of this is a scene that portrays the death of a character, which is then followed by a musical interlude of upbeat, fun music. The audience identifies with the death scene, but is then detached from it by the inappropriate music. This results in the audience reflecting on the death from a distant position where they can consider the social and moral implications.

- **Gestus**: This means capturing the essence or main theme of a production in a single element. Anything from a facial expression to a lighting state could be 'gestic' and capture the essence or main theme of a production. Brecht would take many photographs of his productions to ensure that every image was gestic.

- **Spass**: This means 'fun'. Spass was important to all Brecht's productions, and he learned a lot from the *commedia dell'arte* tradition. He felt that comedy and a sense of fun would enhance the play's serious social, moral or political message.

- **Modelbook**: Brecht advocated a modelbook approach to his productions, where he would write a detailed plan for a whole production, along with hundreds, if not thousands, of photographs. This meant other directors (or indeed his future self) could return to a production and copy it. He felt copying was an important creative element of the theatre. He felt that once the original had been copied, then details would develop through critical experimentation. Many of these modelbooks still exist, including one for his production of *Antigone*.

A Brecht production concept

If you choose Brecht as your practitioner you must be able to refer to his theories in your own production concept. You should make reference to how you would use Brecht's key ideas and conventions to develop a production concept that is educational, challenging and entertaining. Below is an overview of the conventions of a Brecht production concept that you can adopt and adapt for your written exam.

- **Acting**: Brecht believed that actors should 'show' real, observed behaviour rather than imitate it. This very difficult skill was perfected by Helene Weigel in many of his productions. A good example is her silent scream in Brecht's production of *Mother Courage and her Children*. The behaviour was observed from a photograph of a Singaporean mother mourning the death of

Brecht

her child, but the silence in the performance meant that it was shown, not imitated. This idea of showing was developed in rehearsal by speaking the parts in third person or the past tense.

- **Venue**: Any space is encouraged that breaks the idea of the fourth wall (the imagined divide between the acting space and the auditiorium). For example, Brecht used a revolving stage for his production of *Mother Courage and her Children*.

- **Set**: Sets should be constructed according to the needs of the actor and no more. An empty space should be filled with just the necessary props. (Brecht often detailed these and they were historically accurate depending on the needs of the production. If he needed a curtain, it was a half-curtain on a string across the stage.) Actors should not leave the stage unless it is necessary for the gestus of a scene. Transitions should take place in full view of the audience.

- **Lighting**: The light source should be in full view of the audience. Brecht preferred a harsh, bright, white light as a form of verfremdungseffekt. The auditorium should remain dimly lit to remind the audience of their surroundings and encourage them to actively think about the events of the play.

- **Music**: The composer Kurt Weill was a long-term collaborator with Brecht and created music that served as its own independent response to the themes of the play. The music should occasionally create the opposite atmosphere to the stage action as a form of verfremdungseffekt.

- **Costume and make-up**: Costumes should be made from authentic fabrics to support the social standing of the character. The colour of the costumes should be carefully chosen to reinforce the gestus of every moment. Make-up is applied in such a way that it is clearly visible and resembles a mask. Costume changes take place in front of the audience.

Legacy

Brecht is an influential figure in the development of modern theatre. He has been a strong influence on the director and theatre practitioner Peter Brook (1925–) and his idea of The Empty Space. The playwright and theatre artist Tim Crouch (1964–) has taken the idea of verfremdungseffekt to extremes in his productions. The desire for a theatre that offers an entertaining social and political education can be seen in the work of many modern playwrights, including Lucy Prebble's *Enron* (2009) and Lucy Kirkwood's *Chimerica* (2013).

Complicite

Practitioner: Complicite

Formed: 1983.

Artistic director: Simon McBurney.

Born: Cambridge, UK – 25 August 1957.

Occupation: Theatre director, Actor.

Vision for theatre: Theatre is a collaboration between performers, audience, director and designers. It should stimulate the senses. Theatre must never be the same. It must always evolve.

Style: The company is reluctant to define a style as it believes this would restrict future creativity. It describes its work as having a distinctive, visually rich stage language, which layers physically beautiful performances and tightly choreographed ensemble work with innovative lighting, sound and video design.

Comedy, physical theatre, total theatre and innovation

Complicite's artistic director Simon McBurney trained at Jacques Lecoq's drama school in Paris (1981–83). Lecoq influenced McBurney's physical style and encouraged the idea of ongoing creativity and evolution. Around the same time, McBurney met director Annabel Arden and together they teamed up with fellow Lecoq students Marcello Magni and Fiona Gordon. They formed Théâtre de Complicite, which at first made physical comedy and won the Perrier Comedy Award at the Edinburgh Fringe Festival in 1985.

The first major evolution came in 1989 when they were offered a 15-week season at the Almeida Theatre, London. After a fractious development process, they created an original adaptation of Friedrich Durrenmatt's *The Visit*. Their interpretation of this classic play held weight with critics and their mime skills were transformed into a more mature 'physical theatre' style. The group slightly reconfigured at this point, renaming itself simply 'Complicite' and appointing McBurney as artistic director. He has remained in the role ever since. Despite having an individual as its only constant member, Complicite has kept collaboration at its heart. New work always evolved and developed in response to the people involved in each project.

This evolution has continued throughout the company's history, moving from comedy, to physical theatre, to a 'total theatre' style where every element of the production is integrated to serve the story. Complicite's interest in production elements and its relationship to the performer is the foundation for its most recent projects. Most of the company's work is devised, and each production brings a drastic shift in style and approach. The vast number of associates who work with the company contribute to a collaboration that begins afresh with every new idea.

Key ideas

There is no standard formula for a Complicite production as the company always looks for new, innovative ways to communicate with an audience. An examination of its vast number of productions does highlight recurring ideas that feature in the majority of productions.

- **Physicality**: The actor's body is a primary tool used to create character and the world of the story. The work is demanding, requiring energy and precision from performers. A highly trained awareness of the body must be combined with a playfulness that makes the experience live and fresh every time. Complicite often uses the seven levels of tension to change the tension of a scene and spark it into life. This is a scale of muscular tension that an actor embodies to support characterisation and includes: catatonic; relaxed/Californian (soap opera); neutral/economic (contemporary dance); alert (farce); suspense (melodrama); passionate (opera); and tragic (for example, the end of *King Lear* when he is holding Cordelia in his arms).

- **Collaboration**: A collaborative spirit is at the heart of every stage of Complicite's work. Development of a work is undertaken as a group; the highly physical or technical performances require trust and cohesion between performers and technicians. However, the most vital collaboration is that between audience and performer. Performers must approach their relationship with generosity to make the audience feel at ease and open to the ideas of the production. Occasionally the trust between actor and audience is tested with abrupt, surprising or even aggressive interactions if these reinforce the ideas of the production.

- **Technological innovation**: A Complicite production satisfies the senses through innovative video projection and sound design. The instruments of technology are often integrated as part of the experience, making them visible to the audience. The performance of *The Master and Margarita*, for example, integrated a camera and its operator who roamed the stage, filming the action, projected on a large screen visible to all. In another production, *The Encounter*, sound collages were created with onstage microphones, including a binaural microphone and mixing equipment – the audience being able to experience every detail through headphones.

Complicite

Top tip

If you use 'binaural microphone' in your exam, it might be useful to explain that this type of microphone has two inputs that replicate human hearing. Binaural microphones are often placed in the position of ears on a dummy head. McBurney was influenced by the use of binaural microphones in the work of theatremakers Lundahl and Seitl.

- **Evolution and momentum**: Every production evolves and changes with each new performance. There is an ongoing sense of experimentation and a continual reassessment of audience responses. This change and adaptation highlights and celebrates the live nature of the theatre. As a production evolves it gathers a momentum and rhythm of its own. This rhythm is essential for propelling the audience through the story.

- **Dreams, memory and consciousness**: These are recurring themes that are explored by Complicite. These themes inform the content of productions such as *The Three Lives of Lucie Cabrol, Mnemonic, The Master and Margarita* and *The Encounter.* They also inform the form of productions: dream-like experiences are created with choreographed movements, lights, sound and video projection; memory is explored through non-linear narratives and the foregrounding of recording technology. These themes are particularly relevant to 21st-century living, where people are always attempting to capture a memory or a dream through social media, even though life continues to move forward.

A Complicite production concept

If you choose Complicite as your practitioner you must be able to refer to its theories in your own production concept. You should make reference to how you would use Complicite's key ideas to develop a production concept that stimulates the senses through collaboration between actor and audience, and the use of innovative technology. Below is an overview of the conventions of a Complicite production concept that you can adopt and adapt for your written exam.

- **Acting**: Actors must be versatile and fully aware of their bodies as a tool for communication. They must have the awareness and presence on stage to bring the audience into the world of the story with the subtlest of looks. In Complicite shows, performers frequently play more than one character, and also often bring their own experiences and personal stories into the narrative.

- **Venue**: To date, most Complicite productions have been staged end-on, and this arrangement is particularly good at supporting the creation of vivid stage images. The venue must have the technical capabilities to manage the needs of the production.

- **Lighting and projection**: Lighting must be dynamic and support the rhythm and momentum of the production. It is used to create atmosphere and mood for the different worlds explored by the story. Projections must support the story and themes of the production. Technology can be placed in full view of the audience.

- **Sound and music**: Sound and music should be used to highlight the rhythms of the story. They could support the energy and atmosphere or counter it. Technology can be placed in full view of the audience.

- **Set, costume and props**: The physicality of the actor is of primary importance and these elements must support this. They must serve the needs of the story and be fully integrated with sound and lighting design. Simplicity is used if it serves the clarity of communication. But the same can be said for elaborate, large-scale sets that draw on the tradition of magical realism where the everyday collides with the fantastical.

Legacy

The Complicite company is a trailblazer of the British theatre, influencing the shift from text-based to visual theatre. The company has had a huge influence on the rise in number of devising companies. Its work has influenced the Kneehigh theatre company as it made the transition from regional theatre to national theatre (see pages 113–15 in this section). Complicite's influence can also be seen in the visual theatre of Headlong and the physicality of Theatre O. However, it is Complicite's desire to change and evolve that means its work will remain challenging and inspirational to theatre artists for years to come.

Practitioner: Kneehigh

Formed: 1980.

Artistic directors: Mike Shepherd and Emma Rice.

Occupations: Theatre director and Designer.

Vision for theatre: Theatre should be a memorable, community event that takes place in a charged space, where stories are shared with a spirit of joyful anarchy.

Style: Kneehigh claims not to have a formula as the company feels this would restrict the creativity of new projects. But it takes inspiration from the storytelling tradition and magical realism, where everyday worlds are created with a twist of the fantastical.

Cornwall and beyond

Shepherd, from Cornwall, had failed several auditions in London. This experience motivated him to return home to make his own theatre. As a result, in 1980 Kneehigh was founded. It began as a response to the Cornwall countryside and was a playful interaction with the elements. Early performances took place in their natural surroundings – for example, the end of a woodland path, cliff tops or in the open-air Minack Theatre, near Penzance. This exposure to the elements gave the company's performances a wildness and an anarchy.

Kneehigh began by making theatre for the community in the community – performing in schools, village halls and marquees. The audiences and their environment led the company to create theatre that drew on storytelling traditions. The story is central to Kneehigh's work and these stories respond to their Cornish environment. The spirit of the country village and the community is brought to every show, with performers treating the audience with the generosity of a friend confiding in trustful intimacy. This way of treating the audience is combined with a playful, wild anarchy that creates conflict and intrigue. The actors achieve this relationship with the audience because of the camaraderie between members of the company.

Despite its cultural and spiritual home being Cornwall, Kneehigh has become a touring company of national and international renown. It has not sought a fixed residency, although it has acquired a portable tent theatre space known as the Asylum – a place of refuge and anarchy.

Key ideas

Kneehigh's ideas evolve and adapt with each new production. The company is reluctant to declare a methodology or conventions it follows; it feels that a rigid approach would restrict the ability to make every production live and fresh. A closer look at the company's production history and records of its process does reveal patterns that repeat and could be identified as central ideas. But who knows what Kneehigh may come up with in the future!

- **Wondertales**: Storytelling is at the heart of a Kneehigh production. The story, not the play, is the priority and the actors can be considered story-servants. Its most famous productions (for example, *The Red Shoes*) are created out of fairytales or what it has come to refer to as wondertales. Wondertales provide the company with a world of theatrical ideas to adapt and create into a production. The skill of the traditional storyteller is expanded and exploded into a multi-sensory production.

- **Superstructure**: Every story has a superstructure. These are the themes and major narrative arcs that the production must present. All elements of the production come together to support the communication of the superstructure. The production is developed collaboratively and emerges through rehearsals, but is tied together by the superstructure: What story are we trying to tell? Why are we telling this story?

Kneehigh

- **Multimedia and puppetry**: Kneehigh wants to transport the audience to a world they didn't expect. This is achieved through the use of live music, recorded sound, projection and puppetry. The approach allows them to create magical worlds that help to tell the story. It also makes the theatre accessible and relevant to contemporary audiences. The company's production of *Brief Encounter* used a huge, cinematic video projection and the sound of recorded Cornish waves to create the dream-like memory of the protagonist.

- **The event**: Kneehigh wants the theatre to be a memorable event. To achieve this, the company takes its productions beyond traditional performance ideas. The event starts before the performance and goes on after it. For example, the actors remain in role to serve audience members their refreshments post-performance. This notion of the 'event' is being explored further with the introduction of the Asylum, the company's own versatile space. The performance is just one element of the event, with shows followed by music and dancing.

- **The charged space**: This is important for the success of Kneehigh's irreverent and playful productions. The charged space is created with a welcoming, communal and sociable atmosphere. It is aesthetically pleasing, creating a child-like spirit of investigation and discovery. There is a story to the space that forces a sense of enquiry that supports the story of the performance. The charged space is accessible to the elements. Many of Kneehigh's early productions were outdoors and 'site-specific', responding directly to the environment and the elements. Current productions take place in the Asylum, which lets in natural light and amplifies the sounds of rain and wind.

A Kneehigh production concept

If you choose Kneehigh as your practitioner you must be able to refer to the company's theories in your own production concept. You should make reference to how you would use Kneehigh's key ideas to develop a production concept that is a community event that delights in joyful anarchy. Below is an overview of the conventions of Kneehigh's past productions that you can adopt and adapt for your written exam.

- **Acting**: Kneehigh considers actors to be story-servants. They are multi-skilled performers who use dance, music and acting to help tell the story. The characters of Kneehigh productions have an instability that the actor must capture. This encourages a sense of the live experience for the audience. The performers must remain in the present moment and acknowledge the presence of the audience. There is no 'fourth wall' (the imagined divide between the acting space and the auditorium), as the actor's role is to share the story with the audience in a trusting, mutually rewarding experience.

- **Venue**: A large tent that is exposed to the elements. Natural light is used by Kneehigh to create elemental atmosphere – such as when the sun sets.

- **Lighting and projections**: Technical lighting is key to creating the world of the story, defining space and creating atmosphere within the worlds of the story. These will complement and enhance the use of natural light. Each show should be designed as an integrated part of the devising/rehearsal process. Video projections will allow for dream-like worlds to be created.

- **Set and props**: The sets should be aesthetically pleasing and follow constructivist principles where one or two simple structures represent the worlds of the story. Height and depth should be fully utilised to stimulate a sense of wonder in the audience. Sets and props are often inspired by magical realism, as they point to the realistic and everyday but have an exaggerated and magical quality.

- **Sound and music**: Recorded sound effects should be used to create atmosphere and support the world of the story. Both live music and recorded music can be used. The sound design and music often give productions the feeling of a festival or a concert.

- **Costume**: Kneehigh looks for inspiration in the traditional clothing of its Cornish heritage. The company also creates costumes inspired by magical realism, as they can be identified as everyday but have one or two elements that are exaggerated and fantastical.

Legacy

Kneehigh continues to make work and has grown into a company with a national and international reputation – largely because it takes inspiration from its own history and surroundings. Its legacy is yet to be known, but one of its joint artistic directors, Emma Rice, became the artistic director of the Globe Theatre in London in 2016. In a similar way to Kneehigh, the Globe has to respond to the elements and celebrates the playfulness and anarchy of the live theatre experience. Kneehigh's legacy will be the model it provides regional and touring theatre companies for capturing a spirit of local community and communicating it with a large audience.

Joan Littlewood

Born: London, UK – 6 October 1914.

Died: London, UK – 20 September 2002.

Occupation: Theatre director, Actor, Radio broadcaster.

Vision for theatre: Theatre should both present community and be a community where all participants are equal. It should be playfully disciplined and structured anarchy. The theatre is live interaction.

Style: Theatre Workshop: A Theatre of Community – the fluidity and performance of everyday life should be captured through psychological research combined with movement and rhythm in the space.

Littlewood

Communism, Theatre Workshop and community

Littlewood was a working-class girl whose experiences of class divisions in the UK during the first half of the 20th century helped to form her communist ideals. She felt that the theatre should not ignore the 'real' world, but instead reflect it.

Littlewood's communist ideals and her frustration with the 'bourgeois' establishment and its middle-class, materialistic values led her to create a political theatre that appealed to the working classes. She was never in charge of a theatre group, as she preferred to be part of an equal and collaborative ensemble. Her group started as the Theatre of Action, before developing into the Theatre Union and finally becoming the Theatre Workshop (1945–). The workshop idea was chosen because it captured the way its theatre was created out of research, training and collaboration. Its research was vast; its methods were influenced by Constantin Stanislavski, Vsevolod Meyerhold, Rudolf Laban, Adolphe Appia and Bertolt Brecht. It also drew inspiration from film, music hall and street entertainment. Theatre Workshop was a touring company until it found a home at the Theatre Royal, Stratford East, London. Despite it remaining an equal ensemble, Littlewood was the main director. Her reputation grew with original stagings of classics and ground-breaking productions of Shelagh Delaney's *A Taste of Honey* (1958), along with Theatre Workshop's own devised *Oh! What a Lovely War* (1963). It is during these years that she formed her ideas on theatre and developed her working methods.

Key ideas

Littlewood's ideas grew out of experimentation and led to the ideas of other practitioners being merged together to make a style that would influence future British theatre makers.

- **Performing community**: Littlewood believed in the ensemble: a group of equal partners creating and collaborating to make theatre. This emphasis on the group allowed the performances to capture a sense of community that was truthful. The presentation of groups was important in Theatre Workshop productions. The group would have a strength and unity in its position on stage in contrast to traditional hierarchies. Synchronisation combined with a real, improvised camaraderie, inspired by the music hall, gave the idea of an organic, live mass – a real community on stage.

- **Improvisation**: Littlewood saw the theatrical in everyday life. She thought that people performed all the time and therefore changed all the time. She wanted to capture this fluidity of everyday life in her productions. Her anarchic spirit led her to change details of a production at the last minute to make the actors live in the moment and not become stale. Improvisation was a major part of the training she offered at the Theatre Workshop and remained a big part of the group's approach throughout production runs.

- **Mixing Stanislavski and Laban**: Littlewood wanted to capture a character's psychology through movement long before Stanislavski's ideas on physical actions had been translated into English. She placed great emphasis on the super task (key theme) of the production, and worked with the ensemble to explore and research the characters so that they supported it. She divided the plays into accessible bits and identified each character's tasks. Littlewood encouraged the practical exploration of these bits and tasks, and used Laban's ideas to develop the physical, living character. Laban was a dance theorist who developed a 'movement analysis' in which each character's direction and quality of movement was explored: up/down; left/right; heavy/light; flowing/stuttering. Through this method of working, Littlewood was able to create a precise rhythm that drove productions forward.

- **Biomechanics and eurythmics**: Littlewood used Meyerhold's idea of 'biomechanics' to emphasise the importance of clear, economical and precise movement. Littlewood combined this with eurythmics, a theory from the music teacher and composer Emile Jacques-Dalcroze that suggested the human body was the original instrument. Littlewood used it to encourage a sense of rhythm in the everyday movements of characters. Movement and rhythm were fully integrated with the space and communicated themes to the audience.

A Littlewood production concept

If you choose Littlewood as your practitioner you must be able to refer to her theories in your own production concept. You should make reference to how you would use Littlewood's key ideas to develop a production concept that captures and emphasises the idea of community. Below is an overview of the conventions of a Littlewood production concept that you can adopt and adapt for your written exam.

- **Acting**: Littlewood trained her own actors in a method of performing that combined the psychological realism of Stanislavski, the awareness of rhythm and movement of Meyerhold, and the playful interaction with the audience of Brecht. Trust and teamwork are essential to her approach because the cast is an ensemble – a group of equals.

- **Venue**: The Theatre Workshop's home was an old Victorian theatre in Stratford East – the Theatre Royal. This 'home' meant the financial security of the group was assured. However, Littlewood much preferred the community venues where the group toured because they did not place barriers between the performers and the audience.

- **Set and lighting**: Littlewood adopted Appia's idea of the set as a three-dimensional space, fully integrated with atmospheric lighting. Her sets followed the constructivist tradition, with minimal sets of one or two structures that represented the world of the play. An example that epitomises her approach to set is her production of *Operation Olive Branch* (1953), an adaptation of *Lysistrata*. Here, different levels were connected with simple block steps; ramps were lit to emphasise the edges of the structure and provide a dark atmosphere.

- **Sound and music**: Realistic sound effects should be used to establish the world of the play and reinforce the key themes of the production. Littlewood used live singing and recorded instrumental music to both complement the action and contrast it.

- **Costume and props**: Costume should be designed in response to the key themes of the production. Costumes can be simple, using specific textures and colours. When needed to communicate themes clearly, they should be realistic and historically accurate. A similar attitude applies to props. Neither should interfere with the pace and rhythm of the production.

Legacy

Littlewood battled against the British establishment theatre from her first experiences at the Royal Academy of Dramatic Art (RADA) in 1932 to her final frustrations with Theatre Workshop actors being poached by the West End. She was a strong and 'in-yer-face' woman who did not fit in with the male-dominated theatre in the UK. However, this did not stop her work with the Theatre Workshop or her ground-breaking application of European practitioners having a huge influence on British theatre. She was a contemporary of Peter Brook (1925–) and inspired his experimentation and ensemble approach. Her methods of training actors were used as the template for teaching at the East 15 Acting School. Perhaps her most notable legacy is the theatre company Kneehigh (1980–), which sees Littlewood and the Theatre Workshop as inspiration for its versatile approach to a 'community' theatre that has grown to become one of the UK's major creative forces. Littlewood's trailblazing approach has led to British theatre being full of companies that devise work and adapt classics with the sense of ensemble developed by the Theatre Workshop.

Practitioner: Punchdrunk

Founded: 2000.

Artistic director: Felix Barrett.

Occupation: Theatre director and Designer.

Vision for theatre: Theatre should focus as much on the spectators (audience members) and the performance space as on the performers and narrative. The spectator must be immersed in the world of the play so they discover their own meaning and narrative through an imaginative journey.

Style: Immersive theatre blurs the lines between life and performance. The performer and spectator exist together in the world of the play. Punchdrunk also uses the term 'site-sympathetic' to describe its work.

Dens, installations and immersive theatre

As a child, Felix Barrett enjoyed building dens and creating his own adventure stories. Aged 12, he discovered the attic in his home, with its dark, eerie atmosphere and relics from the past. He proceeded to rearrange what he found into a maze of objects from his family's past. Barrett's

punchdrunk

wonder at the magic of hidden spaces was given substance when his Drama teachers at Alleyn's School, Dulwich (Matthew Grant and Geoff Tonkin) introduced him to the Romanian director Silviu Purcărete. As a 17-year-old, he was intrigued by Purcărete's use of space in rehearsals. (The director would take his actors, with candles, to a large, disused area and ask them to improvise a scene.) In the same year, Barrett visited Robert Wilson and Hans Peter Kuhn's installation *H.G.* at Clink Street Vaults, London. Both of these experiences, along with a study of the theatre practitioner Edward Gordon Craig, inspired his final A level work: a post-apocalyptic installation piece.

Barrett continued to explore installation while studying Drama at Exeter University from 1997 to 1999. The course was experimental and practical, giving Barrett the opportunity to test his theories. His investigations focused on an interest in what the spectator felt rather than what they saw. He wanted to explore the blurring of life and performance. This led to his final-year practical assessment: a version of Büchner's *Woyzeck* presented in an old Territorial Army barracks. The performance included two of the fundamental ideas that became Punchdrunk's style: the use of masks to make the spectator 'invisible' and blur with their surroundings; and the looping narrative where a 20-minute version repeated for three hours.

Barrett graduated and quickly formed Punchdrunk (initially with Joel Scott and Sally Scott, although he took sole control within a year). Since then he has built a team of core collaborators that includes Maxine Doyle as choreographer and associate director. The company's spirit of investigation continued as it experimented with the limitations of what came to be known as 'immersive' theatre from 2005.

Key ideas

After a decade of experimentation, Punchdrunk began to work with an established set of ideas to create engaging immersive experiences for the spectator. The key ideas remain set because immersive theatre is a fragile style that requires a careful combination of elements to ensure the illusion is maintained.

- **The space as a character**: A show cannot begin to be developed until an appropriate space is found. It is then explored like Purcărete's company and new ideas are generated. The space becomes a collaborator and ultimately a key character in the production. The company works from classical texts and conducts extensive contextual research, which is brought into the space. This material is combined with performer improvisations in order to create potential spectator experiences.

- **One-on-ones**: A Punchdrunk production is developed on a large scale with many participants. Contrasting the scale of the worlds Punchdrunk builds, spectators can encounter moments of intimacy through one-on-one scenes with performers. The spectator is encouraged to explore the world alone and discover for themselves different characters. As the spectator discovers a new space, they meet a character that occupies that space. The character may then invite a lone spectator to share a scene, a moment or a secret, sometimes behind a locked door, which complements the story and encourages further exploration.

- **A masked spectator**: Although not obligatory to every Punchdrunk performance, at the beginning of many productions the spectator is masked ceremoniously as part of their entrance into the world. This ensures they remain as background figures that complement the performance rather than break the illusion. Productions, such as *The Drowned Man* (inspired by *Woyzeck*) or *Sleep No More* (inspired by *Macbeth*) use the masked spectator to create an other-worldly presence that features in the source material. The masked spectators become the ghosts that haunt the psychologically disturbed protagonists.

- **Dance**: Punchdrunk primarily uses dancers as performers in its shows (although not exclusively). Dance allows for an improvisation and fluidity of performance that the spoken word does not. Dancers can adjust their movement to respond to the spectator, while action merges with transition to create a sense of an unbroken world. At the end of group-choreographed moments, the performers disperse, moving through the space at different paces so as to scatter the gathered spectators.

- **Sound and atmosphere**: Any spoken language is precisely chosen, while the sound design provides a consistent score to the productions, akin to that of a film soundtrack. The space is filled with speakers that have instrumental and atmospheric music playing through them. The loud volume of sound is intense for the spectator, and the rhythms of the music propel the world forward, building to different climaxes. This intensity of sound is complemented by the dark, hazy atmosphere created by the lighting design. The shadows and darkness hold secrets to be explored.

- **Looped narrative**: Classic texts are used as a starting point for productions, but the encounters in the texts are more important than the words themselves. Punchdrunk captures the essence of the world of the play and its narrative arc, and loops it. The looping allows the spectator to see multiple strands of the narrative as the performance goes on and they explore further. Spectators then have individual experiences of the narrative from different characters' perspectives.

A Punchdrunk production concept

If you choose Punchdrunk as your practitioner you must be able to refer to its theories in your own production concept. You should make reference to how you would use Punchdrunk's key ideas to develop a production concept that blurs the line between life and performance. Below is an overview of the conventions of a Punchdrunk production concept that you can adopt and adapt for your written exam.

- **Acting**: Dancers should feature alongside actors, as their physical awareness of space allows them to adapt to an ever-changing environment. The quality of movement and individual gestures can quickly communicate character and allows for a fluidity and pace that gives the performance a forward momentum and urges the spectator to explore. Specifically selected spoken text should be used sparingly for maximum impact.

- **Venue, set and props**: New venue spaces (these can be non-traditional theatre spaces) should be found for each performance. The architecture of the spaces should inform the production, and be dressed with artefacts and minute details that allow the spectator to investigate the space. For example, drawers could be filled with photographs, desks covered with letters and so on. The set and props should be created in elaborate detail, allowing the spectator to touch and feel every part. Importantly, nothing should be extraneous; all items should further the narrative or inform the audience about a character.

- **Sound and music**: The quality of sound and music should drop into the spectator's subconscious. Sound and music should induce reactions because of the physical effect they have on the body. The tones and pitch of the sound should resonate with the whole body, not just the ear. Individual rooms could have their own sound design that blurs with the omnipresent sound of the whole space.

- **Costume**: These should be precisely designed to complement the realistic cinematic world of the production. The costumes should accentuate the movement and fluidity of the bodies of the performers.

Legacy

Punchdrunk is inspiring the current generation of theatre makers to experiment with the potential of theatre. Emerging companies like Slung Low and Tin Box Theatre cite Punchdrunk as an influence, while established companies like Headlong have learned from Punchdrunk's methods. The company's influence has been felt across the arts, with music concerts, fashion events and cinema adopting its immersive style.

Punchdrunk

Practitioner: Constantin Stanislavski

Born: Moscow, Russian Empire – 17 January 1863.

Died: Moscow, Soviet Union – 7 August 1938.

Occupation: Actor, Director, Theatre practitioner.

Company: Moscow Art Theatre.

Vision for theatre: Theatre should entertain the audience and make them think about humanity. There should be a highly charged atmosphere that causes infectious emotion.

Style: Realism focuses on the internal psychology of the characters. It allows an audience to recognise and associate with the characters on the stage.

Moscow Art Theatre (1897–)

Stanislavski was born into a wealthy family devoted to theatre. He inherited his parents' love of theatre and acted in many productions from a young age. In 1888, he found the Society for Art and Literature and developed his ideas for theatre. These ideas became fully explored and developed when he founded the Moscow Art Theatre with Vladimir Nemirovich-Danchenko. Stanislavski was in charge of the actors while Nemirovich oversaw the literary side of the production. They worked closely with the writer Anton Chekhov and produced premieres of many of his great plays.

The Moscow Art Theatre succeeded in bringing together many ideas on theatre that already existed – for example:

- an emphasis on the ensemble rather than individual actors

- realistic, researched set and costume.

It brought them together with the main aim of facilitating an acting style that communicated human truth.

Key ideas

Stanislavski is often misunderstood as being a director focused primarily on the mind of an actor. In fact, his ideas developed over the years to focus on external physical actions that show the inner psychology of a character. He wrote more than 800 pages about the process of acting, but never wanted it to be purely theoretical or scientific. He wanted acting to be demanding but playful and he often chose simple terms to describe his ideas. These terms have been complicated through years of translation and interpretation.

- **Physical actions**: This is, put simply, anything observable the character does – for example, opening a door or grabbing someone's arm. Many physical actions join together to become a string of actions, with one leading to another. Stanislavski believed that a role would simply emerge from improvising a character's physical actions. He even wanted his actors to improvise the physical actions of a play before reading it. They had to base their improvisations of physical actions on anything they knew about the play. Take King Lear as an example: he is a king; therefore, he sits on a throne. Sitting on the throne is the first physical action. Stanislavski would allow the cast to read the play only after the actors had worked out and improvised a string of actions for their character. He would ask the actors to compare the physical actions they had improvised with the physical actions in the text. If these actions were the same, then the role had been created. If they were different, the director supported the actor to merge the improvised actions with the actions of the text.

- **Actor training**: Stanislavski wanted to train actors in his system of acting. His training would allow actors to find themselves inside every role they played. He did not want actors to play clichéd characters; rather, he wanted them to find parallels between their own selves and the character. He felt this would be more genuine and truthful for an audience. Stanislavski developed strategies to help actors who could not discover a role through improvised physical actions. These were ways in which the actor could explore the contents of their own mind to discover the external behaviour most appropriate for that character. First, the actor must identify the 'Given circumstances' – that is, the who, what, where, when and why created by the playwright for the character. Second, the actor must use the 'Magic if' to ask what they would do 'if' the given circumstances were really true. Finally, the actor must use their 'emotion memory' – in other words, any personal memories that link to the character's given circumstances. These should spring to mind spontaneously with improvisations, but if they don't they must be consciously thought up to strengthen the truth of the character.

- **Bits, tasks and the super task**: Stanislavski taught his actors to divide the play into smaller, more manageable bits. The size of these bits was dependent on what the actor could manage. Each bit would have a task – an obstacle to overcome. Physical actions are used to complete a task. Every bit leads to the next bit. Every task leads to the next task. The super task is simply the central theme of the play. All bits and tasks support the super task.

- **Tempo-rhythm**: This is simply the rhythm of a character, the play or the production. Stanislavski wanted his actors to discover the appropriate pattern and pace of a role through playful exploration.

A Stanislavski production concept

If you choose Stanislavski as your practitioner you must be able to refer to his methodologies in your own production concept. The conventions of his stage productions aimed to hide his methodologies, as he wanted the audience to see the human characters as real and truthful. You should make reference to how you would use Stanislavski's key ideas to develop a production concept that is realistic. Below is an overview of the conventions of a Stanislavski production concept that you can adopt and adapt for your written exam.

- **Acting**: Stanislavski believed that actors should present a truthful and realistic human character. The actor should not play the character, as this leads to clichés. They should always be themselves and find parallels between the character and their own personal emotions, memories and wants. No two performances should be the same, as the actor should live the role with a fresh approach each time. Successful performances cause infectious emotions and can only be described in terms of 'stage presence' or the 'x-factor'.

- **Venue**: The Moscow Art Theatre had a proscenium arch stage. A proscenium arch creates a frame that reinforces the idea of the fourth wall (the imagined divide between the acting space and the auditorium). The audience should be a passive witness to the action.

- **Set**: Stanislavski's sets presented realistic three-dimensional worlds that could be fully inhabited by the characters. He was opposed to the normal convention of re-using old painted sets. His designs were heavily

The proscenium arch stage at the Moscow Art Theatre.

influenced by the German Meiningen Court Theatre Company (1866–90) and its historically accurate scenery that replicated real rooms. He was also inspired by the company's use of multi-level and depth of staging, which allowed the action to flow. Smooth transitions were achieved by the actors remaining in role as the scene changed.

- **Lighting and sound**: This should try to create lighting states and sound effects that reinforce the reality of the set.

- **Costume, make-up and props**: This should be historically accurate to help the actor embody the role; the props should support the given circumstance of the characters.

Legacy

Stanislavski is one of the most influential figures in the development of modern theatre. He directed actor Vsevolod Meyerhold (1874–1940) in the Chekhov productions. Meyerhold went on to become an influential theatre practitioner in his own right. It was on his advice that Stanislavski developed his use of improvisation to develop a role. Jerzy Grotowski (1933–99) was another theatre practitioner heavily influenced by the idea of 'physical actions'. He created his own physically demanding theatre style that has, in turn, influenced modern physical theatre and immersive theatre companies. Perhaps Stanislavski's most famous influence was based on a misunderstanding of his methods. The Moscow Art Theatre toured the USA in 1923, and the actor and director Lee Strasberg (1901–82) was captivated by the emotionally intense and psychologically driven performances. Strasberg went on to develop the popular idea of 'Method Acting', which is more focused on the psychological world of a character than Stanislavski's emphasis on physical action. Stanislavski's theories have also influenced the work of many living directors, including Declan Donnellan (1953–) and Katie Mitchell (1964–).

Developing a production concept

This section will give an overview of the content and vocabulary that will be required for your exam response. It will focus on general terminology that can be applied to any 21st-century theatre production. There will be additional connections made with specific practitioners and particular texts to give some ideas for potential directions in which to take your production concept.

Your production concept will be rooted in the theories and methodology of one of the practitioners, but any ideas must be fully justified with explicit reference to the extract from the play provided in the exam. This extract will be the focus of your essay, so you must also make explicit reference to the following when justifying your ideas:

- the play as a whole
- the overall themes and ideas of the play
- the original performance conditions
- the social, historical, political and cultural context of the text.

The ability to link your understanding is important in this section of the written exam. Your original performance concept will make up the majority of words in your essay, but it is also essential that you use appropriate connections regularly to justify your choices.

Below are brief introductions to the different elements of a production that might come up in the exam.

Directing acting

It is easy to generalise about acting in a production concept, especially when you are having to continually make connections with broader contexts. You must avoid these generalities at all costs and take every opportunity to develop detailed ideas for directing acting. There are infinite variables within acting that allow for very specific interpretations of texts. You must be able to articulate how you will combine the different elements of acting to support your interpretation. You must also consider venue and stage space, entrances and exits, the relationship with the audience, relationships between characters, and acting conventions where each practitioner will have their own established approach to acting.

Interpretation of key roles

One of the major decisions you will have to make is how you will interpret the roles in your production concept. The decisions you make will inform the tone and atmosphere that you create in the production. The director has a responsibility to both the text and the audience. You must make sure the author's intentions are respected while creating an engaging production for a contemporary audience. Carefully consider the impact your interpretation of key roles will have on the meaning of the production. You can choose any historical period to set your play. You must be able to justify your decisions and ensure that the author's intended meaning is retained regardless of the era you choose to set your production.

ACTIVITY

Research the social, historical, political and cultural context of the text and write a list of key words associated with this context. Do these words remind you of a current news story? Try to find parallels between the context of the text and the context of your audience. For example, words that you could associate with the context of *Woyzeck* (1836) are: trapped, restricted, poverty, desperation, aftermath of war. These have parallels with the Calais Jungle Camps (2016) that house refugees, asylum seekers and economic migrants. You can then expand these initial parallels and find similarities with key roles in the production.

Characterisation

There is a vast number of variations when making characterisation choices. The variables that arise from combining voice, movement (and stillness), non-verbal communication (including vocalisation) and text are truly limitless. You have to make sure that the examples you give in the exam are detailed and show an awareness of the character within the whole text. There are lots of ways to describe voice, movement and non-verbal communication and you must be comfortable with this terminology when discussing your production.

Voice

The way you choose to direct the actor's articulation when speaking the lines of the play can contribute to the communication of status to an audience. An emphasis on the consonants gives words the clarity and emphasis of a high-status character. Furthermore, the over-articulation of consonants can communicate aggression, while the articulated vowels can communicate pain and anguish.

Exam tip

Make explicit reference to a specific moment in the extract text that you are given in the exam when discussing characterisation. Then describe your characterisation choices for one or two additional moments from the whole text that will show the examiner that you are aware of the importance of character development and continuity of role.

Steven Berkoff

Berkoff uses over-articulation and extended word sounds to create a stylised form of speech that exaggerates the characteristics of different roles. This links to expressionism as the distorted effect reinforces the main character's perspective on the world.

The choice of pitch can have a real impact on the audience. Shifting pitch can pick out important words or phrases, while sudden changes in pitch can jar with the audience and create emphasis. Pitch will have a subliminal quality that communicates a sense of masculinity or femininity to the audience, which can affect meaning.

Antonin Artaud

Artaud wanted the actor to revert to ritualistic and primal vocal qualities. He emphasised the importance of subliminal communication as he thought meaning would infect the audience. He proposed the use of extreme variations in pitch so that sound would have a physical impact on the audience. Imagine how you wince at a high pitch or shudder at a low pitch.

The decisions you make about pace of speech are integral to a production and tie in with all production elements. The pace of speech communicates different levels of control for a character and can give a sense of emphasis. The way you direct an actor to control pace around a climax in the play can be the making or breaking of an interpretation.

Constantin Stanislavski

Stanislavski placed great emphasis on the pace and patterns within an actor's performance. The pace of vocal delivery was of great importance when drawing the audience into the world of the play and carrying them along with it. He used the term 'tempo-rhythm' to describe the pace and patterns in a production.

A pause can hold so much meaning and must be carefully directed. Pauses go hand-in-hand with other non-verbal communication choices and have a great impact on the meaning of the language spoken. You may choose to include pauses to give psychological depth to the character, but equally a pause could be used to break the fourth wall and interact with the audience.

Waiting for Godot

Beckett created a world that challenges an audience's sense of narrative and time. The use of pause and silence can be integrated into the characterisation of Vladimir and Estragon to accentuate the theme of waiting.

The way you direct the tone of an actor's voice will emphasise differences between characters and highlight conflicts. The tone of voice can communicate sub text: the true meaning beneath the spoken language. It can also contribute to the communication of climaxes in the narrative.

Hedda Gabler

Ibsen was an innovator of realism, and the quick dialogue that he writes in *Hedda Gabler* is full of sub-text that reveals the social differences. Hedda is a ruthless manipulator and the actor's choice of tone will have a great impact on the subtlety and dynamism of characterisation that is so important to the success of the play.

The stress and emphasis of words can have great impact on an audience. Your choice of how actors will **inflect** the language will communicate status and can associate characters with particular words.

The School for Scandal

Sheridan satirises and mocks the social attitudes of the upper classes in *The School for Scandal*. Actors performing characters in this play will have to use emphasis for comic effect. The choice of inflection will reveal how some characters fail to fit with the social standard, despite their desperate attempts to fit in.' Volume (a continuum of loud to quiet) is a crucial quality of voice that you must direct carefully. Quiet voices can emphasise the jeopardy and danger of a scene, while loud voices can show authority or overt conflict. But inverting these standard 'rules' can also communicate meaning with an audience.

Antigone

Sophocles places Creon and Antigone up against each other. Their role as king or woman sets up clear status roles. Volume can be used to assert control and status during the scene when Antigone challenges Creon's decision. Creating contrasts in volume will reinforce the contrasts in the text. Consider how a quiet voice for Antigone may emphasis her control, while a quiet voice for Creon could exaggerate his disgust.

Movement and stillness

The **pace of movement** (continuum of fast to slow), similar to the pace of voice, is integral to the whole production. The way you direct the actor's pace of movement can have a huge impact on the communication of the narrative and the energy of the production. Pace of movement can be used to capture variable levels of control for characters.

The **direction of movement** is closely linked with spatial behaviour. The direction that you choose for an actor to move in can determine their status and communicate relationships with other characters. Direction combined with variations of voice can create interesting contrasts that will communicate complex characterisation to an audience. Consider how a threatening tone and a loud volume could be complemented by a backwards movement.

Joan Littlewood

Littlewood was particularly interested in the movement of the actors within the space. She developed Laban's ideas of movement analysis with her actors so that direction, weight and flow all supported the meaning of the character.

Taking it further

Laban Movement Analysis (LMA) is a method and language for describing, visualising, interpreting and documenting all varieties of human movement. Find out more about Laban's ideas of movement analysis *in Laban for Actors and Dancers* (1993) and the illustrated *Laban for All* (2004) by Jean Newlove.

The **size of movement** (a continuum of big to small) that you direct an actor to make can communicate the confidence of a character. It can also emphasise a character's awareness of precision and detail. Discovering the size of a character's movements can be the beginnings of stylised and exaggerated characterisation and could lead you to other voice, movement and non-verbal choices.

Doctor Faustus

The central relationship of Mephistopheles and Doctor Faustus created by Marlowe has a lot of potential for interesting and complex movement choices. The presence of magic and the fact that Mephistopheles is a devil expand the possibilities. But subtle choices and interesting combinations could be the most effective way of communicating their relationship.

- Mephistopheles' movements could mirror those of Doctor Faustus', but with subtle exaggerations in their flow and size.

- During the scenes of playfulness and mischievous practical jokes, Doctor Faustus could adopt some of the fast and light movements of Mephistopheles.

Flow (a continuum of free to restricted) is a very important element of characterisation as it is often the physicalisation of a psychological state. Characters will make major shifts in a production and this psychological change can be communicated with careful awareness of the way the character flows. Free-flowing movement shows a connection between movements and a sense of control, whereas restricted flow breaks up movement and reveals uncertainty.

Punchdrunk

Punchdrunk uses dancers in its productions because their quality of movement can draw the spectator into the world of individual characters. The flow of movement is vital to their quick communication of a character's psychology. The flow of a performer's body also interacts with the space in a way that uses the immersive environment to engage the audience and create impact.

The **weight of movement** (a continuum of heavy to light) can help to create archetypal characters, but can also be the foundation for more complex characterisation. The weight of movement can also support the creation of mood and atmosphere, with heavy movements associated with sadness, while light movements are associated with happiness.

Lysistrata

Aristophanes presents a battle of the sexes in his comedy. Archetypal characters are used to enhance the comedy. The weight of movement for different characters helps to communicate the contrasts and the comedy. Cinesias' heavy movement could be used to reinforce his sexual frustration, while Myrrhine's light movement could show her feminine power.

The **control of movement** (a continuum of stable to unstable) can communicate intensity and strength. You can direct your actors to have stability of movement at moments they are in a commanding position, while unstable movement could show a moment that they are off guard or weak. Subtle variations in control of movement can give a sense of danger and conflict for an audience.

Woyzeck

Büchner's Woyzeck becomes swiftly more unstable throughout the play. Directing your actors with specific control movements will help reinforce the instability of Woyzeck. The moment he sees Marie and the Drum Major dancing allows for interesting contrasts between the control of the dancing couple and Woyzeck's lack of control.

The orientation (choice of where the body is facing) of a character can communicate both power and fear. This is another movement choice that is closely linked with non-verbal communication. The meaning of a line can change if spoken with an orientation of the body.

Bertolt Brecht

Brecht carefully controlled every aspect of movement on the stage to ensure that every moment, every stage image was gestic. This means that every moment should capture the essence or the meaning of the play as a whole. The orientation of the characters would have played a crucial role in communicating meaning and relationships. He also emphasised the importance of stillness over needless movement.

A vital part of movement characterisation is knowing when to direct an actor to remain still. Stillness, like a vocal pause, can be loaded with meaning. Stillness, in the face of aggression, can communicate great power to an audience.

Non-verbal communication

Non-verbal communication can be a vital method of reinforcing the language of the text or communicating subtext. You should experiment with non-verbal communication that supports or contrasts the verbal. These choices will add to the subtle and continual communication of meaning with an audience.

Spatial behaviour (proxemics)

The spatial relationship between characters can be controlled to communicate meaning in relationship with the language. Like all the elements of acting, you should not see it in isolation because it works in tandem with other forms of communication. Close proxemics can be used to mean both affection and aggression.

Kneehigh

Kneehigh attempts to create a charged space for its performances and has created site-specific work in the past. This type of theatre experience relies heavily on the interaction of characters within the space, but they also consider the spatial behaviour between actor and audience.

Facial expression

The face reveals a lot about a character and is the most obvious way of capturing emotion and psychology. You must be able to describe the subtlety of facial expression that you expect from your actors. Meaning can be communicated with the brow, the eyebrows, the eyes, the lips, the teeth and the jaw. But you have to be careful that you don't make the facial expressions too subtle for the space that you use for the production.

Complicite

Complicite has roots in physical comedy and mime. The physicality of the actor is still important for the company, especially in more recent experiments with technology. The company continues to explore new ways of communicating with an audience that complement and challenge the essential elements of human communication.

Gesture

The choice of gestures has a real impact on the meaning of the language spoken. Consider how gestures can complement, or contrast with, what is being said. Choose gestures that work in relation with the gestures of other characters. Be specific in your description of gesture and avoid simply stating the emotion behind the gesture.

Gaze

The gaze of the character is the direction in which they are looking. The gaze of two lovers may be held for slightly longer than the gaze of enemies. Looking down can communicate low confidence and status, while an erratic gaze can communicate an uncertain character.

Non-verbal vocalisations

Any sounds that are not words are non-verbal vocalisations. They can be used to communicate agreement or disagreement; pain or joy. Consider how the characters that are not speaking in a scene could be responding with vocal noise.

Posture

The way a character holds their body is crucial when establishing character. Posture can be used to establish dominance or show a relaxed attitude. Consider how a character may use a strong posture to disguise other frailties.

The Tempest

Shakespeare presents an exploration of humanity and society in *The Tempest*. The relationship between Caliban and Prospero has become central to modern interpretations. This relationship can be explored through different choices of posture and how they communicate the power dynamic between the two characters.

Touch and bodily contact

The touch of characters can be electric for an audience. Directing when your actors should make contact is a very important as overusing contact can weaken the potential for a connection between characters at a climax of the play.

The Maids

Genet creates a triangular relationship between the characters in *The Maids* based on power and dominance. You must carefully choose when touch and physical contact are used, as they are important to the power dynamics of the relationships. The stage directions will give you guidance and ideas – look at the directions given on pages 40–42 for examples.

look at the directions given on pages 40–42 for examples.

Use of venue and stage space

Your choice of venue and stage space will have a significant impact on the acting style of the production. The proscenium arch will reinforce the imagined division between actors and audience known as the fourth wall. But the proscenium arch stage can also be used for highly visual theatre where a control of stage image is very important. A **thrust** stage is a very communal space where the audience can interact. The amphitheatre gives a strength to the audience as a collective group and also naturally amplifies the actor's voice. The **traverse** stage with the audience on either side of a central stage 'catwalk' reinforces a sense of confrontation and conflict while emphasising the presence of the audience. Immersive space and site-specific work cast the space as an additional character that lives with audience and performer. Whichever space you use for your production, make sure the examiner is made aware of how it will complement and reinforce your direction of the acting.

Entrances and exits

The way a character enters a space can significantly influence an audience's impression of that character. Consideration of where they enter the stage, what they have come from and how they enter should be explicitly communicated to the examiner. The entrance and exit choices form the punctuation for the character's presence on the stage. Think carefully about what impact your choices have on an audience. Ancient Greek theatre established the tradition of symbolic and meaningful entrances and exits, with women using the central entrances while men used the side entrances. Furthermore, the left exit signified the wilderness while the right signified civilisation. Are such symbolic choices translatable for a modern audience?

Relationship with audience

Each writer and each practitioner will have their own approach to interacting with and engaging the audience. Your responsibility as the director is to merge their ideas to form a production that will appeal to a contemporary audience. The non-verbal communication of the actors can be expanded to include the audience. Use this vocabulary to describe how you choose to direct the actor's relationship with the audience.

Relationship between characters

Characters rarely, if ever, exist in complete isolation of other characters. As soon as two characters inhabit the stage space, a relationship is created. Every direction you give an actor about the voice, movement or non-verbal communication of their character will affect the performance choices of other actors. Every action will have a reaction. Always refer to the possible combinations of acting choices and how they will communicate relationships with the audience.

Glossary

Thrust
A stage that extends into the audience area, with seats on three sides of a peninsula-shaped acting space.

Traverse
A form of staging where the audience is either side of the acting area. See also the table entitled 'Variety of stage spaces' on page 132.

Top tip ☑

Remember that the proscenium opening was of particular importance to the realistic playwrights of the 19th century, such as Ibsen and Shaw, for whom it was a picture frame or an imaginary fourth wall through which the audience experienced the illusion of spying on characters.

Conventions

Each practitioner will have their own established approach to acting. You must consider how these conventions can reinforce the characters, themes and ideas of the play. You need to carefully match the conventions of your practitioner with the conventions of theatre that are linked to the play's genre, style and original performance conditions.

Ancient Greek theatre had its own conventions that were important because of the spirit of competition within which they were written; for example, one actor played all the main parts and two assistant actors played the smaller parts leading to character doubling. Marlowe and Shakespeare wrote in response to the conventions of the stage of their day, so boy actors played the female roles and they used direct address in asides and soliloquys. They also established new conventions that still influence theatre today; for example, they introduced the use of more realistic blank verse with iambic pentameter rather than the less realistic rhyming verse. Sheridan parodies social convention through the use of theatrical conventions of melodrama and comedy. Genet and Beckett challenge the conventions of theatre with confrontational choices that turn the audience's attention on the very idea of performance.

Directing design

It is important to see your design choices in the practical context of a production. The examiner will be looking out for ideas that are possible, so you must consider how your design choice impacts on other elements of the production. If you choose to direct design for your response then you must be comfortable with the vocabulary of all the design elements. Look at past productions of your chosen practitioners and the original performance conditions of the play for inspiration. Make sure you explicitly refer to things that have inspired your ideas. Even though you are not focusing on acting, you will inevitably discuss how design impacts acting, with specific reference to entrances and exits, the relationships between characters, and the relationship between actor and audience.

Space

The choice of space for your production concept will have an impact on all your other choices as director. Choosing the right space will create an appropriate environment for the play to thrive because it will instantly create meaning in the audience's mind.

Exam tip

Remember this is a question about the text in performance and not a history essay. You must drop in references to the original production that show your understanding and awareness of how the text was first performed. You must always say how they have informed your own creative and theatrical ideas as directors.

ACTIVITY

Research the original performance conditions of the play and find out about your practitioner's preferred space. Identify the key themes of the play that you will be directing. Go through the list of spaces and work out which space will combine the practitioner's style with the original intentions and themes of the play.

Variety of stage spaces
End-on
This is often in a studio theatre where the seats face the stage space at one end. There is no proscenium arch.
Traverse
The audience are positioned on two sides of the space with the performance taking place in the middle.
In-the-round
The audience are seated on at least three sides of, or all the way around, the performance space.
Thrust
The performance space thrusts out into the audience. The audience sit or stand on three sides of the stage space. This is similar to the open-air theatres that *Doctor Faustus* and *The Tempest* would originally have been performed in.
Proscenium arch
The audience sit facing a stage at one end. The stage is framed with a proscenium arch. More and more traditional proscenium arch spaces are adding small thrusts to break the divide between the audience and the performance space. This is the type of space that *Hedda Gabler* and *The School for Scandal* were written for.
Amphitheatre
The audience sit in a large and steep half-bowl shape, with a circular stage at the bottom. The Olivier Theatre in the National Theatre is designed as an amphitheatre. This type of space was invented by the ancient Greeks and would have been the original performance space for *Lysistrata* and *Antigone*.
Promenade and immersive
These can be found spaces or non-theatre spaces. The audience walk through the space to experience the performance. Immersive theatre spaces have been pioneered by Punchdrunk, but Artaud's theories also point to the immersion of the audience.
Site-specific theatre
These spaces are chosen as a key part of the production. The performance links directly to the space that it is performed in. Kneehigh created site-specific theatre in its early days and its work can still be described as site-responsive because of the importance of Cornwall to the company.

Once you have decided upon the space that you will use, you must consider how you want to interact and engage the audience. Kneehigh and Joan Littlewood's Theatre Workshop placed great emphasis on theatre as an act of community.

- How will your actors interact with the audience in the space to create this spirit of community?

Complicite gives away its intentions in its name and wants the audience to be party to the creative process of the performance.

- How will you make sure your audience feels involved within the space rather than a passive onlooker?

All the practitioners give the audience a role in the theatre event and they have particular intentions for their experience. You must be able to articulate your own intentions for your audience in the space in response to your practitioner choice.

Taking it further

Adolphe Appia (1862–1928)

Appia pioneered theatre design and had a huge impact on the theatre of the 20th century. Research the key ideas of his constructivist vision:

- minimal sets with one or two simple structures to represent the world of the play

- lighting that varies in intensity and creates shadow to accentuate the actor with the depth and height of the space.

This style of set design, with its emphasis on the depth, height and width of the space, heavily influenced the design ideas of Berkoff, Littlewood and Kneehigh.

Set and props

The type of set design you choose will be heavily linked to your practitioner. There are four major types of set that each practitioner fits in to:

- **Realistic** recreations of the detailed world of the play – Stanislavski and Punchdrunk both create this type of set, but Punchdrunk allows the audience to touch and investigate the set, whereas the set is separate from the audience for Stanislavski.

- **Constructivist** sets with one or two simple structures that represent the world of the play – Brecht, Berkoff, Littlewood and Kneehigh use this type of set, but Brecht did occasionally choose to keep the space empty.

- **Technological** sets that use projection – Complicite uses this type of set more in its later work.

- **The set is the space and the actors body within it** – Antonin Artaud proposed this type of set for his Theatre of Cruelty. Punchdrunk also responds to the space, but it places greater emphasis on the detail and accuracy of set.

Period

Despite the different approaches to set design, all the practitioners (apart from Artaud) create the detail or imply a period in their set designs. Your choice of period will be heavily linked to your overall interpretation, and you need to consider the context of the text when making a decision.

Historical periods of performance texts
Antigone – 442 BC
Lysistrata – 411 BC
Doctor Faustus – 1580s
The Tempest – 1610s
The School for Scandal – 1770s
Woyzeck – 1830s
Hedda Gabler – 1880s
The Maids –1930s
Waiting for Godot –1940s (no specific time is implied by the text)

Whether you choose to stick with the period of the text or change the period, you will have to research the detail of the historical period. If you choose a more realistic set, then you will have to know the types of objects that can become props in your production. A Stanislavski-style production needs to have props that will support the action and stage business of the actors.

A Punchdrunk-style production will create props that the audience can interact with and which support the story and the world of the play, such as letters or precious trinkets. If you choose a practitioner with a constructivist approach to set, you will have to carefully design the structures that will represent the world of the play. If it is the technological set of Complicite that you need to create, then you will have to consider what the projections will depict and how these images support your chosen period.

Colour and texture

Colour is an important element of set design that can communicate mood and atmosphere to an audience. You must consider what meaning is created by your colour choices and how the colour of the set combines with the colour of costume and lighting. The texture of the set will also hold meaning for the audience. Rough or smooth, metallic or earthy, the texture of the set and the floor will reinforce key themes when combined with all the other design elements.

Entrances and exits

You must research the original performance conditions of your chosen play to develop an understanding of how entrances and exits would have been significant. You will need to consider how entrances and exits are integrated with your set design and how the actors will interact with them (see page 124 in 'Directing acting').

Set changes

The transitions that involve a change of location and sometimes set will be particularly important to show your awareness of the pace of your production.

Punchdrunk does not require any set changes, as the audience move and interact with the space. The other practitioners all attempt to integrate set changes within the narrative of the production, but they occasionally use music to complement changes.

Lighting and multimedia

Lighting is an important way of communicating with an audience, but not all of the practitioners advocate lighting to symbolise and represent particular themes or ideas.

- Stanislavski used natural lighting, while Brecht wanted a stark, bright white light to continually fill the stage and expose the actors.
- Artaud's theories included ideas for lighting technology that was yet to be invented but is now readily available.
- Littlewood and Berkoff use particular angles of lighting that illuminate their three-dimensional structures with shadows which reinforce mood and atmosphere.
- Kneehigh works outdoors or in its Asylum tent, and the natural light of the sun plays a key role alongside state-of-the-art lights.
- Complicite is always experimenting with the combination of cutting-edge lighting and projection.

You will need to carefully plan the lighting for your production concept so that it appeals to a 21st-century audience while responding to the ideas of a practitioner. You must use the following vocabulary to describe your lighting design ideas.

Types of lighting

There are many different types of lantern that are used in stage lighting. Here is a basic selection of commonly used lighting (both halogen bulb and LED).

> **Top tip**
>
> Remember that Stanislavski was concerned about set changes, with the realistic sets taking a while to change, but he decided to have the actors continue in role while the set changed around them.

Selection of lighting

Flood light: Lights a large area with no edge. No lens means no focus.

PAR can: Lights a large area with an edge. Lens allows for some focus.

Fresnel: Small fixture that gives a soft-edged spot of light. Little flexibility in the size of focus.

Profile spot: Long fixture that gives a hard-edge spot of light. Very flexible in the size of focus.

Moving heads: Automated lights that offer flexibility and variation.

Different ways to use lighting

Focus: Different types of lantern and combinations of lanterns can focus the audience's attention on different parts of the stage or on specific characters or props. You should be able to describe the type of lantern and the focus that it will provide. You must then justify your decisions about the focus of the lights by referring to the text, original performance conditions or the chosen practitioner.

Intensity: You must decide how bright you want the lights to be. The intensity of the lights can affect the audience in different ways.

You should also consider how the juxtaposition of scenes with different lighting intensity can communicate a key part of the narrative or a theme of the play.

Colour, mood and atmosphere	You will have to decide on the colour you want for each moment of your production. Colour is created using gels that sit in front of the light source. Modern lighting also uses LED technology to be able to shift more economically from one light colour to the next. The colour of lighting can be a major factor in establishing the mood and atmosphere of your production. Successful productions don't just rely on the lighting, but consider how the colour of lighting combines with the other elements of the production.
Position and direction	Another major factor in creating meaning with lighting is the position and direction of the lights. The subject can be front- or back-lit, the light can come from either side, or the subject can be lit from a high or low angle. The position and direction of light can create shadows that affect mood and atmosphere. The direction of lights complements a constructivist set because it changes how the simple structures are perceived by the audience and gives them variety.
Pattern, shape and projection	Patterns of light can be created by placing **gobos** in front of the source of a light. This is a good way of changing the perceived texture of the set quickly and reinforcing mood and atmosphere. Lighting can be shaped with a hard- or soft-edge quality by using **barn doors** or changing the **shutter** size in the lantern. These methods are being combined with projection technology to establish set changes or change the mood and atmosphere.

Glossary

Gobo
Metal slide placed in the gate of a lantern which throws a pattern.

Barn door
A rotatable attachment consisting of two or four metal flaps (hinged) which is fixed to the front of a fresnel or PAR can-type lantern to cut off the beam in a particular direction(s). Profile lanterns use shutters to achieve a greater degree of control and accuracy.

Shutter
Device in a lantern used to shape beam.

Top tip

Remember that Stanislavski used sound effects to create a realistic world and support the action of the play. Brecht and Kneehigh use live musicians on stage who often sing songs that are separate to the action but support the meaning. Punchdrunk uses atmospheric instrumental music throughout the space to give the audience a sense of momentum as they build to the climax of the experience.

Sound and music

The sound and music that you choose to use will contribute to the mood, atmosphere and world of the play.

You have to consider carefully the music you use because music has a huge emotional impact on the audience. You have to decide whether music will support the expected emotion or go against the emotion of the scene. Sound effects also play an important role in a production and you will have to decide whether you need realistic sound effects or if you want to distort sound to reinforce the mood and atmosphere. Instruments on stage can be used to create a sound effect, and a production in the style of Brecht, Littlewood or Kneehigh may use this idea. Music that is played live or pre-recorded can be amplified and adjusted to create different effects. Use the following vocabulary to describe the sound and music that you use.

Genre: The type or style of music.
Pitch: High or low pitch of the sound or music.
Tempo and rhythm: The pace and pattern of the music.
Volume: High or low volume of the sound or music.
Direction: The position of the live band or speakers in the space.

Costume, make-up and masks

Costume and masks have an artistic part to play in your production concept, but you must also show an awareness of the practicalities of actors wearing them. Historically accurate costumes were used by Stanislavski, Brecht, Littlewood and Punchdrunk, while more ritualistic costume was proposed by Artaud. Berkoff uses simple, symbolic costume that is often black and white, while Kneehigh's costumes are often inspired by magical realism. Masks would have been used in the original performance conditions of *Lysistrata* and *Antigone*, while Berkoff uses make-up that is thick and mask-like. You need to be able to use the following terminology to describe your choice of costume, make-up and mask choices.

Garments

Researching the specific garments that you will use in the production is essential. Items of clothing can indicate character, status and location. You can use annotated sketches in your essays or describe what garments are worn by key characters. Make sure you are able to identify items of clothing added or removed and the moments that these happen. Your social, political, historical and cultural research will support your understanding of the significance of different garments.

Colour

Colour can communicate broad meaning for audiences. You must make sure you choose colour that supports the text but also shows an awareness of your practitioner. Research the meaning of different colours, as they will trigger sub-conscious associations that will inform how an audience feel about a character.

Material

The fabric used to create costumes can also communicate meaning to the audience. It is often associated with different levels of wealth and status because particular fabrics were very expensive to import. This symbolic use of fabric is more predominant in the historical or cultural contexts of Aristophanes, Sophocles, Marlowe, Shakespeare, Sheridan and Ibsen.

Shape

You must be able to describe the key parts of a costume's shape and fit. A costume can have hard or soft edges and it can hug the figure or disguise the body's shape. Consider whether the shape and fit of a costume change during the production, as these changes can support meaning.

Hair and make-up

The design of hair and make-up can communicate the character's control at a particular point of your production. It is also closely linked with cultural ideas of status. You could use realistic make-up to reinforce an incident or injury.

Masks

Masks have a major effect on the performance and movement of your actors. Consider the impact that a mask will have and weigh it against the visual quality of neutralising a face or giving a face an exaggerated expression. Ancient Greek theatre used masks to help to communicate the intensity of emotions in both tragedy and comedy.

Preparing for your exam

Section C: A level sample answers with commentaries

You will be presented with two questions. You must choose one. Both questions will focus on your directorial production concept and offer opportunities for you to discuss how your ideas might be realised in front of a contemporary audience. You should consider all possibilities including how you will direct your actors and designers to create audience impact. The first half of this section deals with directing acting, with brief extracts from answers that cover every text and every practitioner. The second half deals with directing design, with extracts that cover different combinations of text and practitioner. Relevant text extracts will be given at the start of each example answer.

As a director, discuss how you would apply the methodologies of your chosen theatre practitioner to the acting styles used in your production concept.

Your answer must make reference to:

- the overall aims of your production concept in response to the play as a whole
- how your practical ideas will work in performance
- the original performance conditions of your chosen performance text.

(24 marks)

This answer is based on an extract from *Antigone* by Sophocles, from page 40 '*This is the land of my fathers…*' to page 42 '*among the ashes.*' The chosen practitioner is Brecht.

Student A

My production would be inspired by Brecht and would use an empty stage space with a half-curtain at the front. At the start of the production I would have 'Syrian Civil War 2011' projected onto it before it is drawn back. This would move the play away from being a museum piece and instead have it work for us as Brecht would have wanted. This projection will be gestic in that it will conjure the key ideas and themes of bitter and complex revolutions where justice and religion collide that are at the centre of Sophocles' play. I will direct the acting to capture the essence of the play and these themes at every given moment. I will also use Brecht's verfremdungseffekt to move the audience from a recognisable reality to a state of reflective detachment. This idea of verfremdungseffekt was actually inspired by the original performance methods of the ancient Greek tragedians, notably, the interventions of the Chorus.

> Student A has provided a complex integration of the production concept with the practitioner influence and the original performance conditions.

I would direct the actor playing Antigone to create a realistic and emotionally complex character that the audience will recognise. I would direct the actor to speak the opening line of the extract, 'This is the land of my fathers: Thebes, Built by a god', in response to Creon's death sentence with a slow pace and a tone of disappointment and dejection that is gestic of the collision between religion and the injustice. I will direct her to have a lengthy pause at the caesura, 'Built by a god. You see, senators' – this will allow the actor to fill this pause with a look to the floor and rising to make direct eye contact with the Chorus of senators as she is filled with bitterness and a spirit of rebellion. This simple pause and change in eye contact will once again be gestic of the key idea of a bitter revolution. I will direct the actor to gradually increase the pace of the lines with the attacking force of a final stand that naturally brings emphasis to the harsh consonant sounds of 'die his victim' and 'unjustly' and 'justice'.

> The student has repeatedly focused on the acting in relation to the communication of key themes and ideas to the audience.

These vocal choices will continue the gestic quality of the acting in my production. The audience will have recognised and identified with this emotionally realistic speech, but the illusion will be broken by the Chorus who address the audience directly: 'Others have suffered, my child, like you.' I will have the Chorus remain still and move their eyes in synchronisation away from looking at Antigone leaving to making direct eye contact with the audience. Directing the abrupt contrast in this way will create verfremdungseffekt, which means the audience will move from identification with the emotionally realistic acting of Antigone to a state of detachment caused by the Chorus's reminder to the audience that they are watching a play. The combination of this with the gestic half-curtain projection and the gestic acting will support the overall aim of my production to get the audience to actively reflect on the opposites of justice and religion and the complexity of revolutions.

> There is a balanced approach to the elements of acting that allows the student to show how the extract would fit into a broader approach to the production.

Commentary

This is a strong response because it makes perceptive and well-developed connections between the production concept and the text. The examples show a comprehensive knowledge and understanding of creative ideas and their impact on the audience. The practitioner's ideas are perceptively applied to their production concept and specifically the acting. Also, the perspective on original performance conditions research is well thought through and connects to the production concept.

This answer is based on an extract from *The Tempest* by Shakespeare, from page 65 start of Act 2 Scene 2 to page 71 *embraces Stephano*. The chosen practitioner is Complicite.

Student B

My production would be inspired by Complicite and I would use technology to create a magical island environment. This is in the spirit of innovation of the Renaissance theatre of Shakespeare: the Globe stage roof would have been painted with gods, and grand sound effects created from above the tiring house. A large projection screen would fill the back wall of a large, modern proscenium arch space like in Complicite's *The Master and Margarita*. Similar to their production, my actors would interact with the video projections. At the start of Act 2, I would project a video of gathering storm clouds from a low angle so that Caliban is caught in the projection as he enters. His movement would be a combination of ape and adder as he moves forwards as if through the storm cloud. He will be jittery but energetic, and these movements will respond to the images of his language that will flash up in the film projection: firebrand, ape and adder.

> Student B has made the connection with Complicite run throughout the response, and a variety of their ideas are joined together to make a coherent production concept.

The visual illusions will be supported by the use of sound effects that have been recorded with two microphones that replicate human ears listening, similar to Complicite's *The Encounter*. All the sound effects of the island will be pre-recorded, with two microphones positioned as ears on a dummy head that will also be onstage representing Ariel. The audience's seats will be rigged to all have headphones, and the pre-recorded and live 3D stereo sound will be played into them like in *The Encounter*. For example, Caliban will pass the two microphones on dummy head when he says the line 'do hiss me into madness'. He will exaggerate the hiss and this will be loop recorded and repeated to create the 'sing i' th' wind' that Trinculo describes when he enters. The actor playing Trinculo will react to the rumbles of thunder that happen to stage left and to stage right, with the audience hearing the sounds in the appropriate corresponding ear of their headphones. The blurring of the actor with the technology will create a multi-sensory world for the audience that will make the experience intimate and personal. This is similar to the intimate actor–audience relationships that were possible with the thrust stage at Shakespeare's Globe Theatre.

> Acting is central to the idea of the technology-led production, but these examples are not developed with enough detail and flair to make it a strong response to a question that focuses on acting.
>
> The original performance conditions lack the depth of a truly strong response but do show a good awareness of the audience's experience.

Commentary

This is a good response because:

- it makes confident connections between the production concept and the text
- examples show good knowledge and understanding of creative ideas and their impact on the audience
- practitioner's ideas are effectively applied to their production concept and specifically the acting
- comprehensive original performance conditions research is relevant and connects to the production concept.

This answer is based on an extract from *Woyzeck* by Büchner, from p. 36 start of Scene 24 to page 39, end of Scene 25. The chosen practitioner is Artaud.

Student C

As a director, my production will be inspired by Artaud and his Theatre of Cruelty. I want the audience to be infected with the feelings of oppression and violence that Woyzeck feels in the play. I intend to stage my production in a large, disused warehouse space, as this is the kind of space that Artaud wanted for his Theatre of Cruelty. The audience would be sat individually on tree stumps placed randomly around the space so that the actors perform in and around them. This contrasts to the original performance in 1913 at the Kammerspiele in Munich, with a revolve stage that allowed for fast transitions. My production would not require transitions as scenes will bleed into each other and overlap to create an unrelenting performance. To achieve this mash-up of scenes, I would use a large ensemble, with many actors playing single parts.

> Student C shows their knowledge and understanding of Artaud and refers to specific ways their production concept has been influenced by the practitioner.
>
> The staging of the original performance is connected to the idea of transitions in the production concept.

The acting style is influenced by Artaud and will appeal to all the senses rather than emphasise language and intellect. For example, during Scene 24, I would have the Doctor wheel the bodies of the corpses on medical tables that squeak. The Doctor will move in an extremely fast motion as he violently explores the dead bodies. His speech will also be fast, but key lines like 'death by asphixiation' and 'A poor ending, Woyzeck' will be exaggeratedly slow. As this scene takes place, extreme versions of key violent scenes will be taking place all around the space. This will create a nightmare-like experience for the audience.

> Examples are developed with reference to the exam extract and give a sense of the impact of the overall production concept.
>
> The student shows an awareness of the audience that gives production concept continuity.

Commentary

This is a good response because it makes clear connections between the production concept and the text. The examples and key moments are used to justify ideas and their impact on the audience. The practitioner's ideas are competently applied to the production concept and specifically acting. Also, the original performance conditions knowledge is connected well to the production concept.

This answer is based on an extract from *Doctor Faustus* (A Text) by Christopher Marlowe, from page 33 start of Act 3 Scene 1 to page 37 end of Act 3 Scene 1. The chosen practitioner is Punchdrunk.

Student D

My production of *Doctor Faustus* is an immersive theatre piece that has been influenced by the work of Punchdrunk. Doctor Faustus is the main actor in my performance. His character would be played with heightened emotions that swing from excited to scared. I would want him to speak with a fast pace to show a childish excitement.

> Student D introduces their concept and links ideas to the extract, but ideas are left underdeveloped.

Doctor Faustus is an ambitious and scholarly character and this could be shown through his costume and body language. Doctor Faustus in my production would be played to be in his 30s and he would be a little over-weight but strong-looking. He would have an upright body posture as he tries to show his intelligence and superiority, but he would become more hunched as he begins to doubt his pact with the devil. His movement would go from being fast and smooth when he is being mischievous with Mephistopheles, like in the extract, to slow and broken when he realises that he can't avoid hell. The actor playing Doctor Faustus will often break from a scene and address a member of the audience. This type of direct address was popular when *Doctor Faustus* was first performed in 1594. It will make the audience feel like they are in the pact with Faustus.

> Examples are brief. There is focus on physicality and movement, but there is some sense of characterisation.
>
> The direct address of the original performance is connected to the production concept but lacks depth and specificity.

Doctor Faustus was written at a time when knowledge meant power, so I would use the immersive style of Punchdrunk to create this for a modern audience. Every room in the space will have computer stations where the audience can search for knowledge and videos will play to them. These information videos will contribute to the mixture of sound in the space.

> Reference to Punchdrunk is inconsistent and leads to an incoherent overall production concept.

Commentary

This is an average response because it is mostly a sound approach that demonstrates adequate knowledge but only some understanding. The brief examples show some awareness of the impact on the audience. The links to the practitioner's ideas are inconsistent and underdeveloped in relation to acting. The original performance conditions research is sufficient, but connections to the concept are not fully explored.

This answer is based on an extract from *The Maids* by Genet, from pages 56–61. The chosen practitioner is Berkoff.

Student E

The Maids are two sisters who want to kill their mistress. They never get it right and end up fighting between themselves. I don't want any props in my production as everything will be mimed by the actors. This fits my Berkovian style of production and will make it clear that the performance is a performance during the play.

> Reference to the influence of Berkoff is superficial and lacks justification.

This means the space will be completely empty apart from a four-poster bed. The maids will move around and through the posts as they argue with each other. Claire will always change her posture and facial expression when playing Madame to show that she is really posh. The original performance was done in French so I would have my actors speak with a French accent.

> Student E has included brief and insubstantial ideas that fail to connect the production concept with the text.

They will wear traditional maids' clothing because it is black and white and Berkoff liked to use black and white in his productions.

> Reference to the influence of Berkoff is superficial and lacks justification.

I want my production to be funny so I would have men dressed up as women to play the three parts in the play. This is how the original performance happened and I think that it would be funny for an audience.

> The fact about the original performance being performed by men is inaccurate as Genet's proposal for this to happen was ignored by the first director.

Steven Berkoff used a lot of slow motion in his work and I would use it in my production to emphasise key moments. The maids would move towards the phone in slow motion as it rings. I would also make them move in fast motion to create a contrast that will prevent the audience from becoming bored.

> The overall production concept is disconnected and lacks clarity or continuity.

Commentary

This is a weak response because it only offers surface description and struggles to make connections with the text. There are no examples from the extract or the text as a whole. The links to the practitioner's ideas are superficial and brief. The original performance conditions research is inaccurate and irrelevant.

This answer is based on an extract from *Hedda Gabler* by Henrik Ibsen, from page 62 start of Act 3 to page 65 end at stage direction *Hedda shuts stove door and stands.* The chosen practitioner is Stanislavski.

Student F

My production would be inspired by Stanislavski and I would ensure it appealed to a modern audience by having a contemporary setting of the ostentatious 'new money' of Essex. This is in light of the emphasis placed on contemporary works of Ibsen and Chekhov during Stanislavski's time at the Moscow Arts Theatre from 1897. I would have a detailed and precise set built, filled with vulgar extravagance and faux-Victorian features in a modern, proscenium arch space. The downstage area would be a lounge space with furniture, and a fireplace with a wood burner on the downstage right wall. The central upstage area will be a conservatory, divided from the lounge by large glass doors, and a large window is on the stage left wall. Entrances and exits are either side of the conservatory. This set is inspired by Stanislavski's emphasis on three-dimensional, realistic sets that allow the characters to live in the scene, carrying out tasks in response to props. Furthermore, I have created depth with the conservatory space upstage as this was an element of Stanislavski's theatre that was taken from the Meiningen Company's ideas of the 1880s. This depth of space will allow the action of the play to flow smoothly, supporting the fast-paced witty dialogue, as well as the structural inevitability of Ibsen's tragic plot.

> Student F has fully justified the drastic ideas about modernisation for a production concept in relation to the practitioner and the text.

I will direct the actors so that they capture the pattern and pace of Ibsen's play precisely. This is what Stanislavski referred to as the tempo-rhythm and focusing on this will help shape the characterisation choices that the actors make. They will discover these after following Stanislavski's system of exploring physical actions then identifying given circumstances. For example, the actor playing Hedda's physical action at the start of Act 3 would be waking and sitting up, and the given circumstances would be waking after sleeping in the lounge, waiting up with Mrs Elvsted until 4 a.m. for the men to return. This is followed by work on the 'magic if' of these circumstances, and finally their personal emotional memories that are triggered by their exploration. To continue the example, the actor playing Hedda would ask 'what "if" I had just woken up?', 'what "if" my husband had not returned after a party?' and 'what "if" my jealousy was appeased because I was right about the men's drunkeness?' This would lead to emotions of anxiety and joy. This preparatory work is essential for my production, but only informs the final performance of voice and movement.

> The student has established an idea of other elements of the production while repeatedly refocusing and returning to the acting element that is central to the exam question.
>
> Examples take into account preparation of a role that is central to Stanislavski's theories and cleverly weaves these with precise performance outcomes.

This preparatory work following Stanislavski's system will lead to the actor presenting the character at the start of Act 3 with a slow rise from lying horizontal to sitting upright, with the movement supported by her arm. She will then slowly turn her head and look around the room through bleary eyes. This slow movement will be accompanied by the slow pace of speech of someone holding back a yawn. These characterisation choices will support the weakness and frailty with which Hedda wants to be perceived by Elvsted so as to enflame her anxiety. The actor playing Hedda will then begin to thrive in Elvsted's anxiety by having close proxemics and putting an arm around her as she says: 'Now, now, now. There's nothing to worry about.' The actor will use a sympathetic tone of voice combined with a high pitch that begins to communicate her malicious joy at the situation. She will use a fast pace during these lines and leave barely any pause in the dialogue when she says: 'Well obviously the party went on very late –.' This fast pace will contrast her slow pace when she first woke up and subtly reveals the *schadenfreude* she feels towards Mrs Elvsted. This subtle but complex layering of voice, movement and characterisation (alongside the psychological preparation of the actor) will create a stage presence or 'x-factor' about the performance that contributes to the charged atmosphere and draws the audience into the emotional life of the play.

> There is a balanced approach to the elements of acting that allows the student to show how the extract would fit into a broader approach to the production.

Commentary

This is a strong response because it makes perceptive and well-developed connections between the production concept and the text. The examples show a comprehensive knowledge and understanding of creative ideas and their impact on the audience. The practitioner's ideas are perceptively applied to their production concept and specifically the acting. Also, the perceptive original performance conditions research is strong and connects to the production concept.

This answer is based on an extract from *Lysistrata* by Aristophanes, from page 150 stage direction *all the women retire …* to page 153 stage direction *approaching from the opposite direction.* The chosen practitioner is Joan Littlewood.

Student G

My production would be inspired by Joan Littlewood because the play marries political and social issues with the kind of knock-about comedy that appeals to the working classes. My production would be performed in the Olivier Theatre as it is an amphitheatre design similar to the original performance conditions. I would use a stark constructivist set design, with lighting that emphasised the simple blocks of the design with shadow. The set would resemble the front of the Bank of England in London, but the pillars will be simple blocks with a flat roof that Lysistrata can stand watch on. I would set my production during the financial crash of the 1980s in the City of London. This will mirror the original performance conditions as the amphitheatre would have a wooden building known as a skene that would have represented the Acropolis that held the state's money. The men's costumes would be power suits that were the fashion of the time, but with the addition of exaggeratedly large model erections under their trousers. The women would be costumed in colourful cotton dresses with shoulder pads and long faux-pearl necklaces.

> Student G has made the connection with Littlewood and their eclectic ideas run throughout the response and join together to make a coherent production concept.

The chorus of men enter at the start of the extract, struggling to carry their wood. The chorus's movement will interact with blocks of the Bank of England-style Acropolis, and their collective movements will be emphasised by the shadows cast by the stark lighting. Littlewood was a pioneer of combining physical acting styles with psychological acting styles. I will direct the movement of the chorus using a Littlewood-esque combination of physicalised psychology inspired by Meyerhold, basic movement efforts described by Laban and rhythmic movements influenced by Jacques-Delcroze. First, the group of men would physicalise the psychological state of sexual desperation by labouring as if under a weight, but thrusting their crotches delicately with every heavy step. Second, I would direct them to move with the Laban basic effort of thrusting, and these will be direct, sudden and strong while bound. This will give the men the characteristic of being possessed with sudden erratic movements centred around their erections. This will be particularly pronounced as they speak the lines 'I doubt if I have any hope' to 'And then found in the end that I had not'. The innuendo in this speech will be emphasised with the repressed sexuality of the movements. Finally, I would have the men step in synchronisation, but the sudden, erratic thrusts will be improvised and random. This use of clashing rhythmic movement choice will communicate the theme of sexual weakness and the idea that the men are feeble in comparison to Lysistrata and the women.

> Acting is central to the idea of the chorus in the production, but these examples are not quite developed with enough detail to make it a truly strong response to a question that focuses on acting.
>
> The connections to the original performance conditions lack the clarity and relevance of a strong response, but do show a good awareness of the relationship between the actors and the space.

Commentary

This is a good response because it makes confident connections between the production concept and the text. The examples show an assured knowledge and understanding of creative ideas and their impact on the audience. The practitioner's ideas are effectively applied to their production concept and specifically the acting. Also, the comprehensive original performance conditions research is relevant and connects to the production concept.

This answer is based on an extract from *The School for Scandal* by Sheridan, from page 13 start of Act 2 Scene 1 to page 15 end of Act 2 Scene 1. The chosen practitioner is Kneehigh.

Student H

As a director my production will be inspired by Kneehigh. Their emphasis on storytelling and joyful anarchy seem to fit the world of gossip and scandal in Sheridan's play. The theatres of the day were so anarchic that Drury Lane was wrecked by riots five times in the 1700s. I intend to stage my production in Kneehigh's Asylum tent and decorate it in the fashion of the 1770s when the play was set. The audience experience will begin from when they enter the tent, as the actors will mingle with them in character, sharing gossip and scandal. This is similar to the social event that theatre would have been when the first performance took place in 1777 at the Drury Lane theatre, London.

> Student H shows their knowledge and understanding of Kneehigh and refers to specific ways their production concept has been influenced by the practitioner.
>
> The staging of the original performance is connected to the core idea of community and actor/audience integration in Kneehigh's Asylum tent.

The design features, including costume, will be exaggerated in the style of magical realism that is common to Kneehigh productions. The acting style will match the design and be exaggerated to emphasise the comic contrasts in the play. For example, during Act 2 Scene 1 I would direct the actor playing Sir Peter to exaggerate his age by physically stooping and moving slowly. This will contrast the upright posture and faster movements of Lady Teazle. I will direct her to have an exaggeratedly posh accent to keep in with the fashion of London, but when she says 'Lud, Sir Peter!' she will slip into the harsh 'r' sounds of the Cornish accent. She will quickly correct herself with the extremely posh delivery of 'would you have me be out of fashion?' These contrasts and slip-ups will be funny for the audience.

> Examples are developed with reference to the exam extract, with a focus on acting, while details about design support the understanding of the overall production concept.
>
> The student shows an awareness of the audience that gives production concept continuity.

Commentary

This is a good response because it makes clear connections between the production concept and the text. The examples and key moments are used to justify ideas and their impact on the audience. The practitioner's ideas are well applied to the production concept and specifically acting. Also, the good original performance conditions knowledge is connected with the production concept.

This answer is based on an extract from *Waiting for Godot* by Beckett, from page 18 stage direction *Pozzo eats his chicken...* to page 20 'Eleven'. The chosen practitioner is Stanislavski.

Student 1

My production of *Waiting for Godot* will focus on the detail of text and the characterisation. I will direct the actors with techniques from Stanislavski to get the audience to recognise and associate with the characters. The actors playing Estragon and Vladimir will use emotion memory to capture their loneliness and the boredom. Estragon's voice and movement would be quite abrupt and masculine, while Vladimir's would be passionate and sympathetic. These contrasts would be exaggerated when Vladimir says, 'He looks tired' and Estragon replies, 'Why doesn't he put down his bags?' They will be dressed like tramps and they will use the details of their costume to emphasise mannerisms that capture their characters. I would use a small studio space with an end-on stage to allow the audience to see the details of the performance. This is similar to the original performance conditions as it was first performed in the 75-seater Théâtre de Babylone in Paris.

> Student 1 has only mentioned Stanislavski briefly at the start and this seems superficial and lacks any justification.
>
> Reference to emotion memory shows good knowledge, but lacks the understanding of how these would be performed in a production.

The repetition and boredom of the production will be heightened in such a small space, so I would use the pace of the dialogue to keep the audience engaged. Estragon and Vladimir have short sentences when Pozzo and Lucky enter in the extract and I would have these overlap to emphasise their shock. Pozzo's long speech will break this fast pace and replace it with a slower, contrasting pace. Pozzo's actions will be violent and abrupt towards Lucky, but he will barely react, while the facial expressions of Estragon and Vladimir will capture his pain. This will intensify the emotions of disgust and fear for the audience.

> Characterisation is described in general terms and examples are never justified in any depth.
>
> There is some understanding of the text and the original performance, but there is little coherent connection with the production concept.

Commentary

This is an average response because it is mostly a sound approach that demonstrates adequate knowledge but only some understanding. The brief examples show some awareness of the impact on the audience. The links to the practitioner's ideas are inconsistent and underdeveloped in relation to acting. Also, the original performance conditions research is adequate, but connections to the concept are not fully explored.

Section C: Interpreting one performance text, in the light of one practitioner for a contemporary audience

You will be given **two** questions to choose between for Section C. You must choose **one** question focusing on directing acting **or** directing design. The first half of this section dealt with directing acting, with brief extracts from answers that covered every text and every practitioner. This half deals with directing design, with extracts that cover different combinations of text and practitioner.

As a director, discuss how you would apply the methodologies of your chosen theatre practitioner to the lighting design in your production concept.

Your answer must make reference to:

- the overall aims of your production concept in response to the play as a whole
- how your practical ideas will work in performance
- the original performance conditions of your chosen performance text.

(24 marks)

This answer is based on an extract from *Antigone* by Sophocles, from Antigone's speech '*This is the land of my fathers*' (page 40) to '*among the ashes*' (page 42). The chosen theatre practitioner is Joan Littlewood.

Student J

Joan Littlewood's use of three-dimensional constructivist sets that are fully integrated with atmospheric lighting inspired by Adolphe Appia will be the foundation for the ideas for my production of *Antigone*. A set of simple blocks and ramps will lead to a large entrance at the raised level. The lighting will focus on the sides of the structure to exaggerate their shape. This use of side lighting will also be used to reinforce the shape of the actors' bodies in the space. I will use lighting to show differences in power and status between characters in *Antigone*. These distinctions are important as the original performances of ancient Greek tragedies would have clearly denoted power and status through masks, entrance points and stage position in relation to the Chorus. My production won't use masks, but the second two methods will be used in my Littlewood-inspired constructivist set and lighting design.

> This student shows their knowledge and understanding of Littlewood and refers to specific ways their production concept has been influenced by the practitioner.

> The symbolic status and levels created in the original performance are connected to the idea of power created by modern lighting techniques.

The choice of set and lighting will bring out the idea of Antigone's powerlessness in the face of Creon. She will be led away by Creon's guards immediately after he tells her: 'Don't comfort yourself with hope. There's none.' The actor playing Antigone will speak her response as she is led up the stairs backwards. The awkward physicality of her reverse up the stairs will communicate her hopelessness. But the actor will deliver the speech with a strong, defiant tone and visually she will be on a raised level that will give her a visual status in the eyes of the audience. These contrasting meanings will only be effectively communicated to the audience when combined with side lighting that accentuates the three-dimensional form of the actor's body and stage steps and ramps.

> Examples are developed with reference to the exam extract and give a sense of the impact of the overall production concept.

Tiresias' entrance will be significant as his blindness and old age will lead to the actor creating a stooped and physically fragile form that will contrast with Creon's upright and powerful stance. But having Creon on the lower part of the set and Tiresias enter from the raised entrance will communicate his status to the audience. Furthermore, the Chorus will be on the opposite half of the stage to Tiresias, giving the blind prophet the greater weight in the balance of the stage. Creon and the Chorus will be lit from all angles without any shadow accentuating their form. Tiresias will be lit from the side and below to accentuate his form and emphasise his three-dimensional presence in the space. The lighting will connect Tiresias with the structure and thus his environment, which will also communicate his power. This connection will be further reinforced as he is led down the steps by his boy. His movement will be slow and tentative, but this will be in contrast with a confident and forceful voice. As Tiresias moves towards Creon, the lighting that is directed at him will transition to side-lighting to reflect the prophet's influence over the king. This will also begin to communicate the shift in power that comes when Creon later dismisses Tiresias' vision.

> The answer gives generalities to describe lighting and doesn't emphasise how one state will lead to the next.

Commentary

This is a good response because it makes clear connections between the production concept and the text. The examples and key moments are used to justify ideas and their impact on the audience. The practitioner's ideas are well applied to the production concept and specifically acting. Also, the good original performance conditions knowledge is connected with the production concept.

This answer is based on an extract from *Doctor Faustus* by Christopher Marlow, Act 3, the whole of Scene 1. The chosen theatre practitioner is Complicite.

Student K

My production would be inspired by Complicite and I would use lighting to emphasise the actor's body and the tableaux created by the ensemble. Lighting would be the primary method of indicating the shifts of time and magical qualities in *Doctor Faustus*. The production will take place on a proscenium-arch stage so as to frame and emphasise the images created by the combination of lighting and actors. The centre of the stage will be a square platform, raised 20 centimetres, that fills half the area of the space. The purpose of this raised platform is to allow there to be two cross-cut scenes, such as Faustus and Mephistopheles becoming ghostly observers during scenes like the Pope's banquet. There will be a large table in the middle, with a chair behind, designed in the style of a Renaissance writing desk. This will be Faustus's desk, but also the Pope's banquet table, etc. Apart from the costume and the props, the space will appear 'neutral' and white. The back of the space will be a white, plastic half-curtain similar to the one used in Complicite's *Mnemonic*. The purpose of this half-curtain is to create ghostly shadows when people are backlit behind the sheet. It will also create a murky transparency similar to a gauze material when people are front-lit behind the curtain. Finally, the purpose of the white sheet material is to offer a surface for coloured lighting to instantly change the mood and atmosphere of a scene, or as a screen for projections that support the shifts of time in *Doctor Faustus*. My lighting ideas are inspired by the candlelight that would have been used in the indoor playhouses of the original performance conditions. The atmosphere of candlelight suits the demonic atmosphere that is present in *Doctor Faustus*.

The technical focus of the question is grounded in the style of the chosen practitioner with effect reference to Mnemonic *as an illustrative example.*

This gives a detailed and technical vision for how lighting will integrate with other elements to communicate meaning to the audience.

I would direct the actors playing Faustus and Mephistopheles to stand on the desk at the start of Act 3 Scene 1, and there would be no lighting except the projection of the places Faustus describes having visited. The projected images would fill the white half-curtain, with the actors' bodies caught in the projection beam. The pace of the images will give the lighting effect on the actors' bodies a sense of movement. I would ensure that the pace and rhythm of the images complemented the iambic pentameter of Faustus's blank verse that distinguished Marlowe's play when it was first written. During this sequence of projections, stage smoke will gather so as to create a haze effect that will create a ghostly atmosphere. The lighting effect created by the projected images will come to an abrupt end when Mephistopheles breaks the blank verse and speaks in prose – 'Faustus, I have.' It will be replaced with a single PAR-can light from above directed at Mephistopheles and Faustus. This will be the lighting state for the next 35 lines, and during this time the Pope and Friars will gather, barely seen in the shadows of the stage. They will create a still image of their feast seated around the desk that has become their banquet table. Instead of 'placing a robe on Faustus', Mephistopheles will gesture to trigger the next change in lighting state. This lighting state

The original intentions of Marlowe and his use of language are used to justify lighting choices that show a flair and precision in the design choices.

Examples are taken from the extract and show full consideration of the practicalities of the whole production.

will be many additional PAR-can lights from a high angle that will create columns of light. I will use a pale yellow gel on these PAR-cans to create a warm but ghostly atmosphere. The columns of light will be hardened by use of the gentle haze effect of the stage smoke further reinforcing the ghostly atmosphere. The next lighting shift, an abrupt blackout, will happen when the Pope and Friars exit the stage and run away. Faustus's, 'Come on, Mephistopheles. What shall we do?' and Mephistopheles' reply will take place in the blackout. This will create a connection for the audience between Mephistopheles' power and the lighting states. As Faustus speaks the 'How? Bell, book, and candle' speech, lighting will rise up the white, plastic half-curtain. The Friars will enter and sing the dirge behind the curtain while backlit, to create silhouettes and to present them as the haunting figures. Faustus and Mephistopheles will turn upstage and watch the Friars' silhouettes sing the dirge. As it comes to an end Faustus and Mephistopheles will exit and re-enter behind the curtain. I will direct the actors playing the lead pair to stand nearer the light source so their silhouette is bigger than that of the Friars, before proceeding to beat them. This will ruin the haunting silhouette effect and will create comedy for the audience. It will support the idea that Faustus abuses and wastes his power. The use of lighting technology combined with comedy brings together two strands of Complicite's work in a way that supports the atmosphere and narrative of the play while accentuating the language that distinguished Marlowe's play in the original performance conditions.

> Impact on the audience is fully considered in relation to the original performance conditions and Complicite's style of theatre.

Commentary

This is a strong response for many reasons. It makes perceptive and well-developed connections between the production concept and the text. Examples show a comprehensive knowledge and understanding of creative ideas and their impact on the audience. The practitioner's ideas are perceptively applied to their production concept and specifically the acting. Perceptive original performance conditions research is strong and connects to the production concept.

As a director, discuss how you would apply the methodologies of your chosen theatre practitioner to the sound design (including music) in your production concept.

Your answer must make reference to:

- the overall aims of your production concept in response to the play as a whole
- how your practical ideas will work in performance
- the original performance conditions of your chosen performance text.

(24 marks)

This answer is based on an extract from *The Tempest* by Shakespeare, from the start of Act 2 Scene 2 to the stage direction *embraces Stephano*. The chosen theatre practitioner is Punchdrunk.

Student L

My production of *The Tempest* would be an immersive experience for the audience inspired by Punchdrunk. I would adapt a large warehouse space over multiple floors that would become the island of the play. The themes of power and control, as well as the idea of utopias, fit the immersive style experience. I would follow Punchdrunk's convention of masking the audience and will consider them to be the invisible spirits, like Ariel, that fill the island. I would set the play in an abandoned party island venue of the near future, with the remnants of a neon party world making up the different zones that the audience can explore. The experience will begin with the audience exploring the brightly lit abandoned and empty world, unable to find any characters. There will only be an eerie silence of people moving around a museum or a piece of installation art. The lighting will gradually dim as more audience members enter the space, and a light smoke will fill the space to create the mysterious haze effect that Punchdrunk uses to reinforce the illusion of being alone on an individual adventure through the space. The silence will also be gradually filled with the rumbles of a storm that will get increasingly loud and intense. The almost unbearable volume of the storm sounds will mark the start of the performance and the performers will begin to inhabit different parts of the space. Sound and music, like in a Punchdrunk performance, will be vitally important for moving the action forward and propelling the audience through the immersive experience. The intense theatricality and modernity of my immersive production will be in the spirit of innovation of the original performance. *The Tempest* is considered Shakespeare's farewell to the theatre and is overtly theatrical. The latest technology would have been used to create intense and loud sound effects that would have been highly dramatic and engaging for the original audience. Instead of thunder created with a cannon ball running down a large pipe, I will use modern, recorded sound and amplification to present my sounds. Speakers will be concealed throughout the space, with sound and music being constant and fully integrated with the desired pace and rhythm of the immersive experience for the audience. They will explore the space at their own pace and follow characters and story that they are interested in, but a sense of an overall arc of time will be solely communicated through sound and music.

This student gives a detailed and technical idea of how recorded sound and music are an integral element of the immersive style of Punchdrunk.

The original performance conditions are connected to the immersive style of Punchdrunk with a constant focus on and awareness of impact on the audience.

One zone for the audience to explore will be an abandoned strip of bars, and this will be where they can discover Caliban when he enters with wood at what is considered Act 2 Scene 2 in the text, but will be looped and running in parallel with other events in my immersive production. His entrance will be marked by a crack of thunder that will come from a speaker concealed near Caliban's entrance. By designing the direction that the sound comes from I will be able to have some control over where the audience look. The crack of thunder will trigger a distorted and distant sound of bass that is concealed in a nightclub. The details of melody will be subtle and secondary to the bass while Caliban conceals himself. The bass will fluctuate in volume to mirror the thunder of the text, with the volume increase causing Trinculo to creep under Caliban's garment. Stephano will enter from one of the abandoned bars and the sound of a melody will increase and come from the door that he enters from. This will again direct the audience's attention to Stephano's entrance with bottle in hand. The volume of the music will gradually increase and the low bass beat will speed up as the comedic confusion of the 'beast' with 'four legs and two voices' increases. Once Stephano discovers Trinculo, he will lead him back to the inside of the bar where the music appears to come from. Caliban will speak his aside to the audience as he follows them into the bar space. The volume of the music will increase from this space, and some audience members will be encouraged to follow Caliban and the others as they drink in this other space. Other members of the audience will have their attention taken by Ferdinand, who will move through the abandoned strip with wood on the way to another space where Act 3 Scene 1 of the text will take place. This means the end of both Act 2 Scene 2 and Act 3 Scene 1 will be happening at the same time, and the audience will have to decide which character they follow. Those that choose to follow Caliban will experience the intensely loud music of a nightclub that will come from all around this space and envelop the audience. My idea for this all-encompassing and intense music is that the atmosphere induces a kind of drunkenness and rebelliousness among the audience that matches Caliban's drunken rebellion. This is another way that my Punchdrunk-style immersive experience will mirror the original performance conditions because there would have been a greater sense of revelry and anarchy among the groundlings at the Globe than there is in modern, conventional theatres.

> Examples are taken from the extract and show full consideration of the practicalities of the whole production.

> The examples given link to the extract but they are placed with the wider immersive experience of the audience that shows a flair and precision in the design choices.

Commentary

This is a strong response that makes perceptive and well-developed connections between the production concept and the text. Examples show a comprehensive knowledge and understanding of creative ideas and their impact on the audience. The practitioner's ideas are perceptively applied to their production concept and specifically the acting. Perceptive original performance conditions research is strong and connects to the production concept.

This answer is based on an extract from *Woyzeck* by Georg Büchner, Scenes 24 and 25. The chosen theatre practitioner is Bertolt Brecht.

Student M

My production of *Woyzeck* will be inspired by Bertolt Brecht and specifically his ideas of 'spass' or fun and verfremdungseffekt. I intend to make music central to my production, with a band led by the Showman character playing songs in between some of the scenes. My production, like Brecht's ideas, would encourage the composer of the music to simply look at the major themes of the play and capture them in the songs rather than trying to put the story to music. There is some precedent for this with Tom Waits composing songs for Robert Wilson's production of *Woyzeck* in 2000. The important thing about the music in my production is that the tone contrasts the tone of the scene that it precedes or follows. This will create verfremdungseffekt and make the audience think. I would have the Showman and his band permanently on a raised part of the stage and they will create a rock concert-style atmosphere for the audience.

> This response begins with a reference to Brecht and two of his specific ideas, but these remain surface connections that are not fully explained in the concept.

> Reference to songs and transitions remain general but do give some sense of the whole production.

Scene 24 with the autopsy will be preceded by an upbeat song with a fast rhythm. This will contrast the slow, mournful entrance of the dead bodies on medical tables pushed by stage hands dressed as the Doctor's students. It will be a confusing combination that will make the audience reflect on what has happened to Woyzeck. The upbeat nature of the music will also give the whole production a sense of 'spass' and make the experience fun and entertaining for the audience in order to avoid them becoming too emotionally embroiled with Woyzeck's plight. The transitions will take place during the songs and the actors will improvise scenes that lead into the scenes of the play. This will all take place on a revolving stage to ensure that there is a pace to the transitions that doesn't leave the audience bored. This is similar to the use of a revolve in the first ever production of *Woyzeck* in Eugen Kilian's 1913 production in the Munich Kammerspiel.

> The response drifts a little towards acting without much connection to sound and music in parts.

The role of the Doctor was inspired by Büchner's interest in *commedia dell'arte* and so I would make sure he was funny as well. His actions and gestures will be fast and over-exaggerated in Scene 24 as he carries out the autopsy of the body. I will have him tugging and pulling at the insides of Woyzeck and Marie, with bits flying into his face and all over the place. He will run his hands through his long, grey hair, even though they are dirty with blood. I will direct the actor to make him manically enthusiastic for the autopsy. This comedic element will be further heightened when the Captain enters. He is another character that is inspired by the *commedia dell'arte* tradition. I will have the Captain mock the Doctor's analysis before having the status shift to the Doctor as he rushes out of the scene, leaving the Captain without his own diagnoses. During this scene I will have the band led by the Showman create sound effects that will accompany the movements in a

> The final paragraph offers detailed description of the use of sound effects but this lacks depth of justification, choosing to focus on general ideas of the audience being entertained or made to think.

cartoonish way. They will use their instruments as well as found materials in the spirit of Brecht's theatre. One of the band will play great metal on a washboard as the Doctor mimes sawing to *cut briskly through the rib cage*. Symbols will crash together as he *incises again deeply* with his knife. As the Doctor pulls at the insides of the bodies, one band member will pluck at the strings of a bass guitar. When Woyzeck's head is revealed by the Doctor he will shake it about and this will be accompanied by the sound of maracas shaking. The Doctor then punctures Woyzeck's body and makes an incision. The puncture action will be accompanied by the Showman popping his cheek with his finger into a microphone, while the incision sound will be supported by the sound of a swanee whistle. These different sound effects will distance the audience from the clinical and depressing scene of an autopsy and make them laugh, but then consider why they are laughing. The audience will not be passive in my production, and instead I will have the members of the band fully engage with the audience as though they are also viewers of what is unfolding, along with the audience. This will help position the audience as laughing at the Doctor and the Captain rather than with them. Sound and music will play a key role in this removed position almost as a form of narration or chorus commenting on the action.

Commentary

This is an average response. The student has a mostly sound approach that demonstrates adequate knowledge. However, there is only some understanding. There are brief examples that show some awareness of the impact on the audience. Links to the practitioner's ideas are inconsistent and underdeveloped in relation to acting. The original performance conditions research is sufficient but connections to the concept are not fully explored.

As a director, discuss how you would apply the methodologies of your chosen theatre practitioner to the set design in your production concept.

Your answer must make reference to:

- the overall aims of your production concept in response to the play as a whole
- how your practical ideas will work in performance
- the original performance conditions of your chosen performance text.

(24 marks)

This answer is based on an extract from *The Maids* pages 56–61. The chosen theatre practitioner is Constantin Stanislavksi.

Student N

My production of *The Maids* will be inspired by Stanislavski's realism as well as the playwright Genet's ideas about theatre. The space I would use would be a traverse stage, but the stage area will be a complete box with a middle horizontal strip removed, big enough for three rows of audience to see through. The interior of the stage box will be decorated in the precise style of a 1930s French art deco bedroom. This will have the combined effect of creating the four-wall realism of Stanislavski's sets, but will also create the hall of mirrors-style experience that Genet wanted theatre to be. The traverse stage will mean the audience on one side will see the audience on the other as if there were a large mirror. It will also highlight the idea of the audience as a voyeuristic observer that was a feature of Genet's Theatre of the Absurd style.

> The connection between the set, space and audience shows creative flair and is fully justified in relation to the intentions of the writer.

There will be an element of mime involved because of my choice of set. When Claire goes to open a window, she will approach the horizontal gap that the audience look through before being stopped by Solange, who encourages her to open both doors instead. This interjection from Solange takes on a layered meaning that I believe Genet would have appreciated. The surface meaning is underscored with the idea that she is aware of the audience's presence, and rather than mime opening a window and breaking the illusion she would prefer a door to be opened. The play continually blurs the boundary between fantasy and reality. This set and space choice will have a similar impact to Louis Jouvet's original production at the Athénée Theatre in Paris in 1947. The set was praised for being majestic and detailed, while the illusion it created helped the play teeter on the edge of fantasy and reality. I believe my choice of this voyeuristic traverse staging draws the audience into a Stanislavski-style, realistic illusion, but then encourages them to acknowledge the theatricality of the event as befits a Genet play.

> There is an awareness of how set and space will impact acting, with carefully chosen examples that are fully explained in relation to the impact on the audience.

> This paragraph offers a balanced response that shows an awareness of how meaning can be created through set design.

The moment that Solange *runs a comb through her hair* will take place as she sits at Madame's petite art deco dressing table and looks out into one of the audience areas as if she were looking in a mirror. The imagined mirror will allow for the actor playing Solange to bend the rules of this reality. She can bring the audience in on her anxiety about her sister with a sigh and a shake of the head to the audience as she says: 'Claire, don't get carried away, don't be rash.' The actor playing Claire almost acknowledges Solange's relationship with the audience. Her speech in response is full of frustration at her sister for the failings with Monsieur, but it could also be played on a level that she is frustrated that Solange is allowing the audience to discover them. First, I would direct her to take the comb and aggressively comb out knots in her hair before dragging her backwards by the hair into the centre of the space. This will disturb parts of the set, mirroring her breakdown, but as Claire says 'Let's talk calmly. I'm strong', I would direct the actor to rearrange the disturbed parts of the set. This precise interaction with the set for what Stanislavski referred to as 'tasks' would begin to merge the psychology of the maid characters with the set and space. Then there is the added layer that the audience become part of the set when the actors look in the mirror or go to open a window that implicates them in the mad world.

> Examples from the extract are fully integrated with the ideas for the set design of the production.

I have chosen to replace the Louis Quinze furniture that is identified in Genet's stage directions with the 1930s French art deco furniture because it is appropriate to the era of the original performance. It also combines symmetrical straight lines with lyrical curves that make each item seem unique and unusual. This combination of formal and the bizarre fits the duality of the maid characters. The furniture will be a dark mahogany, with the grain panelled to create a checkerboard effect. This choice of colour will give my production a dark atmosphere, while the irregular grain will add to the communication of things not quite fitting in the production. One element of furniture and prop that will be used at a significant moment of duality is the pair of round art deco bedside tables either side of the bed and the telephone. The moment Claire answers the telephone I would direct her to stand upright and servant-like as she speaks to Monsieur through the large receiver about his release from jail. I would contrast this upright quality with her crawling under the bed covers, invading Madame's personal space when she says: 'The judge let him out on bail.' The effect of these little, subtle contrasts in the way they interact with their environment will add to the communication of their duality and make the play humorous for the audience.

Commentary

This student has given a strong response to the question. They make perceptive and well-developed connections between the production concept and the text. The examples chosen show a comprehensive knowledge and understanding of creative ideas and their impact on the audience. The practitioner's ideas are perceptively applied to their production concept, and specifically the acting. Finally, perceptive original performance conditions research is strong and connects to the production concept.

This answer is based on an extract from *Hedda Gabler* by Henrik Ibsen, the whole of Act 2 Scene 1. The chosen theatre practitioner is Steven Berkoff.

Student O

My production of *Hedda Gabler* would be inspired by Steven Berkoff and specifically his Kafka series of plays. The themes of control and the self versus society seem to be similar in both and I would use some of Berkoff's techniques to communicate the idea that Hedda feels trapped. I would use a proscenium-arch space as the stage, and the image created by a combination of the actors, the set and the lights will be important. My set would be a large, metal frame of a cube that fills the stage space. There will be no walls to the cube and the audience will be able to see the black back wall and the side flats of the stage. The upstage side of the cube will have a fireplace and a wood burner that will be suspended by a reinforced wood burner chimney that connects with the top of the cube. There will be furniture from the period when the play is set, in the 1880s, around the space to suit the action of the text. The empty shell of a cube will represent Hedda feeling caged and trapped in a life that doesn't suit her.

> This response begins with a reference to Berkoff, but this choice of combination of practitioner and play is never justified in a way that gives a sense of the whole production idea.

My production would focus on the actors' bodies creating tableaux that emphasise themes and ideas to the audience. Furthermore, I will direct the actors to create all the sound effects with their voices; thus the actors become the set and environment. This is an idea inspired by Berkoff's *The Trial*, where everyday elements in Joseph K's life are exaggerated and distorted to communicate the idea that he is trapped. An example of how I would create this would be the first scene when Hedda arrives home from her honeymoon. I would have the ensemble sitting around the edge of the cube structure, whispering and hissing lines that are spoken by her husband's irritating aunt. Lines like 'And has the young bride slept well in her new home?' will be repeated and echoed by the ensemble while Hedda positions herself in the back corner of the cube. The combination of these sounds and Hedda's stage position will communicate the nightmare experience that Hedda feels she is having.

> Ideas about the actors' bodies creating tableaux and sound effects seems like an add-on that is not fully explained in relation to how they suit this specific play.

Hedda's position within the large cube grid will communicate her power and status in relation to other characters. This is important in my production because the original production of *Hedda Gabler* would have used social conventions of the era to communicate the power and status relationships of characters. Costume and set would have held much more significance at the first performance at the Residenztheater in Munich in 1891. A good example of how I will use the set space is the relationship between Hedda and Judge Brack. Their first encounter in the play will put Hedda on an even footing with Judge Brack, with her flirtatiousness even giving her the edge of power. I will communicate this by having the actor playing Hedda standing still at the front of the cube while Brack moves about behind her to get her attention. This will contrast the use of the space at the end of the play when Brack tells her about the true circumstances of Loevborg's death. Here I will direct the actor playing Brack to dominate the front centre of the stage while Hedda struggles to remain standing, propping herself up against the downstage corner of the cube. The visual clarity that is provided by a cube structure allows for quick communication of status and power with the audience.

> The response is more about the spatial interaction of actors, without enough detail about specific interactions with the set.

The actor's relationship with the objects and furniture of the set will also hold significance for the audience in my production. Ibsen's text has a lot of sub-text beneath the quickfire dialogue on the surface. I would communicate this sub-text to the audience by precisely directing the actor's non-verbal relationships with the objects and furniture of the set. An example of this is when Hedda approaches Mrs Elvsted during Act 2 Scene 1. I will direct Hedda to stand directly behind Mrs Elvsted, who sits nervously on the edge of a stool. Hedda will hold Mrs Elvsted's shoulders and move down to her level to look directly in her eyes when Hedda is trying to seem sincere and supportive. But when she says, 'I know what's happened', she will stand up and look out over Mrs Elvsted towards the audience. This will communicate the sub-text of Hedda's delight at Mrs Elvsted's painful situation, despite the words she is saying, communicating her concern. This scene would not have the sound effects of the ensemble because the silence and stillness is important at the start as the audience begin to fully understand Hedda's mischievousness.

> There is a lack of detail about the set that is, in part, connected to practitioner choice, but the student does not take the opportunity to describe the organisation of furniture and what impact this could have on the meaning of scenes.

Commentary

This student has given an average response. It is mostly a sound approach that demonstrates good knowledge, but there is only some understanding. Brief examples show some awareness of the impact on the audience. Links to the practitioner's ideas are inconsistent and underdeveloped in relation to acting. The original performance conditions research is sufficient but connections to the concept have not been fully explored.

As a director, discuss how you would apply the methodologies of your chosen theatre practitioner to the costume design (including make-up and masks) in your production concept.

Your answer must make reference to:

- the overall aims of your production concept in response to the play as a whole
- how your practical ideas will work in performance
- the original performance conditions of your chosen performance text.

(24 marks)

This answer is based on an extract from *Waiting for Godot* by Samuel Beckett, from the stage direction *Pozzo eats his chicken* to Estragon's answer '*Eleven*' (pages 18–20). The chosen theatre practitioner is Kneehigh.

Student P

My production of *Waiting for Godot* will be a site-specific piece that takes place on Truro High Street. The site-specific idea and the Cornish location are inspired by the work of Kneehigh, whose early productions were site-specific works in Cornwall. I would also use the magical realism-style costumes that are often part of Kneehigh's shows. *Waiting for Godot* in this style would make interesting connections with street theatre and clowning that I believe will bring out the humour and the pathos of Beckett's play.

> The links with Kneehigh show a strong understanding of the company's ideas while effectively connecting them to the text and the production concept.

Casting will be very important to my production and will have a big impact on the way the characters are costumed. Roger Blin directed the first production of *Waiting for Godot* at the Théâtre de Babylone, and it was his decision to dress Estragon and Vladimir as the tramps that became the norm for the play's future productions. I want them to be dressed as modern tramps for my production, as it will fit the street theatre, site-specific idea. I will cast Vladimir as tall and long-limbed, while Estragon will be short and chunky. Vladimir will be dressed in large, loose-fitting, shabby woollen suit trousers. They will be torn and held up with a piece of rope for a belt. On the top he will have a torn knit sweater that is too big and frayed. His hat will be a trucker-style sport's cap that is filthy and loose because of the broken back clips. The elements of magical realism that are inspired by Kneehigh's style would be captured in the exaggerated size of the garments. Estragon will have a contrasting costume that accentuates his stocky body type. His trousers will be tracksuit bottoms that are too tight and so long that he wears the waistband just below his nipples. He will wear a hooded jumper that is torn and frayed but tucked into the trousers. Over this he will wear an old, padded vest jacket that will accentuate his large size. His hat will be an old, fraying flat cap.

> There are references to Blin's original production throughout and these are integrated into ideas for the student's production concept.

> The costume is described in detail and continually linked to the impact on the site-specific audience.

The costume of Estragon and Vladimir will support the action that I direct for the actors and will draw out the comedy and the pathos. When Estragon says 'you won't be wanting the bones', he can drop to his knees, stretching the fabric of his trousers while unzipping and removing his vest jacket to give himself room for the feast of bones. Similarly, Vladimir's costume will accentuate his '(exploding)' when he says, 'It's a scandal!' His limbs will flail as his baggy garments flap and almost inflate with the pace of the movement. The costume will offer a support to the actors' performance as they draw out the comic moments that are also tinged with pity and sympathy.

The tramp characters will only have subtle elements of the magical realism that is a feature of Kneehigh's productions. But Lucky and Pozzo will have costumes that really play on the magical realism style. Lucky's jacket will be a performing monkey-style over coat, with bright red fabric and gold trim. Pozzo will be dressed as a ringmaster, with exaggeratedly broad jodhpurs and shiny, pristine boots. The buttons on his waistcoat will be extravagant, large and gold.

This answer makes confident connections between the impact of costume on the performance of the extract and how it would communicate meaning with an audience.

The contrast between the pairs of characters will be important for Pozzo and Lucky's first entrance. Lucky enters with a rope around his neck that is held by Pozzo. In my production they will enter from a side street and make quite a long walk to the performance space. Their costumes will make them stand out from the public, and the reference to circus performers in the costumes will give a sense of the relationship and power dynamic between Pozzo and Lucky. This will place the audience/members of the public in a similar position to Vladimir and Estragon, who comment on Lucky as he enters. They will say similar things to Vladimir such as: 'Look', '(Pointing) His neck'. This will use the site-specific nature of my production to immerse members of the public and audience members in the perspective of Estragon and Vladimir.

Commentary

The student has given a good response here, because it makes well-developed connections between the production concept and the text. Examples show an assured knowledge and understanding of creative ideas and their impact on the audience. The practitioner's ideas are effectively applied to their production concept and specifically the costume, which is mentioned in detail. The student has undertaken comprehensive original performance conditions research, which is relevant and connects to the production concept.

This answer is based on an extract from *The School for Scandal* by Richard Brinsley Sheridan, the whole of Act 2 Scene 1. The chosen theatre practitioner is Antonin Artaud.

Student Q

I want to do an Artaudian version of *The School for Scandal* where the audience are placed at the centre of the gossiping and scandal. I will get my actors to interact with the audience when they are not in a scene, whispering about the other actors or other members of the audience. They will be malicious and horrible in the style of Artaud's Theatre of Cruelty. I would actually perform my production in the kind of stately home that is in the play, but I would dirty and rough-up all of the furniture to give it a destroyed feeling. The audience will follow the action in a promenade style and be offered garments that fit the 18th-century era that the play is set in. Large dresses will be handed out and tights will be given out so that the audience blend in with the society of the play. Costume will no longer be a barrier between the actors and the audience, but a way that they are unified in one performance experience. The cast will be dressed in costumes that are dishevelled and destroyed, almost like the ghostly figures in something like the London Dungeon experience. The world that my production will create is as if an apocalypse had happened in the 1770s and these people were growing a society again. The arguments between Sir Peter and Lady Teazle will become physically violent, to complement the verbal attacks and to further increase the atmosphere of cruelty that suits an Artaudian production. Their physical altercations in Act 2 Scene 1 will leave the costumes further ripped and dishevelled. This Theatre of Cruelty interpretation will communicate with the audience the horrible side of gossip and scandal that Sheridan was poking fun at in his original production.

This response begins with a reference to Artaud, but this choice of combination of practitioner and play is never justified in a way that gives a sense of the whole production idea.

The link between Artaud and the play is tenuously hinged on the negativity of gossip and scandal being linked to cruelty.

Ideas about set and location are brief, unrealistic and not achieveable.

The connection with the extract is not appropriately justified and shows little understanding of the importance of dialogue and wit in the original text.

The answer refers to the original production but gives an example of the writing rather than any relevant performance description that informs their ideas.

Commentary

This student has given only a weak response. It only offers surface description and struggles to make connections with the text. The student hasn't provided any examples from the extract or the text as a whole. Links to the practitioner's ideas are superficial and brief. The student has researched only minimal original performance conditions. Unfortunately, the few comments the student has made are irrelevant.

Drama and Theatre AS level
Component 2: Theatre Makers in Practice

SECTION A: LIVE THEATRE EVALUATION

Answer ONE of the following questions in this section with reference to a theatre performance

you have seen. Write your answer in the space provided.

Write the title, venue and date of the performance you have seen in the space provided.

EITHER

1 Analyse and evaluate the contribution of the **sound designer** and their use of live and recorded sound and music in the performance you have seen.

In your answer you should consider:

- key moments in the performance
- your response as an informed member of the audience.

Your answer must give **balanced consideration** between your analysis **and** your evaluation.

(Total for Question 1 = 16 marks)

OR

2 Analyse and evaluate how voice and movement were used to create impact in the performance you have seen.

In your answer you should consider:

- key moments in the performance
- your response as an informed member of the audience.

Your answer must give **balanced consideration** between your analysis **and** your evaluation.

(Total for Question 2 = 16 marks)

TOTAL FOR SECTION A = 16 MARKS

SECTION B: PAGE TO STAGE: REALISING A PERFORMANCE TEXT

Answer BOTH of the questions in this section with reference to the performance text you have studied.

You need to read and refer to an extract from the text you have studied.

Performance texts:

Accidental Death of an Anarchist, Dario Fo

Colder Than Here, Laura Wade

Equus, Peter Shaffer

Fences, August Wilson

Machinal, Sophie Treadwell

That Face, Polly Stenham

> **Exam tip**
>
> In the exam, you will be provided with an extract from your text which you will need to read and refer to in your answer. Here, your teacher will give you an extract to use to answer the question.

3 As a **performer**, what choices would you make in presenting **one** of the **key roles** in the extract in performance?

You should use examples from the extract to support your ideas and your answer should make reference to the performance text as a whole.

(Total for Question 3 = 16 marks)

4 As a **designer**, discuss how you would use **theatrical elements** to create an **appropriate environment** for the performance of the extract.

You should use examples from the extract to support your ideas and your answer should make reference to the performance text as a whole.

(Total for Question 4 = 16 marks)

TOTAL FOR SECTION B = 32 MARKS

TOTAL FOR PAPER = 48 MARKS

Drama and Theatre A level
Component 3: Theatre Makers in Practice

SECTION A: LIVE THEATRE EVALUATION

Answer ONE of the following questions in this section with reference to a theatre performance

you have seen. Write your answer in the space provided.

Write the title, venue and date of the performance you have seen in the space provided.

EITHER

1 Analyse and evaluate the live performance you have seen in light of the following statement:
'Theatre makers rely more on style than content when it comes to live performance.'

Your answer should:

- include analysis and evaluation of key moments from the performance you have seen and the contribution made by different theatre makers

- offer **balanced consideration** between your analysis and evaluation of the performance and your response to the statement.

(Total for Question 1 = 20 marks)

OR

2 Analyse and evaluate the live performance you have seen in light of the following statement:
'The role of the actor is second to the role of the director in modern theatre.'

Your answer should:

- include analysis and evaluation of key moments from the performance you have seen and the contribution made by different theatre makers

- offer **balanced consideration** between your analysis and evaluation of the performance and your response to the statement.

(Total for Question 2 = 20 marks)

TOTAL FOR SECTION A = 20 MARKS

SECTION B: PAGE TO STAGE: REALISING A PERFORMANCE TEXT

Answer BOTH questions in this section with reference to the performance text you have studied.

You need to read and refer to an extract from the text you have studied.

Performance texts:

Accidental Death of an Anarchist, Dario Fo

Colder Than Here, Laura Wade

Equus, Peter Shaffer

Fences, August Wilson

Machinal, Sophie Treadwell

That Face, Polly Stenham

Exam tip

In the exam, you will be provided with an extracts from your text which you will need to read and refer to in your answer. Here, your teacher will give you an extract to use to answer the questions.

3 As a **performer**, outline how you would use **non-verbal** communication to create an impact on the audience in the portrayal of one character in this extract.

Your answer should make reference to the performance text as a whole.   **(Total for Question 3 = 18 marks)**

4 As a **designer**, outline how **one** theatrical element could be developed to enhance appropriately the dramatic content of this extract.

Your answer should make reference to the performance text as a whole.   **(Total for Question 4 = 18 marks)**

TOTAL FOR SECTION B = 36 MARKS

SECTION C: INTERPRETING A PERFORMANCE TEXT

Answer ONE of the questions in this section with reference to the performance text you have studied.

You are the director of a new production concept of the performance text you have studied.

EITHER

5 As a director, discuss how you would apply the methodologies of your chosen theatre practitioner to the characterisation used in your production concept.

Your answer must focus on the section given for your chosen performance text.

Your answer must make reference to:

- the overall aims of your production concept in response to the play as a whole
- how your practical ideas will work in performance
- the original performance conditions of your chosen performance text.   **(Total for Question 5 = 24 marks)**

OR

6 As a director, discuss how you would apply the methodologies of your chosen theatre practitioner to the set design used in your production concept.

Your answer must focus on the section given for your chosen performance text.

Your answer must make reference to:

- the overall aims of your production concept in response to the play as a whole
- how your practical ideas will work in performance
- the original performance conditions of your chosen performance text.   **(Total for Question 6 = 24 marks)**

TOTAL FOR SECTION C = 24 MARKS

TOTAL FOR PAPER = 80 MARKS